Mother is Gold

Mother is Gold

A study in West African
literature

by ADRIAN A. ROSCOE

CAMBRIDGE

At the University Press 1971

Published by the Syndics of the Cambridge University Press
Bentley House, 200 Euston Road, London N.W.1
American Branch: 32 East 57th Street, New York, N.Y. 10022

Library of Congress Catalogue Card Number: 74-149425

ISBNS:
0 521 08092 4 clothbound
0 521 09644 8 paperback

Printed in Great Britain
by C. Tinling & Co. Ltd. London and Prescot

PR
9898
.W4
R6

For Gertie, my Parents and Family,
and all who have taught me

Iya ni wura

Contents

Acknowledgements

I wish to thank Dr J. P. Matthews and Dr N. H. MacKenzie for their invaluable help during the writing of this book. A general debt is owed to Ulli Beier and Gerald Moore, pioneers in this field, and to the following who have given both help and encouragement: W. H. G. Armytage, Francis Berry, Mary Lefebvre, Bessie Jones, and Gladys Rogers.

Thanks are due to the following for permission to quote from copyright material:

Gabriel Okara and André Deutsch Ltd for *The Voice*; Chinua Achebe and William Heinemann Ltd for *No Longer at Ease, Arrow of God,* and *A Man of the People*; Heinemann Educational Books Ltd for *Burning Grass* by Cyprian Ekwensi, *The Imprisonment of Obatala and Other Plays* by O. Ijimere, *Equiano's Travels* edited by Paul Edwards, and *A Book of African Verse* edited by John Reed and Clive Wake; Longman Group Ltd for *Mortality* by M. J. C. Echeruo, material from *A Reed in the Tide* by J. P. Clark, and *Thinking With You* by Tai Solarin; Benedict Ogutu for 'In Memoriam'; Oxford University Press for 'Love's Own Tears' from *The Truly Married Woman and Other Stories* by Abioseh Nicol, for *Owe L'Esin Oro* by Isaac Delano, for *A Dance of the Forests, The Road, Kongi's Harvest, The Lion and the Jewel,* and *The Trials of Brother Jero* by Wole Soyinka, and, with Atheneum Publishers, for 'Nuit de Sine' from *Selected Poems* by Léopold Senghor; Hill and Wang Inc and Methuen and Co Ltd for 'Death in the Dawn' and 'Season' from *Idanre and Other Poems* by Wole Soyinka; Faber and Faber Ltd for *Feather Woman of the Jungle, The Palm-Wine Drinkard* and *My Life in the Bush of Ghosts*; D. C. Osadebay for poems from *Africa Sings*; Penguin Books for material from *Modern Poetry from Africa* edited by Gerald Moore and Ulli Beier; Claude Wauthier for extracts from *The Literature and Thought of Modern Africa*.

Sources of all quoted material are given in the notes to the text, and the select bibliography.

Preface

Focusing on Nigeria, this study sets out to examine some of the new writing in English that has recently appeared in West Africa. It does not attempt to assess the literature of the whole continent; nor does it attempt to examine literary developments in all the West African countries formerly under British rule.

Instead, partly from reasons of personal knowledge, and mainly because the bulk of the literature has one major source, this volume looks most closely at the writing from Nigeria. This does not exclude reference to Ghanaian, Sierra Leonian, or Gambian writers; nor does it preclude allusion – substantial where necessary – to writing from former French territories such as Senegal and Cameroun. Indeed, since writers in the francophone community made an earlier start in the modern period than their anglophone neighbours, and were apostles of the great negritude movement, no understanding of West African writing in English would be complete without reference to them. The development of West African verse, for example, cannot adequately be examined without allusion to Senghor.

The Nigerian focus, therefore, is not exclusive. Nor does every working Nigerian author receive scrutiny. Rather, this volume sets out to assess the most significant work being done in a variety of literary forms, laying a finger on problems, and tentatively mapping the direction in which the new writing seems to be moving.

There are shared problems in African literature and commonly held views about their solution. West African voices are part of a continent-wide debate about a newly emerging culture. The artist's role in society, his difficulties over authenticity, and not least the place in his work of those traditions which have fed his culture and shaped his imagination – these are questions as relevant for the Kenyan, Ugandan, or Zambian writer as they are for the Nigerian. It is no surprise that Okot p'Bitek, the Ugkandan poet, following a line of experiment initiated by Gabriel Okara, a Nigerian, wrote his famous *Song of Lawino* first in his vernacular, Acholi.

ix

A writer in East or West Africa faces an initial problem of language. English is usually his second tongue, acquired after an early education in one of a myriad vernaculars. He wants to use it yet retain the special hallmarks of his own culture. At the same time, while anxious to redefine the African past, he is, in Edward Blishen's words, trying to forge a literature capable of dealing with his own 'amazing, painful and volatile present'. The task is formidable. African writers are meeting the difficulties which language and culture pose by resorting to linguistic experimentation and by tapping a rich heritage of oral literature. What Okara or Soyinka have attempted in West Africa finds echoes among writers elsewhere in the continent.

Discussion is not confined to verse, prose, and drama in their conventional manifestations, but includes forms often neglected by literary criticism. Thus, in addition to examining the verse of poets such as Osadebay, J. P. Clark, Echeruo, Soyinka, and Okara, the prose of Ekwensi and Achebe, and the drama of central figures such as Soyinka, Clark, Ogunde, Ijimere, and Ladipo, this volume acknowledges the importance of those who have contributed to children's literature, to journalism, and to political writing. Ahmadu Bello, Azikiwe, and Tai Solarin win a place among authors of a more conventional mould.

There is a further point. Growing evidence suggests that some literary forms in Africa have a brighter future than others. This is an area of speculation into which the present volume tries to move. The Nigerian evidence which is offered does not differ materially from what is found in other regions of the continent.

A basic critical viewpoint must be established. If an African writes in English, his work must be considered as belonging to English letters as a whole, and can be scrutinised accordingly. Robie Macauley was right, however, to complain of outside criticism that approaches African writing with such 'charity and diffidence that the most inept African writer can be made out as an interesting example of something-or-other'. He pointed to a pitfall which the present study strives to avoid.

September 1970   ADRIAN A. ROSCOE

1. The background

Cultural collision

Janheinz Jahn is probably correct when he argues in *Muntu* that Europeans in general believe, when they trouble themselves to think about the African continent, that Africans are hastily becoming westernised, convinced that they must accept modern civilisation or perish:[1] that if Africans are to avoid the fate of the Australian Aborigines, the South Sea Islanders or the American Indians, they must embrace the European view of the world, and embrace it with the utmost dispatch. Europeans believe this because, as far as they know, there is simply no other choice open. Cheerfully confident in a body of information and attitudes inherited from colonial days and early missionary evangelising, they assert that the African has no choice because he has no cultural traditions of his own, no religious, economic or political background worthy of serious attention, and certainly no history of glory in the creative arts. Hence, says Jahn, 'Europe is alleged to provide the model, Africa to copy it; Europe to be spiritually the giving, Africa the receiving partner. Since Europe is held to be the teacher and Africa the pupil, Europe is to decide when Africa is ripe: ripe for a faith, ripe for action, ripe for freedom. Europe is thought to know what is good for Africa, better than Africa herself.' The lofty advice is summed up in the exhortation to westernise as quickly as possible.

There is also another school of thought, which, perhaps sceptical of the shibboleths of colonialism and refreshingly curious about the lives of alien people in a fast-shrinking world, has heard something of the medieval empires of Ghana, Mali, and Songhai, read of the splendid bronzes of Ife and Benin, or, at the very least, learnt that much of what passes for western dancing had its beginning in the villages and forests of West Africa. Members of this school will admit that at least an African does have traditions of his own, that he does in fact have some kind of choice before him. They are likely to feel, however, that the moment of decision, which is here and now, must involve an 'either-or' choice. Africans must 'accept modern civilization and survive or . . .

1

perish with their own traditions', a view which sees western culture, especially in its technological manifestations perhaps, as superior and, ultimately, as the only road to salvation.[2] In effect, then, this school of thought also believes that there is no real choice: and both schools probably foresee that in a future, distant or near, there will emerge an Africa sweetly and reasonably westernised – a second Europe in a tropical climate.

Certainly the African cannot escape the encounter with two ways of life: his own traditional way and that of his former or contemporary masters. The American psychologist Leonard Doob, who is interested in the broad field of African communications, made this point when he wrote:

> Everywhere the traditional society meaningfully survives. The most urbanized African knows that usually not far away is a village of his tribe where many if not most of the old ways are cultivated and practised. His native language, like that of his children, is an African language ... At the same time even the remotest area in the interior has experienced some contact with the West. Planes are visible overhead and roads are being built and improved ... The government from the capital and missionaries from the West are trying conspicuously to induce or compel the mass of Africans to improve their health, to wear respectable clothes, to increase the cultivation of a particular crop ...
>
> Under these conditions Africans, even if they wished to, could not accept one society and then pay little attention or no attention to the alternative; they simply must experience both societies.[3]

Broadly speaking, then, modern Africa knows two societies and two cultures which it must encounter. But we should not be mistaken about the nature of this encounter. In the literary sphere at least, one can no longer accept Malinowski's view that 'the meeting of cultures in black Africa comes down to the effect of one "superior" culture, in this case European, on a "passive" one.'[4]

Historically, Africa's mood in face of Europe has indeed been passive, and, in so far as she is still prepared to learn from Europe, will continue to be so. But a new cultural mood is developing and its literary manifestations are quickly detected in the poets – those finely calibrated anemometers who are sensitive points in any society. Listen, for example, to David Diop addressing 'a Nigger Tramp':

> Have patience the Carnival is over
> I sharpen the hurricane for the furrows of the future
> For you we will remake Ghana and Timbuktu
> And the guitars shuddering with a thousand strokes

Great mortars booming under the blows
Pestles
Pounding
From house to house
In the coming day.[5]
or, again, listen to him addressing his former conquerors:
But we whose hands fertilize the womb of the earth
In spite of your songs of pride
In spite of the desolate villages of torn Africa
Hope was preserved in us as in a fortress
And from the mines of Swaziland to the factories of Europe
Spring will be reborn under our bright steps.[6]
The tone here (which is the tone of many West African poets in states stretching from Guinea to the Cameroons) could invite many different epithets, but the cultural mood underlying it could not conceivably be called 'passive'. Rather it is assertive, aggressive, optimistic, almost violent. The imagery has the stamp of the prophet, calling up visions of the New Jerusalem; the language is pushed about, bullied and ruthlessly pressed into poetic service. Admittedly, poems by Diop represent the extremist voice of negritude. As this study will show, anglophone writers have not tended to be so aggressive; but, equally, neither could they be described as 'passive'.

But cultures are colliding in Africa and the collision is painful; and it must not be forgotten that the encounter has a background history of humiliating colonialism and slavery. There is a good deal of agony in the African situation and the best writers reveal it. 'No thinking African can escape the pain of the wound in our soul', observes Chinua Achebe, a writer determined to help his society 'regain its belief in itself and put away the complexes of the years of denigration and self-denigration'.[7]

But the very turbulence of the African position, the very storms it has blown up in African minds and souls, has created a situation fraught with the challenge and material that provide inspiration for the literary artist.

Africa's cultural collision has necessarily involved the loss of a certain part of the traditional heritage, while western cultural elements have been absorbed; but, in its literary manifestations, it has resulted in the creation of a body of writing that is at once dynamic, original, independent and indigenous.

Let there be no mistake – modern Africans do have a definite choice of cultures. They are daily faced with some aspects of the western world, and yet, as Doob puts it, this happens in an environment where 'the traditional society meaningfully survives'. The anthropologists and social scientists must be allowed their own views. But, as we range over the problems and progress apparent in a diverse range of material in verse, prose and drama, we hope to show that, in so far as it can be said that a definite decision has been made, at least the *new literature* of Africa will not be a slavish imitation of western models and practice. Having increasingly felt the underlying strength and flexibility of their ancestral culture, and having revalued the claims of its western counterpart, West African writers have apparently decided that they will enter the third quarter of the twentieth century with their own heritage largely intact and with the addition of only those European elements which it seems advantageous to absorb. Thus, though their situation is still painful, they have adopted a stance which is not passive, as Malinowski believed, but, at one level, certainly active, and at another, as in the case of the francophone writers, magnificently aggressive.

Let Césaire, the high-priest of negritude, sum up for us:

As for us and our particular societies, we believe that in the new African culture, in the para-African culture if you like, there will be new elements, modern elements, elements borrowed from Europe. But we also believe that many traditional elements will live on in this culture. We refuse to yield to the *tabula rasa* temptation. I refuse to believe that any future African culture will totally and brutally reject the old order. And to demonstrate what I have just said, let me use an allegory: anthropologists have often described what one of them chooses to call cultural fatigue. The example they cite is worth recalling since it rises to the stature of a symbol. Here is the story: it takes place in the Hawaian Islands. Some years after Cook discovered these islands, the king died and was replaced by a young man, Prince Kamehamela II. Won over to European ways, this young prince decided to abolish the ancestral religion. He and the high priest arranged to hold a big festival during the course of which the taboo would solemnly be broken and the traditional gods annulled. On the appointed day, at a sign from the king, the high priest fell upon the images of the gods, trampling and destroying them, while a great cry was heard: 'the taboo is broken!' Well, several years later, the Hawaians welcomed Christian missionaries with open arms . . . What followed is well known. It belongs to history. It is the simplest and most complete example known of cultural subversion preparing the way for bondage. And then, I ask, is this renunciation by a people of its past and its culture, is this what is expected of us?

I tell you frankly: there will be no Kamehamela II among us![8]

4

Césaire is speaking here in a general sense about the kind of African culture that is emerging. But he is a major poet and his words are thus acutely relevant for the literary sphere also. There has been no *tabula rasa* in this area, and no successful Kamehamela either – and this despite the major concession African writers have had to make to the metropolitan culture in the form of a linguistic vehicle for their literature.[9]

The language dilemma

Speaking at the Leverhulme Conference on Universities and the Language Problems of Tropical Africa at Ibadan in 1961, R. G. Armstrong remarked:

> The serious business of the mid-twentieth century is carried on in four languages: English, French, German and Russian. All other languages lag behind these as vehicles for understanding and participating in the main business of the modern world. To be confined to Spanish is to lag thirty years behind the times in science, engineering, business, and scholarship generally . . . To be confined to Arabic is to lag at least fifty years behind . . .[10]

The speaker's point is clear enough and it puts a finger on a basic weakness which African vernaculars share when they are seen from a technologist's or an economist's point of view. And when Armstrong goes on to mention that Africa is 'a very big continent with large, widely dispersed populations speaking between one and two thousand different languages', one can appreciate that there is also, within Africa herself, a grave problem of communication. It is mitigated somewhat by the fact that large numbers of Africans already speak French or English and are committed to the expansion of these dominant languages through rapidly growing systems of secondary education.

Africans themselves are acutely aware of the problem, though sometimes in rather curious ways. At another conference, for example, this time the second Congress of Negro Writers and Artists, the Malagasy poet Rabemananjara testified to the discomfort of African intellectuals in the linguistic situation forced on them by a departed colonialism: 'Truly,' he said, 'our conference is one of language thieves. This crime, at least, we have committed ourselves. We have stolen from our masters this treasure of identity, the vehicle of their thought . . . the forbidden cave where they have hidden the loot taken from our fathers . . .'[11] The uneasiness Africa feels echoes the discomfort which men like Gandhi felt. The Indian leader's answer to Macaulay's support of education in English is in much the same vein as the comment from Rabemananjara:

> Is it not a painful thing that, if I want to go to a court of justice, I must employ the English language as a medium, that when I become a barrister, I may not speak my mother-tongue and that someone else should have to translate to me in my own language?
>
> Is it not a sign of slavery? Am I to blame the English for it or myself? It is we, the English-knowing Indians, that have enslaved India. The curse of the nation will rest not upon the English but upon us.[12]

The language riots on the Indian sub-continent and in Belgium are familiar enough and they testify to the very special place which language can have in the hearts of men. But if the position of English in India is now rather uncertain, despite the support it enjoys from scholars and writers, its future on the African continent, especially perhaps in the West African states, seems assured and recent history there suggests that it is safe alike from the twin forces of political upheaval and tribal rivalry. Here, claims Professor Mahood, who knows West Africa intimately, 'English has virtually established itself ... as a West African language'.[13] The Ghanaian writer George Awoonor-Williams pointedly observes that 'English, French and Portuguese have been *transplanted* into African societies'.[14]

English, then, has already put down roots in West African societies; it has been born anew; and amongst a people who believe that language has sacred properties to be treasured and nourished, it is already enjoying a rich and extravagant existence of its own.

The history of English in Africa is fairly long, though Miss Mahood's note that *Hamlet* was performed off the coast of West Africa just nine years after its composition is perhaps not a very useful starting point.[15] Certainly, when West Africa's first university was opened in Freetown, Sierra Leone, in 1827, the medium of instruction was, naturally, English, and the first members of a Negro élite in Britain's colonies went forth with a training in the mother tongue. Thus, when *The African and Sierra Leone Weekly Advertiser* first appeared in 1855 it was printed in English, despite its African editorial board. Between 1860 and 1870 two other newspapers, *The African Interpreter and Advocate* and the *West African Liberator,* enjoyed brief lives, again as English-language publications. The first newspaper to appear on the Gold Coast, the *Accra Herald,* was published in 1857 and it, too, appeared in English. As the advantages of a world language became apparent, as missionary and economic activity increased, English in West Africa gradually established itself until it reached the position which it now enjoys as a *lingua franca* and the medium of higher education and diplomacy in all the former British territories.

These are some of the reasons why the present generation of African writers have chosen to write in the metropolitan language. Other reasons, besides the desire for an international audience, have a political background. Take, for example, the career of a member of the first generation of West African journalists – Attoh Ahuma. Ahuma, who founded the Aborigines Rights Protection Society, perhaps the first nationalist organisation in the colony, was editor-in-chief of the *Gold Coast Echo* and afterwards of the *Gold Coast Leader*. This is important, for it shows that the introduction of English into the affairs of the West Coast was at an early stage related to the birth and growth of indigenous political liberation movements; and there seems to be overwhelming evidence for Claude Wauthier's view that these movements throughout Africa have been an important incubator of the cultural renaissance we are now witnessing.

Meanwhile the indigenous languages have suffered. Education policy in the colonies, which in British territories allowed vernacular teaching in the primary schools, while insisting on English at the secondary level, contributed in no small measure to the retardation of vernacular languages, for use either in creative writing or in political education. Wauthier cites the experience of Dr Nnamdi Azikiwe, the nationalist leader who became the first President of Nigeria, who in 1937 founded a number of newspapers in both English and the vernaculars, clearly with political aims in mind. He quickly discovered that the vernacular press was useless, quite simply because the education system had ensured that those 'capable of reading and writing their own language' (who were, in any case, very few), 'would read and write primarily, and often far better, in English.'[16]

With English as not only the one language through which the ambitious African could obtain a truly solid academic grounding, but also as the only means of communication between the myriad tribes and clans of each colonial state (a *lingua franca* doing much the same job that Latin did in medieval Europe), it was hardly surprising that the colonialist's language quickly took root and flourished. There seems little doubt that, in West Africa at least, its future is safe and secure.

We should remember, too, that the West African states comprised pre-literate societies. Jahn's argument that drum language was the only sensible means of 'writing' in areas where termites guaranteed paper only the briefest existence, is perfectly valid, but does nothing to alter the fact that written language, appearing early in Arabic and later in French and English, took root only slowly. And then the results were

7

disappointing. Attempts to introduce an alphabet into the Vai language in Liberia and the Bamoun language of the German Cameroons were early failures. Nor has the introduction of the Arabic alphabet fared much better. According to Wauthier, its application to Kanuri, Hausa, Songhai, Bamana, Wolof and Fulani has failed to carry over into writing the richness and vitality which, scholars tell us, these languages possess.

Of the Fulani experience, Lavergne de Tressan writes:

The so-called scholars who used the Arabic characters were automatically muslims and the subjects dealt with were generally islamic religious texts in verse. The results are deplorable: bad transcription, a lexicology limited to abstractions with wholesale borrowings from Arabic, disfigured, shortened and inverted syntax, alien to the spoken tongue ... The comparison between the pathos of the Arabic-Fulani so-called mystical religious songs and the light, rhythmic prose of the Fulani shepherd songs is particularly significant.[17]

Certainly Dr Azikiwe's experience is sufficient to show that a West African artist in *written* literature must, in the present circumstances of a largely pre-literate population, use the metropolitan language if he wishes to be heard, understood, and appreciated by a large international, as well as national, audience. Not surprisingly, therefore, vernacular writing is still extremely small in quantity, if not always in quality. Scholars may anxiously point to the richness, precision and flexibility of African languages, in much the same way that Jesperson lamented the unappreciated virtues of Anglo-Saxon; but the evidence is overwhelming that the advantages and historic strength of English in what was formerly British West Africa ensure for it an increasingly dominant position over the vernacular languages.

We have mentioned the birth of an anglophone African press in Sierra Leone, in 1855. There is evidence, too, that a certain kind of written language was earlier enjoying a spartan life of its own further along the coast in Nigeria, as this letter cited by Wauthier, from the King of Bonny to His Majesty King George IV, testifies:

Brudder Georges ... send warship look um what water bar ab got, dat good, me let um dat. Brudder send boat chopum slave, dat good. E no send warship, for cappen no peake me, no lookee me face. No, No, No; me tell you, No; Suppose you come all you mont full palaver, give a reason whye do it ...[18]

This is an early example of pidgin English, which has enjoyed, and continues to enjoy, an active life all along the West Coast of Africa: it is the bane of purists among expatriate English teachers, the linguistic currency of traders in a dozen different states, and the medium of a modest quantity of written literature.

The problem a second language raises for authors is acute. They face the task of giving artistic shape and form to their creative impulses in a language not originally their own, a language whose very essence bears the marks of a culture and history which they have not been able fully to share. In circumstances such as these, how can an African writer give completely satisfying expression to his innermost vision and response to experience? In other words, how can an African, writing in English, convey his authentic voice and spirit? How, indeed, can he remain African? Will his immersion in the English language simply mean a further dose of the cultural bleaching which people in the West believe is inevitable for Africa? Will it result in a species of schizoid culture, some kind of modern bastardy, neither right African nor right European, but mixing black and white to produce the dullest of greys? The problem is complex and, certainly, it is not a problem which the early writers of Canada, Australia and New Zealand had to face. But one initial hint why Africans in such numbers should be making literary virtues out of linguistic necessity comes from Balachandra Rajan, the Indian novelist most militantly engaged against the language patriots of his country. Here he defends the use of a second language for Indian writers:

> Let me add that language is both a friend and an enemy, as the soil is and as the elements are. The resistance one encounters in it may be a promise of creative strength; it does not necessarily mean that one should turn to a more pliable alternative.[19]

Sew the old days

> We dwell with satisfaction upon the poet's difference from his predecessors, especially his immediate predecessors; we endeavour to find something that can be isolated in order to be enjoyed. Whereas if we approach a poet without this prejudice we shall often find that not only the best, but the most individual parts of his work may be those in which the dead poets, his ancestors, assert their immortality most vigorously.

> No poet, no artist of any art, has his complete meaning alone. His significance, his appreciation is the appreciation of his relation to the dead poets and artists.

> What is to be insisted upon is that the poet must develop or

9

procure the consciousness of the past and that he should continue
to develop this consciousness throughout his career.

T. S. ELIOT

The central idea running through these extracts from 'Tradition and
the Individual Talent' is not new; nor is Eliot the only twentieth-century
writer to have subscribed to it, for Chesterton was expressing it when he
prophesied that 'When the great flowers break forth again, the new
epics and the new arts, they will break out on the ancient and living
tree.'[20] It is also an accepted truth in Africa. 'The tree can grow only by
sinking its roots into nourishing soil', the Senegalese writer Birago
Diop reminded his daughters when dedicating to them his first collection of stories.[21] 'Young palm trees grow on old palm trees' runs a
proverb from the Cameroons, asserting the truths which Eliot carries in
his elegant prose in a more metaphorical, more African, kind of way.

Convinced that exciting creativity in the present can only be achieved
by returning to cultural roots lying deep in the past, West African writers
are voicing an enthusiastic readiness to make the journey, even if, as Eliot
says, it can only be done 'by great labour'. Evidence is provided by the
poets themelves. The songs which his mother taught him inspired the
Ghanaian poet G. Awoonor-Williams to write, and he is strongly
convinced of the abundant material and inspiration awaiting those who
will turn to indigenous sources. 'I should take my poetic sensibility . . .
from the tradition that feeds my language,' he says, 'because in my
language there is a lot of poetry, a lot of music, and a lot of the old literary
art – even though not written.'[22] His conviction becomes a theme of his
verse and in a poem called 'Rediscovery', a title which is descriptive of his
whole poetic effort, he looks forward to what he calls 'the new chorus of
our forgotten comrades/and the halleluyahs of our second selves'. In
another poem, which uses the moon as an emblem for the spirit of his
ancestors, he writes: 'Reaching for the Stars we stop at the House of
Moon/And pause to relearn the wisdom of our fathers.'[23] The Ghanaian's poems constantly rehearse the same theme. 'In our beginnings lies
our journey's end,' is the burden of a piece called 'Salvation', which ends
with the lines:

> And in the season of search
> When the discoverers land on far off shores
> And the others who took the big boats return
> We shall find our salvation here on the shore, asleep.[24]

Similarly, faced with Africa's present state of cultural turmoil – graphi-
cally drawn as 'between the anvil and the hammer/In the forging house
of a new life' – he invokes the aid of his forebears:

10

Sew the old days for us, our fathers
That we can wear them under our new garment,
After we have washed ourselves in
The whirlpool of the many river's estuary – [25]

The point is frequently made in such a way that almost any aspect of Africa's cultural salvation could be intended. In 'My God of Songs Was Ill', however, it is definitely the problem of poetry that Awoonor-Williams considers. Betray or neglect your poetic heritage and the result will be poor art: this is the message of a poem celebrating the joy and inspiration of a renewed encounter with the ancestral tradition. It concludes:

The cure god said I had violated my god
'Take him to your father's gods' he said in my tongue.
So I took him to my father's gods
But before they opened the hut
My god burst into songs, new strong songs
That I am still singing with him. [26]

Awoonor-Williams usefully demonstrates the current eagerness among West African writers to sink a taproot into the soil of their own artistic traditions. It is a most important phenomenon to which this study will constantly be calling attention as it examines the work being done in the three major literary forms of poetry, prose, and drama. It also appears to be the decisive *literary* answer to a question once posed by the Nigerian poet Mabel Segun at the end of some verses entitled 'Conflict':

Here we stand
infants overblown,
poised between two civilisations,
finding the balance irksome,
itching for something to happen,
to tip us one way or the other,
groping in the dark for a helping hand
and finding none.
I'm tired, O my God, I'm tired,
I'm tired of hanging in the middle way –
but where can I go? [27]

In the francophone states, however, the disciples of negritude long ago discovered where their artistic salvation lay. Indeed, Janheinz Jahn defines the very concept of negritude in terms which make this abundantly clear. It is, he writes, 'the practical application of the extremely obvious knowledge that every artist achieves his best work when he attaches himself to his own tradition'. [28] Hence Césaire's paeans of

11

praise for Old Africa and Senghor's constant invocation of his ancestors; hence, too, the determined effort by francophone scholars to rehabilitate African history and culture. The anglophone writers have now also discovered and accepted this 'extremely obvious knowledge' and are pursuing their artistic calling in the light of it. To use the powerful image of a Somali poet, they are writing in the modern world with 'one ear bent to the sleeping centuries along the dark road of time'.[29]

2. *Progress in verse*

From Equiano to Clark

In the Nigerian town of Abeokuta, the birthplace of Amos Tutuola
and Wole Soyinka, funeral ceremonies are still occasions for the
chanting or singing of elegiac verse. The bereaved might hear a poem
such as the following, which, in richly figurative language, subtly
preaches a familiar African lesson, that the ancestors, though buried
and gone, remain the most powerful allies of the living:

> The leopard has eyes of fire
> The tale of the leopard never sleeps;
> But mightiest of all are its claws –
> its hidden secrets.[1]

Alternatively, the mourners might be offered this fleeting glimpse of
the next world, which, in reality, is the chanter's poetic way of
announcing that the deceased died a happy death, an old man who is
leaving behind a great harvest of children:

> I saw the king of the river and the king of the sun.
> In that country there were palms
> So heavy with fruits,
> They bent beneath their weight
> They died beneath their burden.[2]

On numerous festive occasions the Yoruba of Abeokuta will hear,
too, the artistry of the Ijala or hunters, chanting poems in praise of the
duiker and the buffalo, the bushbuck and the baboon, the trees and the
gods. In the Preface to his illuminating study *The Content and Form
of Yoruba Ijala,* Dr S. A. Babalola tells us that in traditional Yoruba
life

> almost every special occasion — worship, homage, greeting,
> merriment, mourning, petition, etc. — is celebrated in poetry ...
> Oral poetry is part of everyday life among the Yoruba. For
> example, as the children do obeisance before their parents, first
> thing in the morning, the parents burst forth into *oriki* recitation
> in commemoration of their ancestors whose achievements their
> young descendants are to be inspired to emulate. And as the

13

farmers toil on their farms or as the craftsmen ply their different trades, they dispel the tedium of physical exertion by chanting snatches of *ijala* or *esa* or *rara*.[3]

It seems clear that oral verse among the Yoruba (and doubtless among all the tribes of West Africa) belongs to a tradition of immeasurable wealth and antiquity; the scholar who would explore it faces a voyage over a boundless ocean. Professor Berry of the London School of Oriental and African Studies has made the point succinctly: 'After a hundred years of collection and scholarly effort,' he says, 'we are ... in reality only at the beginning.'[4]

West African poetry in English, however, has enjoyed no such long and distinguished history. When, in 1957, Olumbe Bassir published *An Anthology of West African Verse,* its finest pieces were translations from the French writing of Birago Diop, David Diop, and Léopold Senghor, negritude poets whose work had been well-known since the thirties. The situation has changed dramatically since 1957. An atmosphere of literary ferment has developed in Nigeria, and so rapidly that none of the truly significant anglophone poets can be found in Bassir's anthology. Moore and Beier's *Modern Poetry from Africa,* with its large proportion of Nigerian verse, illustrates how swiftly the scene has changed between 1957 and 1963.[5] There is now in print enough verse by English-speaking West Africans for an attempt to be made at a critical examination of its history and development; and this is what the present chapter sets out to do.

We might begin by examining a stanza or two from Olaudah Equiano, an eighteenth-century slave and one of the earliest known Africans to write English verse. By virtue of his education in the West, however, we find a style of writing quite indistinguishable from the English poetic convention of the last quarter of the eighteenth century. The stanzas, poor, but pious and sincere, are taken from Equiano's *Miscellaneous Verses or Reflections on the State of my mind during my first Convictions: of the Necessity of believing the Truth and experiencing the inestimable Benefits of Christianity.*

> Well may I say my life has been
> One scene of sorrow and of pain;
> From early days I griefs have known,
> And as I grew my griefs have grown:
>
> *
>
> Dangers were always in my path;
> And fear of wrath, and sometimes death;

14

While pale dejection in me reign'd
I often wept, by grief constrain'd.

*

When taken from my native land,
By an unjust and cruel band,
How did uncommon dread prevail!
My sighs no more I could conceal.[6]

The autobiographical strain continues for another twenty-five stanzas, all equally sincere, and all equally dull. The style owes nothing to Africa. Yet the continent *is* present in the writer's mind, for he retains the memory of his enslavement; and we know from historical sources that Equiano was a militant abolitionist who became personally involved in the attempt in 1787 to establish a haven for freed slaves at Freetown in Sierra Leone. His verse is uninteresting except as a useful starting point, though in view of his known championing of the African cause in Britain, one might argue that he is the first West African to use the metropolitan language against his masters, a weapon which later generations of African spokesmen were to use so skilfully.

After Equiano's work, the next landmark of interest is the publication in 1957 of Bassir's *An Anthology of West African Verse;* and though the two are separated by roughly 170 years, there are, as far as English writing is concerned, few signs of poetic development. We must remind ourselves perhaps that Bassir's anthology is a colonial document, appearing three years before the great turning point of political Independence; for, though its writing often anticipates the happy day of liberation, even at times growing indignant at the humiliation of servitude, the pages tell vividly enough a story of tutelage, cultural uncertainty, and imitation of the metropolitan tradition. Take, for instance, the poetry of Dennis Osadebay, who, wrote Bassir, 'typifies the strain of West African middle-class persons from among whom spring the political and social leaders on whose shoulders the responsibility of national liberation falls'.[7] Osadebay, who studied in Britain and was called to the English Bar, provides a clear example of a colonial poet who, despite his claim that the underlying theme of his verse is the 'Urge in the heart of the African to be free', is unsure of the direction in which he wants his art to move. His poem 'Young Africa's Plea' spells out his confusion and uncertainty:

> Don't preserve my customs
> As some fine curios
> To suit some white historian's tastes.

15

There's nothing artificial
That beats the natural way,
In culture and ideals of life.
Let me play with the whiteman's ways
Let me work with the blackman's brains
Let my affairs themselves sort out.
Then in sweet rebirth
I'll rise a better man,
Not ashamed to face the world.
Those who doubt my talents
In secret fear my strength;
They know I am no less a man.
Let them bury their prejudice,
Let them show their noble sides,
Let me have untrammelled growth,
My friends will never know regret
And I, I never once forget.[8]

The inferiority syndrome, that most devastating result of colonialism, is here in all its glory. There is a plea not to preserve Africa's customs as curios for the white world, revealing in the poet a nostalgic attachment to a heritage he believes to be vanishing; there is his plea for 'untrammelled growth' and a request to those people who doubt his talents to show the noble side of their natures. But if he feels a genuine nostalgia for his customs, meaning, in part, love and respect for them, why does he feel 'ashamed to face the world'? What *is* this 'untrammelled growth' he talks about and where is it meant to lead? And what precisely is meant when he speaks of playing 'with the whiteman's ways', but working 'with the blackman's brains'? One suspects that it all points to bewilderment; and this suspicion seems to be most strongly confirmed by those forlorn words which lie at the heart of the piece. 'Let my affairs themselves sort out', he cries, 'Then in sweet rebirth I'll rise a better man' – lines that ignite a flicker of hope but carry a world of despair. The mixed emotions of this colonised Nigerian are expressed in a style which, though not so imitative as Equiano's, nevertheless still owes nothing to Africa. There is no picture of the homeland, nothing to suggest the existence close at hand of an ancient poetic art laden with metaphor and teeming with imagery. Indeed, apart from a sense of his confusion, the dominant impression which the reader gains from Osadebay's work is one of embarrassment about his heritage and attraction towards Europe. When, in 'Young Africa's Resolve', he asserts:

16

On library doors
I'll knock aloud and gain entrance;
Of the strength
Of nations past and present I will read.
I'll brush the dust from ancient scrolls,
And drinking deep of the Pyrrean stream,
Will go forward and do and dare.[9]

one feels sure that it is European civilisation which he is anxious to explore, not the civilisation of his forebears. It is the Pyrrean stream from which he will drink, not the stream of wisdom that has flowed down the centuries from his ancestors. He does not appear to be thinking of Old Mali, Ghana, Songhai, or Timbuctoo.

Another piece, 'Thoughts at the Victoria Beach, Lagos', illustrates again how thoroughly Osadebay has been captivated by English poetic models:

The Waters stretched from the tropic shores
And seemed to kiss the sunlit skies afar;
The waves riding in majesty,
Glided to and fro like lords of the silvery bar.
The oft washed sands gave forth a smile
To beautify the sphere and heaven extol;
The noble palm and mangrove trees
Stood with their heads aloft as the waters roll.
Poor mortals – birds and beasts and men –
Ran here and there in vain attempt to keep
Their lives from the quenching winds of death,
And sought in vain to solve the mysteries deep.[10]

Similar verse from nineteenth-century Canadians or Australians is usually dubbed Colonial Romanticism, defined by A. J. N. Smith as a spirit in literature 'that gratefully accepts a place of subordination, and which looks elsewhere for the standards of excellence, being content to imitate, timidly and conservatively, the parent tradition'.[11] The Nigerian poet J. P. Clark likes to call it writing of 'the Palm and Lagoon school'. But, appearing as it does in the late autumn of colonialism, and exhibiting scarcely any poetic trait that could be described as African (the Augustan 'tropic shores' notwithstanding), it might more accurately be described by Wauthier's phrase 'the literature of tutelage'. Further examples of Osadebay's colonial attitude and style can be found in his poem 'The Rising of Africa', where the following is a typical stanza:

Oh! 'Tis Afric! Sable son of kings,
Whose fame the Muse Erato sings;

> Whom Greeks of old beheld a god;
> For whom Fair virgins struck a chord.[12]

or in his piece called 'Africa, Arise!' which opens with the unfortunate stanza:

> Ye noble sons of Afric, rise and shine,
> Show forth your courage and your strength;
> Lift up your banners, raise your great ensign,
> And let your trumpets peal at length
> To tell the world your day is come at last
> And weakness but a thing that's of the past.[13]

How different is the verse from French West Africa collected in Bassir's anthology. It represents the voice of negritude, first raised in the nineteen-thirties; a strident voice, often angry and accusing, but a voice which carries a tone of conviction, of self-knowledge, of fervour for aims that are clear and well-defined. For example, there is neither ambiguity of meaning nor cultural vertigo in David Diop's 'Défir à la Force'; it makes its point bluntly and leaves us convinced of the poet's determination vigorously to champion the African cause:

> You who stoop, you who weep,
> You who one day die without knowing why,
> You who fight, who watch while Another sleeps;
> You who no longer laugh with your eyes,
> You, my brother, full of fear and anguish,
> Raise yourself and cry *No!*[14]

Diop is sure about his view of the White Man, and speaks of Africa's encounter with him in strains of burning indignation rarely if ever found in Osadebay. 'The White Man killed my father', he cries in 'Le Temps du Martyr':

> My father was proud.
> The White Man seduced my mother,
> My mother was beautiful.
> The White Man burnt my brother beneath the noonday sun.[15]

If Osadebay looks on his heritage with mixed feelings of affection and disgust, his attitude is not shared by the francophone poets, who, as disciples of negritude, celebrate their cultural inheritance with strong feelings of pride and admiration. The theme of death and the ancestors is a case in point. In the opinion of Ulli Beier, the German scholar, here is an area of thought in which Africa and Europe fundamentally differ. No understanding of African life is possible without an appreciation of the part which the dead play in it. Beier points to western society's increasing cynicism about the after-life, our traditional horror of death, and the appalling finality which we feel when the dead are separated, now and for ever, from the living. He contrasts this with the cosmology of Africa, the belief 'in the great cycle of birth, death and rebirth' which removes from death its horror and finality. He reminds us of the commonplace sight in Africa of children playing round the tombstone of their grandfather, buried in the garden or beneath the living-room floor – always close to the living whom he can guide and influence.[16] Beier mentions, too, Africa's belief in the rebirth of ancestors into the same family, indicated by such names as 'father has come back' or 'mother has returned'. For the African, then, the worlds of the living and the dead interpenetrate one with the other, as though, indeed, they were the same world. This is a cornerstone of traditional Africa's world view, and one to which we will necessarily return as our study proceeds. It has no place in the poems of Osadebay, but it is strongly present in poems by Diop and Senghor which appear in Bassir's anthology. Birago Diop's 'Souffles' is one remarkable example:

> Listen more often to things rather than beings.
> Hear the fire's voice,
> Hear the voice of water.
> In the wind hear the sobbing of the trees,
> It is our forefathers breathing.
> The dead are not gone forever.
> They are in the paling shadows,
> And in the darkening shadows.
> The dead are not beneath the ground,
> They are in the rustling tree,
> In the murmuring wood,
> In the flowing water,
> In the still water,
> In the lonely place, in the crowd;
> The dead are not dead.
>
> *
>
> Listen more often to things rather than beings.
> Hear the fire's voice.
> Hear the voice of water.
> In the wind hear the sobbing of the trees.
> It is the breathing of our forefathers,
> Who are not gone, not beneath the ground,
> Not dead.
>
> *
>
> The dead are not gone forever.
> They are in a woman's breast,

19

A child's crying, a glowing ember.
The dead are not beneath the earth,
They are in the flickering fire,
In the weeping plant, the groaning rock,
The wooded place, the home.
The dead are not dead.

*

Listen more often to things rather than beings.
Hear the fire's voice,
Hear the voice of water.
In the wind hear the sobbing of the trees.
It is the breathing of our forefathers.[17]

It is clear that Diop is not only working with one of the fundamental beliefs of his people, but is doing so in a style whose repeated invocations and parallel phrasing strongly echo indigenous poetic practice. In Senghor's verse, too, as Beier's essay shows, the ancestors are an abiding concern, a source of help and solace to whom the poet can turn in times of doubt and anguish. Often they are symbolised by masks, as they are in Senghor's well-known poem which begins:

Masks! Oh Masks!
Black mask, red mask, you black and white masks,
Rectangular masks through whom the spirit breathes,
I greet you in silence!
And you too, my pantherheaded ancestor.[18]

In Reed and Wake's fine edition of Senghor's verse we find a piece called 'Nuit de Sine' and in it the lines:

Woman, light the clear oil lamp, where the
    ancestors gathered around may talk as
    parents talk when the children are put
    to bed.
Listen to the voice of the ancients of
    Elissa. Exiled like us
They have never wanted to die, to let the
    torrent of their seed be lost in the sands.
Let me listen in the smoky hut where there
    comes a glimpse of the friendly spirits
My head on your bosom warm like a *dang* still
    steaming from the fire.
Let me breathe the smell of our Dead, gather
    and speak out again their living voice,
    learn to

Live before I go down, deeper than diver, into
the high profundities of sleep.[19]

The difference between the work of these two French African poets and
the writing of Osadebay is plain enough; and it would be fair to say that it
marks the void which once existed between francophone and anglophone
African verse in general. Where one is all doubt and hesitancy, the other
is sure, bold, and thrusting. One blushes at an ancestry it would rather
forget; the other gazes on it with pride, and draws strength from it. The
anglophone poet hovers precariously between two worlds, while his
francophone counterparts, only too familiar with the attractions of
Europe, unequivocally pledge their loyalty to Africa.

The French African poets marched under the banner of negritude,
espousing with fervour all that was African and Negro. Negritude
thus provided the driving force for a school of highly original verse
and offered its disciples some important advantages. Beier makes a
comment on Senghor, for instance, which suggests how negritude has
helped this poet to preserve his cultural identity even in the face of a
certain degree of western assimilation:

> However much he has absorbed of European culture, however
> much he may have assimilated it outwardly, he remains an
> African in some of his most basic attitudes. His conscious
> identification with the movement of *negritude* . . . allows him to
> acknowledge these emotions and responses, which he might
> otherwise try to suppress.[20]

Negritude gave French African verse a power and maturity that
British Africa could not match. It gave colonial poets the urge to turn
their attention in the only direction where both psychological release
and artistic success could possibly lie – towards Africa itself, with its
cultural heritage and its own special traditions of art. Negritude
restored, too, those twin blessings of dignity and integrity which are
so necessary for the creation of enduring art.

And yet during the past decade the negritude poets have produced
little. 'There have been signs that the wellspring of Negritude is
running dry', wrote Moore and Beier in 1963, adding by way of
illustration that no less a poet than Birago Diop (who, however, could
be called a poet manqué) had produced 'only one slim volume of
verse in twenty years'.[21] The special conditions into which negritude
was born have changed. With most of the movement's cultural and
political objectives now achieved (the former were initially far more
important than the latter), to continue struggling would be an empty
exercise in fighting shadows. Other fronts must be opened up, yet
those worthy of the Muse's attention seem difficult to find. Former

leaders of the movement, notably Senghor himself, are now pre-
occupied with a flood of workaday problems which negritude's
political victories have brought to their doors. The present situation of
French West African poetry is explained by Mohamadou Kane, a
scholar from Senegal:

> Too taken up by the fight against colonialism, our literature
> seems to have lost sight of the need to prepare for the future: too
> conditioned by its involvement, it subordinated everything to it.
> The crisis it is going through now can be seen in the all too rare
> number of genuine literary works and in the silence of the 'great
> ones', often absorbed by political activities to the exclusion of
> everything else ... The present situation is the result of a crying
> need for new inspirations. A lot of old-time tenors seem to have
> had their day...[22]

There were, in any case, some elements in negritude which, by their
nature, could neither be tolerated nor remain vital for long. Senghor
admits that there was a certain youthful headiness about it; negritude
was 'intoxicating' and its disciples (including himself) were seized
with a racialism which betrayed 'African-Negro humanism'. It also
'led to deadlock by imposing cold war between races and continents,
between man and man'.[23] In an era when political freedom has been
won throughout the whole of French West Africa, and when negritude's cultural claims are widely respected, an afterstorm calm
prevails which calls for new poetic directions. It is as if the negritude
poets, emerging in triumph from the raucous din of war, have been
stricken dumb by the onslaught of silence. They are left puzzled and
uneasy, uncertain now which way to march.

As we shall see, it is largely because the British West Africans
are more familiar with this atmosphere, and, therefore, better
equipped to work in it, that 'the centre of poetic activity', in Moore
and Beier's words, 'seems to have shifted from Senegal – Paris to
Nigeria'.[24] To discover why the anglophone West Africans enjoy
this advantage it is necessary to understand something of the
difference between the major forms of European colonialism under
which the Guinea lands have lived. Such complex historical
phenomena are not easily susceptible of analysis. But in an essay
entitled 'Inglaterra, Francia, España', the historian Salvador de
Madariaga gaily cleaves his way through the labyrinthine
intricacies of imperialism to lay bare some of the dominant
features of three great European empires.[25]

According to de Madariaga, while the driving force behind Spanish
imperialism was religious, the French Empire was the child of a very

different impulse. 'French imperial growth', he argues, 'manifests itself as a systematic attempt to establish in the world a fine intellectual order.' While Spain had struggled for a spiritual principle, French policy, always secular, always indifferent in matters of religion, showed what he calls 'a tendency to organise the world into a kind of solar system, with Paris as its centre and sun'. The French Empire was thus to be a vast intellectual conception, 'un beau spectacle à ravir la pensée' rather than an extension of Christ's kingdom on earth. A belief in her own intellectual supremacy drove France forward; this, together with a highminded desire (which she still perhaps cherishes) 'to shine the light of her genius over the whole world'.

Alongside this intellectually ravishing spectacle of French imperialism, alongside this glimpse of a world illumined by 'le rayonnement de la France', de Madariaga stresses the more empirical nature of the British effort. Here there was no dominant passion, no intellectual vision, and, in consequence, no intransigent conditions, no preordained scheme of things. De Madariaga illustrates his point. Such rugged adventurers as Drake, Raleigh, Clive, and Cecil Rhodes were typical embodiments of British colonial empiricism: what is more, they were men who felt 'the impulse to expand, though one couldn't say that they saw this expansion clearly as a plan, as a future order'. They were empire-builders who resembled 'the buds of a vigorously potent tree or the limbs of a young and healthy body'. Far from imposing one standard pattern of rule on its far-flung territories, the pragmatic spirit of British colonialism allowed it to tailor styles of government to suit ethnic and cultural idiosyncrasies. In West Africa a policy of indirect rule was generally followed; but elsewhere Britannia's sway ranged from the pomp and luxury of the viceregal court of India down to the 'republican simplicity of the Australian Commonwealth'. Empirical, and invariably confined to the sphere of action, British colonialism involved itself mainly in economics; in things rather than people. There was a fair measure of liberalism, says de Madariaga, but always the inspiration was economic. And as for the much-vaunted British virtue of tolerance, he gives us these sobering remarks to ponder:

> The familiar English neutrality towards indigenous religions and repect for local forms of belief and worship is merely an oversight, resulting from the essentially economic orientation of English colonial activity. There is, at bottom, a good deal of indifference in this neutrality, just as there is, in English impartiality towards different sects and races, a huge gap – vertically – between coloniser and colonised.[26]

It may be true that British tolerance of local cultural forms sprang from indifference and not from enlightened benevolence; but we must insist that this 'tolerance' *is* a fact of British colonial history, and one, fortunately, which has worked to the advantage of writers in former British West Africa.

Now France's urge to shine the light of her spirit over colonial peoples assumed an instrumental form in her policy of assimilation, which, in Michael Crowder's words, was 'based on the revolutionary doctrine of the equality of man and at the same time on the assumption of the superiority of European, and in particular French, civilisation'.[27] Faced with men whom they considered barbarians, the French 'believed it their mission to convert them into Frenchmen. This implied a fundamental acceptance of their potential human equality, but a total dismissal of African culture as of any value'.

We can accept that a basically intellectual vision of empire underlay Gallic colonialism and still accommodate a fascinating claim by Crowder that only in Senegal, a small country enjoying long historic links with France, was the policy of assimilation applied with any degree of vigour and depth, and then only among those 'fortunate' Africans who lived in the *communes* of Dakar, Gorée, Rufisque, and St Louis. In splendid schools here, says Crowder, Africans sat side by side with the children of the large French community, enjoyed the same rigorous teaching and competed in the same examinations. Thus in tiny Senegal, a brilliant African élite was created deeply imbued with the spirit of French culture and civilisation. They were men who could distinguish themselves as Deputies in the French Assembly and were indeed assimilation's most resounding successes. What is obvious needs to be emphasised. Their assimilation was necessarily a cultural and intellectual process; and when, in the thirties, they eventually reacted against it, their protest, too, was cultural and intellectual. This was negritude, carried like a torch from Senghor's encounter with Césaire in Paris and thrust into the dormant heart of the African consciousness. It was not against their strict training that negritude's founders were reacting, but against the basic assumption underlying both this and the whole policy of assimilation – that Africans were a benighted people possessing neither history nor culture. Hence the sudden urge to return to roots from which assimilation had effectively cut them off; hence the protest literature of the Senegalese writers, Senghor, David Diop, and Birago Diop; hence the determined scholarly effort to rehabilitate African history; to prove, for example, that Egypt of the Pharaohs was a Negro civilisation; hence, in 1947, the founding by Alioune

Diop, yet another Senegalese, of *Présence Africaine,* a journal open 'to all contributors of good-will (white, yellow or black), who might be able to help define African originality and . . . hasten its introduction into the modern world'. Anxious to prove Africa's worth and dignity to their European masters, and to the white world at large, negritude's disciples took the French language in which they had been so conspicuously well-trained and used it as a vehicle for a great outburst of literary protest and assertion.

Elsewhere along the Gulf of Guinea, in Nigeria, Ghana, Sierra Leone, and the Gambia, Pax Britannica was producing far less excited reaction. Content to exercise the national genius for keeping decent law and order, and, with the notable exception of the missionaries, tolerant of, or indifferent to, indigenous culture, British rule left Africans pretty much as Africans. In the absence of rigorous cultural domination such as the French had imposed on Senegal, there was no cause for a culturally-centred protest, and indigenous art lived on largely undisturbed. Education was made available rather than imposed; and one should remember also that British rule in West Africa was of more recent vintage than the French presence in Senegal, which had dated from the eighteenth century. Cultural domination cannot be carried through overnight.

Reaction to British colonialism assumed political rather than cultural forms, a neat reversal of the francophone experience. It is a commonplace of modern African history that liberation movements were stronger, and developed much earlier, in Nigeria and Ghana than in Guinea, Mali, Senegal, and the Ivory Coast. But political leaders here, such as Azikiwe and Nkrumah, tended to be full-time politicians and not literary men (though Zik and Awolowo made gestures in this direction). When they seized their master's language to use as a weapon against him, it was for political journalism (witness Azikiwe's chain of newspapers), not for verse and prose fiction. French West Africa, on the other hand, was graced by the presence among its élite of men like Senghor who were distinguished both as statesmen and artists. And in Senegal especially, the example of Senghor quickly gave literary endeavour a stamp of respectability. Creative writing in the British states, however, could not so easily be identified with political eminence and high government office. Nor did the French writers make a significant impression on their anglophone neighbours, for communications were poor, translations were not widely available, and a knowledge of French, as a third tongue, could hardly be widespread in countries where, even now, complete fluency in two languages is rare.

25

Briefly, then, under a more empirical and 'materialistic' style of colonialism, British Africans reacted against political rather than cultural domination. The colonial power, while placing fetters on political freedom, did not set out deliberately to tamper with the African mind. It did not officially attempt to produce black Englishmen. Had it done so, worthwhile verse in English would have begun earlier and without doubt would have echoed the furious cries of negritude. Osadebay's work, given definite direction by commitment, would have gained in power; and instead of drawing on French translations, Bassir could have filled his anthology with good English writing. Without the intellectual provocation which French colonialism had brought to bear, it is not surprising that when creative writing in any quantity eventually appeared in the British territories, it was remarkable on the whole for its mature lack of bitterness and for what Ezekiel Mphahlele once called its 'overall steady pace and sedate mood', so different from the wild clamour of negritude. Clearly, even a late start can have its compensations.

But why did the upsurge of creative writing in English occur at all? It would be easy to suggest that growing nationalism in British West Africa created an exciting atmosphere, in which young talent felt called upon to come forward and give vent to patriotic sentiment. The truth is almost certainly more mundane. We are too ready to suppose that literary phenomena such as this must have a lofty and quasi-mystical explanation; and we are not ready enough to search for clues among people and institutions. We anxiously scan the heavens for the truth which stands on the earth before us. An atmosphere of excitement in West Africa there might have been; young talent might well have felt the call of national duty (though there is little evidence for this in the literature); but young talent, however richly endowed, needs careful training if it is to fulfil its promise.

Hence we should not be surprised that the spurt of literary activity which has marked the past decade in Nigeria can be traced largely to the University of Ibadan and to a group of its teachers who were sensitive enough to feel the rich literary potential of the Africans entrusted to their care. Under Professor Mahood, the English Department in particular gave its gifted students strong encouragement to write, though without offering formal courses in creative writing. Nkem Nwankwo, author of the novel *Danda,* said that he spent his time in Ibadan 'writing voraciously', and in an editorial introduction to *Nigerian Student Verse,* a slim volume published in 1960, the British scholar Martin Banham captured the spirit of the place when he roundly asserted that the stimulation of a national literature 'is as

26

much the job of a University as the formulation of some new scientific law'. The list of Nigeria's writers who were trained at Ibadan is long, and includes the novelists Achebe, Amadi, Nwapa, Munonye, and Nwankwo, and the poets Soyinka, Clark, Segun, Aig-Imoukhuede, and Okigbo.

From the middle of the fifties, Ibadan became increasingly a centre of literary activity. To stimulate this development even more, the University set up a syllabus in African literature while students exercised their talents in *Horn,* a thriving poetry magazine established by the poet J. P. Clark. Of major importance, too, was the presence in Ibadan of Ulli Beier, the German scholar who has exerted so remarkable an influence on both English and vernacular writers in Nigeria. Yoruba vernacular literature, and the drama especially, owes him a very great debt. Beier seized every opportunity to encourage indigenous writers and saw the need for physical channels through which his encouragement could be spread more widely. He was the moving spirit behind the establishment of Mbari Writers and Artists Club, which now has branches throughout Nigeria; and it was largely at Beier's instigation that *Black Orpheus* was founded, the English-language equivalent of *Présence Africaine,* in which Nigerian writers, and indeed writers from across the continent, found an outlet for their verse, short stories, and literary experiments. It was in the pages of *Black Orpheus,* too, that the beginnings of African literary criticism first appeared. Mbari soon established its own publishing house, thus helping to satisfy an important need, and making known thereby the work of the Nigerian writers Clark, Soyinka, and Okigbo, Ghana's Awoonor-Williams, Gambia's Lenrie Peters, and South Africa's Alex La Guma. *Nigeria Magazine* played an important role too. Writers and scholars like J. P. Clark, O. R. Dathorne, Robert July, Paul Theroux, and Mabel Segun, contributed work to this journal as well as to *Black Orpheus.*

These, then, have been some of the human and institutional influences attendant on the recent birth of Nigerian literature in English. Although to some extent caught between two worlds, the writers concerned were almost free to examine one world from the relative security of the other. Their writing, and particularly their verse, marked a definite break with the literature of tutelage. Here was verse as mature as Senghor's yet in a way more independent, for these men wrote out of themselves as individual Africans, formed no school and set no store by racial protest or group response. But before we examine the literature of those writers who were educated at Ibadan, we must turn first to Gabriel Okara, ironically one of the few

27

established Nigerian poets who did not train at Ibadan, and yet one of the most accomplished craftsmen of this new generation.

An Ijaw from the Niger Delta area and one of the older members of the modern group of Nigerian poets, Okara did not receive a university education but trained as a bookbinder prior to taking up a post with the then Government of Eastern Nigeria. Okara's verse was first published in 1957, in *Black Orpheus* ('We were pleased to discover Gabriel Okara for the first number', wrote its editor, Ulli Beier) at a time when Wole Soyinka, Chinua Achebe, Christopher Okigbo, and John Pepper Clark were unknown.[28] Mbari Publications, however, which with *Black Orpheus* has been a continual source of encouragement for African writers, has not yet brought out a collection of Okara's verse, so that he seems neglected in a way that lesser figures are not.

An item in *Cultural Events in Africa,* No. 34 (September 1967), mentions an announcement by the poet Christopher Okigbo that he and Chinua Achebe had set up a publishing house, Citadel Books Limited, in Enugu and planned to publish a collected edition of Okara's works. The announcement was made in a letter dated 29 May 1967. Soon after, the civil war broke out and *The Times* of London (24 October 1967) reported that Okigbo was killed during the Federal Army's seizure of the university town of Nsukka.

The superior quality of Okara's work seems to lie partly in its overall intensity of mood. Here is a committed poet, utterly sincere in all he brings to the poet's task and clearly anxious to persist in the cultivation of his poetic sensibility. His fellow poets are perhaps more prolific, at times more technically adventurous; but for the most part they lack the fine richness of soul, the pervading sense of an inner life and a constant preoccupation with the basic themes of life and death, which are the dominant features of Okara's work. A withdrawn, melancholy figure, Okara has something of the Celtic colour of soul, with its sensitivity and large resources of sadness, yet without the Celtic sense of humour. The lyrical 'I' means the collective 'we' for Okara and his private experience is felt to be one that is shared by his compatriots. He is Nigeria's best example of the poet singing in solitude yet singing for his fellow men.

His poetic objectives are clear enough. 'I think the immediate aim of African writing', he once said, 'is to put into the whirlpool of literature the African point of view, to put across how the African thinks.'[29] Given this aim, he was still faced with the problem of achieving it in a way that preserved his artistic identity as an African. Like all poets, he had to find his own voice, and his wide reading in

28

western literature made this a difficult task, though it equipped him
with the apparatus of a recognisably modern idiom. When, in 'Were I
to Choose', he writes

> When Adam broke the stone
> and red streams raged down to
> gather in the womb,
> an angel calmed the storm;[30]

one can almost hear the magisterial voice of Dylan Thomas sounding
forth with 'Before I Knocked and Flesh Let Enter'. Admittedly, the
poem continues with such tropically flavoured lines as 'the har-
mattan/of days has parched the throat/and skin, and sucked the
fever/of the head away'; but it is hard to be authentically African
while using the poetic voice of a Welshman, and Okara had to strike
out on a more independent path. A basic problem was linguistic in
nature. Despite the English language's history in Africa, despite its
having been 'transplanted' into African societies, poets choosing
to use it face a situation in which the poetic diction and imagery
provided for the home tradition are at odds with the features of their
own inner landscapes which have been shaped by an entirely different
culture and environment. One way of bridging this gap, which means
in effect the creation of a new, Africanised English idiom, is to use a
device which, for want of a more accurate term, we will call
transliteration. Okara decided that he would write his verse in his
native Ijaw and then translate it literally into English, the second
version being considered the primary work of art. 'To Paveba', a
poem which charts a characteristic movement in Okara's verse from
hope through joy to ultimate disillusionment, and which illustrates his
skill with symbols and structural organisation, usefully demonstrates
some of the marks of this experiment:

> When young fingers stir
> the fire smouldering in my inside
> the dead weight of years roll
> crashing to the ground
> and the fire begins to flame anew,
>
> *
>
> The fire begins to flame anew
> devouring the debris of years –
> the dry harmattan-sucked trees,
> the dry tearless faces
> smiling weightless smiles like breath
> that do not touch the ground.
>
> *

29

The fire begins to flame anew
And I laugh and shout to the eye
of the sky on the back of a fish
and I stand on the wayside
smiling the smile of the budding trees
at men and women whose insides
are filled with ashes who
tell me, 'We once had our flaming fire.'

*

Then I remember my vow.
I remember my vow not to let
my fire flame any more. And the dead
years rise creaking from the ground
and file slowly into my inside
and shyly push aside the young fingers
and smother the devouring flame.

*

And as before the fire smoulders in water,
continually smouldering beneath
the ashes with things I dare not tell
erupting from the hackneyed lore
of the beginning. For they die in the
        telling.

*

So let them be. Let them smoulder.
Let them smoulder in the living fire
        beneath the ashes.[31]

'The eye/of the sky' may well recall Greek practice; perhaps also the
Old English *daeges eage* and such Shakespearean references as 'There
serve your lusts, shadow'd from heaven's eye' (*Titus Andronicus*
II.i.130) or 'There's nothing situate under heaven's eye/But hath his
bound, in earth, in sea, in sky' (*Comedy of Errors* II.i.16). But it is the
Ijaw way of referring to the sun, too; and while there are these
precedents for it in European literary history, it is doubtful if Europe
can offer any modern parallels. It strikes us as a 'primal' way of
looking at the world, as though in Okara we are witnessing a familiar
poetic cycle beginning anew. It derives directly from the act of
transliteration; and, as we shall confirm later in our study of Okara's
prose, so also do the constant references to 'inside', the idea of years
being dead and of smiles being weightless. This last reference is a
familiar case of the Ijaw evaluating abstractions in terms of substance
or lack of it; but all three are basic aspects of Ijaw thinking and they

emerge by way of a device which allows the poet adequately to render authentic indigenous experience, 'to put into the whirlpool of literature the African point of view, to put across how the African thinks'. Through transliteration Okara has created a new idiom and found his own voice.

Okara likes to work with symbols, which he uses as signposts to the basic ideas his poem is investigating. Notice here the symbol of fire: 'young fingers stir/the fire smouldering in my inside', 'the fire begins to flame anew', 'the fire smoulders in water' and so on. Clearly, this represents warmth, vitality, growth, expectancy, elation. When the fire is stirred up it leads to the sudden gushing abandon of the third stanza:

> And I laugh and shout to the eye
> of the sky on the back of a fish
> and I stand on the wayside
> smiling the smile of budding trees . . .

Sharply opposed to the symbol of fire is the symbol of the ashes, representing quite clearly, death, despair and decay. Okara speaks of men and women 'whose insides/are filled with ashes', and of the fire 'continually smouldering beneath/the ashes'. Associated with this symbol is the idea of dryness; it is the dryness of infertility and death, the dryness that comes with age, when the sap of life and vitality is draining away. Hence, the 'dry harmattan-sucked trees', 'the debris of years', 'the dry tearless faces', and 'the dead weight of years' that 'roll/crashing to the ground'.

These symbols, then, point up the basic ideas of the poem, but they also neatly balance each other, satisfying an almost Augustan desire in Okara to build into his verse a symmetry that comes from a balance of opposing forces.

The poet, presumably, warms briefly to professions of love from a young lady – or rather he allows himself to entertain amorous thoughts about her – and then must remind himself that human love is, after all, mortal, just like human life; it will lead, inevitably, to the coldness of the grave. Now his choice of symbols enables Okara to render this basic idea imaginatively, because it makes possible a fine paradox; for, while it is in the nature of fire to give warmth and for its warmth to promote health and joy, so, too, is it in the nature of fire to consume, to kill, to destroy – a revelation that quickly comes to the poet after the old men and women, shrivelled and dry, have warned 'We once had our flaming fire'.

The final lines contain an unsatisfactory resolution, and the poet offers it in a mood of brooding resignation:

> So let them be. Let them smoulder.
> Let them smoulder in the living fire
>   beneath the ashes.

Notice that it is thematically, and, therefore, artistically, appropriate that the final line should bring the two symbols together, since there is, after all, the closest possible relationship between the fire and ashes. The central situation, we have said, seems to be one of love; but the meaning of this poem surely eddies out beyond this. Such, Okara seems to conclude, is the strange duality of human life, that joy and sorrow, happiness and tragedy, stand so close together.

Okara's use of transliteration does not confine him to purely African topics. Indeed, in 'The Snow Flakes Sail Gently Down', the poet's reaction to a snow scene, one finds some of Okara's most beautiful writing. Constructed around a picture of falling snow that is balanced by a dream of home, the poem is a strange mixture of elements tropical and northern. Its diction captures the quiet gentleness of falling snow, sibilants and controlled alliteration combining to create an effect of great smoothness:

> The snow flakes sail gently
> down from the misty eye of the sky
> and fall lightly lightly on the
> winter-weary elms. And the branches,
> winter-stripped and nude, slowly
> with the weight of weightless snow
> bow like grief-stricken mourners
> as white funeral cloth is slowly
> unrolled over deathless earth.
> And dead sleep stealthily from the
> heater rose and closed my eyes with
> the touch of silk cotton on water falling.[32]

As in 'To Paveba', Okara's success in this poem owes much to a balance of opposing elements; there is here, once again, a concern with the ideas of life and death that provide the infrastructure for what is, on the surface, a poem dealing with nature. Thus, in the first stanza, the landscape is pictured as a funeral scene of delicate and hushed beauty. The icy hand of winter has, for the moment, killed the earth and is now spreading over the corpse a vast 'funeral cloth' of snow; the 'winter-weary elms', meanwhile, bend slowly and reverently under their white mantles, like so many mourners paying dutiful homage to the earth.

In the second stanza, however, the theme of death is forgotten. The

poet dreams of Africa, fertile Africa basking in the sunshine. Birth
and growth become his theme:

> Then I dreamed a dream
> in my dead sleep. But I dreamed
> not of earth dying and elms a vigil
> keeping. I dreamed of birds, black
> birds flying in my inside, nesting
> and hatching on oil palms bearing suns
> for fruits and with roots denting the
> uprooters' spades. And I dreamed the
> uprooters tired and limp, leaning on my roots –
> their abandoned roots
> and the oil palms gave them each a sun.

Instead of bent 'winter-weary elms', he sees tall, upright palm trees
'bearing suns/for fruits' and with roots tough enough to dent spades.
The contrast is carefully planned. There is a contrast in colour, too,
for the nesting birds, symbolically black for the homeland, stand out
starkly against the poem's prevailing backcloth of white established
by the first stanza.

There is in this poem the typical Okara progression from sad
reality to an upsurge of joy and a return to reality once more. Thus,
after dreaming of Africa with its fruitfulness and life, the poet
awakens to the silently falling snow and, as it were, the triumph of the
death symbols:

> Then I awoke. I awoke
> to the silently falling snow
> and bent-backed elms bowing and
> swaying to the winter wind like
> white-robed Moslems salaaming at evening
> prayer, and the earth lying inscrutable
> like the face of a god in a shrine.

The image of the elms is the most effective in the poem. Aware of this
and conscious of the need for artistic unity, Okara uses it on two
occasions – at the beginning and at the end, the two key points in the
poem. But the poet's skill and sensibility go further; when the image is
repeated Okara seizes an opportunity to enrich his work by a subtle
change in the simile accompanyng it. In the first stanza, the elms'
branches, 'winter-stripped and nude', were said to 'bow like grief-
stricken mourners'; in the last, however, it is not the branches but the
'bent-backed elms' themselves that sway to 'the winter wind like/
white-robed Moslems salaaming at evening/prayer'. The image has
been slightly modified and expanded and in the process has, indeed,

been improved, for the hauntingly resonant 'salaaming' – surely a splendidly poetic word – adds a fine touch of the aural to an image essentially visual in nature.

With his language problem largely solved, and calling to mind his declared objectives, it is not surprising to find Okara focusing his attention on specifically African problems, especially on the painful situation in which he and most Africans find themselves – caught between two worlds and yet somehow having to reconcile them. In poems which discuss this dilemma, Okara is apt to use a series of locally culled images to mirror his turbulence of mind and soul. 'Piano and Drums', a poem whose title comprises symbols of the two worlds in conflict, outlines for us the nature of the poet's problem:

> When at break of day at a riverside
> I hear jungle drums telegraphing
> the mystic rhythm, urgent, raw
> like bleeding flesh, speaking of
> primal youth and the beginning,
> I see the panther ready to pounce,
> the leopard snarling about to leap
> and the hunters crouch with spears poised;
>
> *
>
> And my blood ripples, turns torrent,
> topples the years and at once I'm
> in my mother's lap a suckling;
> at once I'm walking simple
> paths with no innovations,
> rugged, fashioned with the baked
> warmth of hurrying feet and groping hearts
> in green leaves and wild flowers pulsing.
>
> *
>
> Then I hear a wailing piano
> solo speaking of complex ways
> in tear-furrowed concerto;
> of far-away lands
> and new horizons with
> coaxing diminuendo, counterpoint,
> crescendo. But lost in the labyrinth
> of its complexities, it ends in the middle
> of a phrase at a daggerpoint.
>
> *
>
> And I lost in the morning mist
> of an age at a riverside keep

wandering in the mystic rhythm
of jungle drums and the concerto.[33]

The drums which Okara can hear are beating out the 'mystic rhythm' of Africa, a spiritual pulse whose throbbing links the poet to his own, and the race's, childhood, with its 'simple/paths', its 'suckling' reassurance and its spontaneous harmony with the natural world; a link, too, with a dimly receding line of forebears. The poet next records his inescapable encounter with a modern world of strange and 'complex ways' – a world symbolised by the piano. The flood of nostalgia for a past evoked by the drum gives way to his response to a new order that has its attractions, too. The piano speaks 'of far-away lands/and new horizons with/coaxing diminuendo, counterpoint,/crescendo'. It briefly evokes a rather Romantic nostalgia that proves to be superficial and short-lived; for the 'complexities' it presents are labyrinthine, and the attractions of a world that had to be listened to end 'in the middle/of a phrase at a daggerpoint'. Clearly, if the poet could choose, he would live in the traditional world which has produced him. But it is a basic fact of life in present day Africa that no such choice is open to him. He can enjoy neither polarity exclusively, no matter how strongly attached he feels to either of them; neither the world symbolised by the drum nor that whose emblem is the piano. He remains, as he puts it in his marvellously allusive image, 'lost in the morning mist/of an age at a riverside ... wandering in the mystic rhythm/of jungle drums and the concerto'.

One might detect a curious discrepancy here, in that a poem containing Okara's lament that he is 'lost' between two worlds is itself a convincing manifestation of his ability to accept his situation, hold the two worlds, artistically, in a sort of precarious balance and even bring them towards synthesis. What was once written of the nineteenth-century Canadian poet D. C. Scott, an artist facing similar problems, could equally have been written of Okara: [He] 'is ... obsessed with the need to hold in synthesis the extremes of experience; he is constantly probing the nature and process of change – the Moment of Becoming ...'[34] This last expression seems acutely relevant here for it suggests the approach of a new order, in Okara's case one compounded of the old world and the new, where a neo-African culture will emerge; a culture which, like Okara's verse, is an exciting blend of western and indigenous elements but which, nevertheless, preserves its essentially African identity.

In the white Commonwealth and in the United States a major problem in the development of writing recognisably distinct from

British literature was the artist's imaginative adjustment to a land-scape which had never formed the environment of writers in the metropolitan tradition. The African experience has been somewhat different. While in the vernacular traditions the landcape of the continent has always been a perfectly normal ingredient, this has not always been true of African writing in English. Colonialism, with its mischievous effects on the psyche of the educated African, tended to generate writing that looked away from the continent towards the home of the ruling power. It created a situation in which a poet like Osadebay was apt to ignore, or only half acknowledge, the despised fact of Africa. Local description was rare, couched in the diction of an alien tradition, and unevocative of an authentic sense of place and time. In the French states negritude in the thirties directed the artist's attention to his own people and traditions; but the verse which emerged was often stylistically polemical rather than concretely descriptive of the landscape. One cannot scream loud and long at the white world and still spare much effort for the private contemplation of one's own environment. Hence, there was a need in West Africa, not to make an imaginative adjustment to an alien landscape (which was the need of Australian, American, and Canadian poets), but to *celebrate anew* a landscape which poets had largely forgotten. The situation is now being remedied. From the pens of the anglophone poets a more personal style of poetry is emerging, which, free of slogans and flag-waving, directs our attention towards the details of physical Africa and the natural phenomena that inform it. Indeed, in J. P. Clark's work it seems that this, rather than an Africanised style of language, is his particular answer to the problem of authenticity. Take, for example, his slight poem 'Streamside Exchange', a simple dialogue, in a rural African setting, between a child and a bird:

> Child: River bird, river bird,
> Sitting all day long
> On hook over grass,
> River bird, river bird,
> Sing to me a song
> Of all that pass
> And say,
> Will mother come back today?
>
> Bird: You cannot know
> And should not bother;
> Tide and market come and go
> And so has your mother.[35]

36

or again, his poem 'Night Rain':

What time of night it is
I do not know
Except that like some fish
Doped out of the deep
I have bobbed up bellywise
From stream of sleep
And no cocks crow.
It is drumming hard here
And I suppose everywhere
Droning with insistent ardour upon
Our roof thatch and shed
And thro' sheaves slit open
To lightning and rafters
I cannot quite make out overhead
Great water drops are dribbling
Falling like orange or mango
Fruits showered forth in the wind
Or perhaps I should say so
Much like beads I could in prayer tell
Them on string as they break
In wooden bowls and earthenware
Mother is busy now deploying
About our roomlet and floor.
Although it is so dark
I know her practised step as
She moves her bins, bags and vats
Out of the run of water
That like ants filing out of the wood
Will scatter and gain possession
Of the floor. Do not tremble then
But turn, brothers, turn upon your side
Of the loosening mats
To where the others lie.
We have drunk tonight of a spell
Deeper than the owl's or bat's
That wet of wings may not fly.
Bedraggled upon the iroko, they stand
Emptied of hearts, and
Therefore will not stir, no, not
Even at dawn for then
They must scurry in to hide.

So let us roll over on our back
And again roll to the beat
Of drumming all over the land
And under its ample soothing hand
Joined to that of the sea
We will settle to sleep of the innocent and free.[36]

The poems are examples of young talent soaring on trembling pinions. Clark has no settled style yet, and the second piece especially has a whiff of undergraduate days about it, giving an impression of good material inadequately controlled and organised. More to our purpose, however, is the direction in which the poet's imagination is turned. The setting of the first poem, undoubtedly taken from Clark's own Ijawland in the Niger Delta; the carefully pictured details of the second – the rain, the sleep mats, the wooden bowls and earthenware, diligent mother moving items about the floor, the owl and bat wet and forlorn on the iroko tree – these all indicate the poet's sensual and imaginative harmony with the rural life of Africa. But this in itself is not so significant as the more crucial fact that the poet's attention *is in fact* turned towards that life, a life which he has shared and is prepared to regard as worthy of his art. Despite the poet's university education there are no signs of cultural neurosis here. Clark is not a poet *déraciné*, and when he chooses a subject for his verse he evidently does not feel the pull of an alien landscape at his back; not for him the sad confusion of Osadebay. His work stands, too, at the opposite pole from the rant of negritude's more extreme outbursts: from Diop's 'Bitter memories of extorted kisses', Léon Damas' 'my hatred thrived on the margin of culture', or Césaire's 'Hurray for those who never invented anything'. Clark evidently feels no compulsion to write in this vein. As certain poems show, he is sensitive to Africa's pains, but by and large he enjoys inner peace and contentment, enjoys celebrating the harmony which he feels between himself and his African environment.

Clark's engagement with the local scene stems directly from his professed interests. He sees himself as a private poet anxious to communicate with an audience. Hence his concern for 'nature and actuality', which, he believes, 'provides the personal link between each poet and his audience'.[37] His poetic rendering of familiar aspects of the African scene – 'Fulani Cattle', 'Agbor Dancer', 'Tide Wash', 'For Granny' and the 'Water Maid' are examples additional to those already quoted – are, in his words, 'attempts to realise natural concrete subjects ... for the reader in a personal memorable way ... in the unconscious hope of adding some fresh dimension to life'.[38] Let us, finally, examine Clark's short poem 'The Year's First Rain', a piece mimetic of the first mighty encounter between parched Earth and the opening storm of the rainy season and aptly rendered as a cosmic sexual union:

> Rain comes . . .
> After long surcease in desert
> Rain comes,
> Hot-breathing, alert
> And swift to thunder-rolls and claps
> With kestrel-together-leaf flaps.
> And earth all the while waiting, waiting inert,
> Fallow and burdened with stone,
> Shudders to her rump,
> Tingles to the trump
> Of the long-missed one.
> Now with more than tongue can tell
> Thrusts he strokes her, swamps her,
> Enters all of him beyond her fell,
> Till in the calm and cool after
> All alone, earth yawns, limbers her stay,
> Swollen already with the life to break at day.[39]

This is a well-organised piece, and the gradual filling out of the lines in mimesis of the storm's development is skilfully done. More important for our discussion, however, the poem aptly illustrates how an African poet as 'liberated' as Clark can work with a local theme and yet do so in a style which echoes the metropolitan tradition. We have noticed Osadebay's reliance on British poetic diction and heard Okara imitating the voice of Dylan Thomas. The pull of the British tradition remains strong, for Clark here is obviously feeling the influence of Hopkins, a poet whose deliberately rude handling of language for special effect might be expected to appeal to a young free spirit like Clark. A further hint of an attachment to Hopkins comes in *A Reed in the Tide,* Clark's most recent book of verse, which includes a poem called 'Ibadan Dawn (After 'Pied Beauty')'. In the present poem with its kestrel image, its hyphenation and alliteration, there are strong and unmistakable echoes of 'The Windhover'.

Clark's artistic directions seem to be settled – he is eager to celebrate the details of the African landscape; but he still acknowledges European masters and enjoys imitating them. Unlike Okara, he does not seem concerned about developing a distinctly African poetic idiom. A young poet, developing rapidly, he is not yet so sensitive a craftsman as Okara, his fellow Ijaw. With Clark, one does not feel, yet, as one certainly feels with Okara, that he is anxious to view mankind *sub specie aeternitatis*; that when he writes he is trying, in Carlyle's memorable words, to 'plant for Eternity'.

Home growth

We have already mentioned Okara's attempt to create a new African idiom by working through his native Ijaw. Faced with the same problem, other poets have experimented in a different direction. Frank Aig-Imoukhuede felt that pidgin English might provide a solution. Here was a truly popular medium, with an ancestry in West Africa that made it almost a home growth, indelibly stamped with the linguistic idiosyncrasies of the people. Surely an indigenous poetic idiom could spring from roots such as these. Debate will no doubt continue; but in the meantime, Aig-Imoukhuede's poem 'One Wife for One Man' reveals the strengths and limitations of this experiment. Here are three stanzas from it:

> I done try go church, I done go for court
> Dem all day talk about di 'new culture':
> Dem talk about 'equality', dem mention 'divorce'
> Dem holler am so-tay my ear nearly cut;
>> One wife be for one man.
>
> *
>
> My fader before my fader get him wife borku.
> E no' get equality palaver; he live well
> For he be oga for im own house.
> But dat time done pass before white man come
> Wit 'im
>> One wife for one man
>
> *
>
> Suppose, self, say na so-so woman your wife dey born
> Suppose your wife sabe book, no'sabe make chop;
> Den, how you go tell man make'e no' go out
> Sake of dis divorce? Bo, dis culture na waya O!
>> Wen one wife be for one man.[40]

There is evidence here which points to the antiquity of this form of English, for words such as 'palaver', 'sabe', 'waya', and elsewhere in the poem, 'una' and 'pickin' are clearly of Portuguese derivation: Anglo-Saxons are apt to forget that Portuguese caravels were carrying traders, colonisers, and evangelists along the West Coast of Africa a decade before the end of the fifteenth century and almost sixty years before the birth of Shakespeare. But age alone will not endow so crude a language as pidgin with the richness and flexibility needed for literary art. Its disadvantages are not hard to unearth.

Could pidgin ever carry those qualities of resonance and subtlety which we have come to associate with great literature? The answer must be in the negative, although its possibilities for evoking a measure of pathos have been recognised, as these stanzas from our much-maligned friend Osadebay testify:

> Sometam I think about dis life
> And de trouble blackman see;
> Poor blackman, he must face big strife,
> Or fall down on him knees,
> When he must get some little good,
> Or put for him belly scanty food
>
> *
>
> I give my blood and life for you,
> But you no member me;
> My heart be clean, my word be true,
> My body no be free;
> Why must my feet be in your chain
> And you must chase me with your cane?
>
> *
>
> I no get gun, I no get bomb,
> I no fit fight no more;
> You bring your cross and make me dumb,
> My heart get plenty sore.
> You tell me close my eyes and pray,
> Your brudder thief my land away.[41]

But apart from this limited asset, the quaint illiteracy of pidgin makes it useful only for light-hearted comic verse or for tragi-comic effects, as in the plays of Soyinka; in any case, the majority of West African writers, who are sensitive lest they should acquire a 'Tutuola image', will be anxious that no further African 'curio' is seized on by the western world. In addition, among the growing ranks of lettered Africans pidgin is held to be the badge of the illiterate; and the illiterate is often cruelly despised. Even among the half-educated school of writers centred on Onitsha market, pidgin is a subject of mirth and derision, always given to the conservative old illiterates who are held up to ridicule. The Onitsha writers know that their audience will find pidgin English amusing. The point is important, for if Aig-Imoukhuede is thinking of pursuing his experiment, he will lack an audience to take him seriously. And the unschooled majority will never know his work, quite simply because they are illiterate and know pidgin only as a spoken, not as a written, language.

But the seriousness of Aig-Imoukhuede's experiment must not be understimated. He is one more example of an African poet who is eager to use English as his medium and yet find a voice which is at once African and genuinely his own. He would agree with Senghor's view of African writers that 'In so far as they are aware of African culture and draw inspiration from it, they rise to international status. In so far as they turn their backs on Mother Africa, they degenerate and are without interest.'[42] But his search for a highroad to artistic salvation has led to disenchantment with negritude's writers, who, he feels, have set up a fixed formula for poetic success and taken to absurd lengths their homage of all things Negro. He accepts the importance of roots, but rejects the negritude writers' way of expressing them. They do not provide an answer to his problem. Their style, moreover, represents, he feels, 'a strain that's both forced and unnatural'. Aig-Imoukhuede's dilemma, his attack on the francophone school and his plea for poetic freedom can all be found in some loosely formed verses called 'Negritude' which he published in an undated issue of *Black Orpheus* (No. 10). They are worth quoting in full, not because of some imagined poetic distinction, but because they provide, in a frankly autobiographical vein, an authentic account of a basic situation which this chapter has been discussing. The poet here is his own best commentator:

> Poor black Muse, since we must, under newlaid
>   laws worship at your altar
> Before true acclaim and recognition can come
>   our way, I have no other
> Course than to dance to puppet tunes and
>   'gainst all conscience
> Force on your new-tuned ears melody that's
>   strange and strained,
> Sounds claimed by some to symbolise the
>   throbbing passion of bonded peoples
> But which in their final effects create,
>   a face full of pimples,
> Slavering obscurities both inane and
>   incomprehensive . . .
> Yet I want to be known. I want my name
>   amongst the host of Afric's Prophets,
> To breathe out deep musings and fresh
>   feelings of the long-forgotten past.
> I already know your conditions; so you
>   apostles, here I come spewing groans
>   from the deep forest negritudine.

Deep down in Afric's forest by the stringy
   streams of Odindom (I hope this is a
   nice choice?)
There my spirit groans for the sweet silent
   past; the dead ancestral spirits
Awake all the native spirit in me, with
   throbbing drums and the music of freedom –
Boom-bam boom-bam room-boom-boom-bah
Tam, tam, boom boom hoompa hoompa hoomph!
By the waters of Odorono (a new variation of
   it!) hoompa hoomph

*

Spirits awaken lethargic souls taram pam
   boom –
No!
I cannot continue in a strain that's both
   forced and unnatural
The sounds, if you think they're 'negritudine',
   make the 'idiot boy' of me.
O Ne – negri – gri, gri-tud-thud! (does
   that sound well?) – tudes!
Why can't you leave the black Muse alone?
   Must you make rules
And thus standardise and commercialise that
   which differs from prophet to prophet?
I want to be known myself but this is not
   the means to that end
I don't care what people think of my verse,
   for what I write is me – negritudine
   or not.

The pidgin experiment, then, was a serious attempt by Aig-
Imoukhuede to solve a familiar African problem. Its results, however,
do not suggest that it can become a medium for interpreting Africa to
the world with any degree of poetic richness and complexity.

A comparative exercise

The abundant signs of increasing confidence among anglophone poets
in the validity and richness of their own background go some way
towards vindicating a claim made by the Ghanaian poet Kwesi Brew in
his poem 'Ancestral Faces', which describes a visit to modern Africa by
a group of his forefathers, and ends with the words:

43

They gazed,
And sweeping like white locusts through the forests
Saw the same men, slightly wizened,
Shuffle their sandalled feet to the same rhythms,
They heard the same words of wisdom uttered
Between puffs of pale blue smoke:
They saw us,
And said: They have not changed![43]

One can most vividly illustrate the difference between the literature of tutelage and the best neo-African writing by comparing two representative poems on virtually the same subject. One poem, Osadebay's 'Thoughts at the Victoria Beach', we have already seen; it was written between 1930 and 1950, and here again are its opening lines:

The Waters stretched from the tropic shores
And seemed to kiss the sunlit skies afar;
The waves riding in majesty,
Glided to and fro like lords of the silvery bar.
The oft washed sands gave forth a smile
To beautify the sphere and heaven extol;
The noble palm and mangrove trees
Stood with their heads aloft as the waters roll.
Poor mortals – birds and beasts and men –
Ran here and there in vain attempt to keep
Their lives from the quenching winds of death,
And sought in vain to solve the mysteries deep.

The other poem is Gabriel Okara's 'One Night at Victoria Beach' written about 1961. One detects immediately something of the vast changes that have taken place:

The wind comes rushing from the sea,
the waves curling like mambas strike
the sands and recoiling hiss in rage
washing the Aladuras' feet pressing hard
on the sand and with eyes fixed hard
on what only hearts can see, they shouting
pray, the Aladuras pray; and coming
from booths behind, compelling highlife
forces ears; and car lights startle pairs
arm in arm passing washer-words back
and forth like haggling sellers and buyers –

*

Still they pray, the Aladuras pray
with hands pressed against their hearts

and their white robes pressed against
their bodies by the wind; and drinking
palm-wine and beer, the people boast
at bars at the beach. Still they pray.

*

They pray, the Aladuras pray
to what only hearts can see while dead
fishermen long dead with bones rolling
nibbled clean by nibbling fishes, follow
four dead cowries shining like stars
into deep sea where fishes sit in judgement;
and living fishermen in dark huts
sit round dim lights with Babalawo
throwing their souls in four cowries
on sand, trying to see tomorrow.

*

Still, they pray, the Aladuras pray
to what only hearts can see behind
the curling waves and the sea, the stars
and the subduing unanimity of the sky
and their white bones beneath the sand.

*

And standing dead on dead sands,
I felt my knees touch living sands –
but the rushing wind killed the budding words.[44]

Despite the fact that they are both written in English, these poems
might well originate from entirely different parts of the world. Examining the first piece stylistically, a practical criticism class might reasonably assume that it came from a minor figure writing early in the
nineteenth century, but using the faded diction of the eighteenth. In
view of the reference to 'tropic shores' and 'The noble palm', they might
further suspect that the author was an Englishman recalling a visit to an
unspecified area of the tropics. Despite Osadebay's dedication of his
collection 'To The Heroes and Heroines of New Africa and to All the
Friends of Africa', Africa as a particular locale, noisy with people
and strife, does not appear. Significantly, the poet is looking out to sea
with his back turned on the continent. He is standing on African soil
but will not see Africa. Perhaps his account is more concerned with
what J. P. Clark calls an attempt 'to prove Young Africa had become
the equal, if not the better, of the Englishman at his own language'.[45] If
so, one need only add that, to succeed in this exercise, the African
behind the poetic mask must remain firmly hidden and suppressed.

45

Okara's poem is quite different; for here is the work of a man free enough to write out of himself and give untrammelled vent to his sensibility – a twentieth-century African responding to his situation without having to turn a blind eye on his own background; without feeling obliged to please or imitate the representatives of the metropolitan tradition. Osadebay went down to the beach and looked away from Africa; Okara went there specifically to look *at* Africa. He knew that here in the coastal towns, especially in capital cities like Lagos, the sensitive front line between Old Africa and the western world can be found. Phrases like 'cultural synthesis' and 'the moment of becoming' have most meaning here, for this is where the struggle between the two worlds is most easily discerned; this is where Okara can most easily see in miniature the basic condition of his country, and indeed of his part of the continent. This is precisely what his glimpse of the beach in Lagos gives him: a telescopic view of modern West Africa in all its pain and confusion.

The idea of the old and the new in conflict is skilfully woven into the texture of the poem. The old order is portrayed in the rather weird picture of the Aladuras shouting their prayers into the wind, their insistent chant being echoed by the poet's monotonous and constantly repeated words 'they pray, the Aladuras pray'. The past is called up, too, by the reference to dead fishermen, the ancestors whose bones give new life to 'dead sands', whose surviving influence reassures the poet, just as we have seen it reassure men like Senghor and Diop. The living descendants of these long dead fishermen are found indulging in the time-honoured pastime of using the divining board to try and peer into the future. They are the living representatives of Old Africa and their pastime serves to emphasise a strongly spiritual quality which Okara associates with the old order.

The old dispensation is balanced by the poet's sketch of the new order, which we cannot fail to recognise as a version of the western world resplendent in all its crude and shoddy glory. Unlike the old dispensation, it is frankly materialistic in nature, and is seen in 'compelling highlife', a bastardised form of traditional music, in the glare of car headlights, in noisy folk drinking at makeshift bars, and in couples who are courting with a vulgarity Old Africa, past or present, would never countenance. These last are lovers whom Okara acidly describes as 'passing washer-words back/and forth like haggling sellers and buyers'. Alongside representatives of the old order stands this sordid modernism, which imitates the worst and most superficial elements of western culture and spurns the claims of an indigenous past. And yet, Okara believes, it is this very past which clutches the seeds of hope for the future; here lies the potential spring from which the dead sands of the present will be watered.

Stylistically, Okara is the master of his idiom, dominating the language and making it work to fine poetic effect. Unlike Osadebay, he has won his freedom and found his poetic voice; he does not lie passive before the idols of an alien convention. Take, for example, the question of imagery. In one poem the images are static and carry only a faint imprint of a specific locale; in the other they are alive with movement and sound which call up the environment from which they arise. The image of the waves is a case in point. As Osadebay saw them, they 'Glided to and fro like lords of the silvery/bar', an image culled apparently from legal ceremonial, though the reference to 'silvery' is puzzling. There is little sense of movement here, except of a restrained, dignified sort. For Okara, however, the waves do not behave so decently. In an image combining the forces of sound, simile, and mimesis, they 'Curling like mambas strike/the sands and recoiling hiss in rage/washing the Aladuras' feet.' The image is clear, violent, and African, and carries with it the immediacy of the graphic present. It flows (literally and figuratively) into the central image of the poem, which is the inset of the Aladuras chanting their evening prayers. Like the poem of which it is part, the image is felt to be working on two levels; for the washing action of the waves as they sweep over the Aladuras' feet is at once plainly realistic and yet potent with spiritual significance, thus lending support to one of the basic issues of the poem. Notice, too, how constant repetition (strongly reminiscent of African oral practice) creates a suitable atmosphere for the spiritual side of the poem by giving a 'monotonous' tone to the verse, suggestive of ritual, litanies and incantation.

Okara's work is 'liberated' in a way that Osadebay's is not; and this freedom is vital, for it allows him as an African to hold the glass up to his own experience, to his own people and his own times. There are other liberated poets in West Africa, too; but, for the most part, they do not share Okara's acute perception of Africa's basic problems, nor, more importantly, the exquisite sensitivity of his response to them. Few are yet capable of shaping an image quite so magical as, say, Okara's 'And I lost in the morning mist/of an age at a riverside'. Few can load their verse with quite so much tension, keep their material so tightly under control, and draw so lucid a line of poetic argument. When comparing Okara with other West African poets, with, for example, J. P. Clark, one might quote the words of Eliot in 'Tradition and the Individual Talent' to put a finger on their essential difference: 'the mind of the mature poet', he says, 'differs from that of the immature one not precisely in any valuation of "personality", not being necessarily more interesting, of having "more to say", but rather by being a more finely perfected medium in which special, or very varied, feelings are at liberty to enter into new combintions.'[46] Okara's mind is an instrument of this order of refinement; and through it West African verse in English has been helped to maturity. He has, however, certain rivals in Nigeria: one is that prodigiously talented poet Wole Soyinka.

Soyinka as poet

It was a day of darkness, in the midst of a year of plague. Some time before his birth, the mother's body was marked by the terrible signs of disease, and when the child first entered 'upon the vast concavity of the Cimmerian night', the door of the little house in which he was born was scrawled over with the fatal cross of red, while the mournful tolling of a bell heralded the approach of the ghastly, creaking tumbril that did service for a common hearse.

Thus wrote Marcel Schwob, in his *Vies Imaginaires* (1896), about the birth of the Jacobean dramatist Cyril Tourneur. He might have guessed, in equally spine-chilling detail, about the birth of Wole Soyinka, a poet with all the gloomy disenchantment and turbulence of soul of a Tourneur or a Webster. He, too, brought these marks from the womb; they were branded on his soul at the moment of conception; and his experience of life in a brutal world has served only to burn in the marks more deeply.

Soyinka, still young, has shown a capacity for youthful joy – a sensuousess, a rich laughter, a playful irony. We have had that rollicking essay 'Salutations to the Gut', written in honour of Opapala, the god of food and all gourmands; we have had the ironic humour of 'Telephone Conversation' and the mirth of *The Lion and the Jewel*. But it is clear now that these were mere *jeux d'esprit*, lighthearted interludes in a career whose underlying mood has grown increasingly dark. The main landmarks of Soyinka's career have been *A Dance of the Forests, The Road, Kongi's Harvest,* and his collection of verse, *Indanre and Other Poems* – all of them brilliant expositions of a profoundly pessimistic view of the human condition.

Comparisons between Soyinka and the dramatists of Jacobean London are often heard; on the whole, they are just. Victorian parallels are less frequently drawn; yet there is a sense in which the Nigerian poet stands comparison with that eminent Victorian Matthew Arnold. Soyinka, it is true, is never found yearning for days gone by when 'life ran gaily as the sparkling Thames': romantic nostalgia of this sort he

leaves to less tough-minded contemporaries. But he would applaud
Arnold's diagnosis of 'this strange disease of modern life,/With its sick
hurry, its divided aims'; and the final stanza of 'Dover Beach', with its
'ignorant armies', and its central image of a 'darkling plain' (where the
participle forecasts *increasing* gloom) might have come from the pen of
Soyinka himself. There is one further similarity: both can, with justice,
be called 'grey' poets.

Soyinka is a poet of twilight zones, be they between night and day or
day and night, life and death, or death and life. They are areas of
transition for which he has an abiding fascination; for they are those
areas in which he can most fully explore certain basic facts about life
and death. *The Road* alone is enough to suggest that no other poet or
dramatist in the English language has explored so extensively, and with
such wrapt fascination, that shrouded middle passage between death,
fleshly dissolution, and arrival in the other world.

Grey, then, is a dominant colour. Soyinka calls a whole section of
Idanre and Other Poems grey seasons; but the colour, in fact, pervades
his work as a whole. In 'I think it Rains', a poem whose tension springs
from its subtle opposition of wet and dry, fruit and sterility, we find the
stanza:

> I saw it raise
> The sudden cloud, from ashes. Settling
> They joined in a ring of grey; within
> The circling spirit.[47]

There is a reference to 'grey essence' in the poem 'Prisoner', which
begins:

> Grey, to the low grass cropping
> Slung, wet-lichened, wisps from such
> Smoke heaviness, elusive of thin blades
> Curl inwards to the earth, breed
> The grey hours,
>
> *
>
> And days, and years, for do not
> The wise grey temples we shall build
> To febrile years, here begin – not
> In tears and ashes, but on the sad mocking
> Threads, compulsive of the hour?[48]

One can see, too, that the ideas implied by this choice of colour are
borne also by words like 'wisps', 'smoke', 'febrile', and 'ashes'. In
'Season', we find 'wood-smoke', 'shadows from the dusk' and 'the
wilted corn plume'. 'In Memory of Segun Awolowo' ends with the
lines

49

> Grey presences of head and hands
> Who wander still
> Adrift from understanding.[49]

It is the 'Lake mists' and veils of 'dawn' that attract Soyinka as he flies over the Luo Plains of Kenya. His 'Death in the Dawn' is a vivid conjuring of greys and twilights, while his eerily cold piece 'Post Mortem' concludes with a ghostly echo of Hopkins:

> let us love all things of grey; grey slabs
> grey scalpel, one grey sleep and form,
> grey images.[50]

Soyinka, who would agree with Pound's dictum about loading the language of verse with as much meaning as it can bear, is often a difficult poet. He dictates the terms on which a reader must approach him; and, apart from an occasional explanatory note, no concessions are offered. To complicate matters further, Soyinka is a poet for whom the traditional Yoruba cosmology is a potent fact in his imaginative life, and, thus, in the art he creates. Without a working knowledge of the Yoruba background, his work cannot fully be understood; and this presents a handicap even to non-Yoruba Nigerians. The Yoruba cosmology, embodied in Ifa, the traditional religious system of his people, constantly underlies his work and has provided growth points for his artistic development. An essential point about Soyinka, then, and one which firmly marks him off from his fellow West African poets, is that *he is still working within a traditional system*; a system which allows him to explore the problems of creation and existence from a philosophical home base. He has not felt obliged to cast off traditional thinking and dress himself in the tattered remnants of alien philosophies. Not for Soyinka the myth-building problems of Yeats or Blake's desperate cry, 'I must create a system or be enslaved by another man's.' And this, perhaps, is why his scorn of negritude has always sounded so confident. Its disciples' prideful strutting was, in any case, a natural target for his satiric mind; a mind that seems always to have been convinced of man's absurdity, his innate imperfection, and the futility of his grandiose assertions. There was something further. More acutely than anyone else, Soyinka seemed to detect an element of the spurious in negritude's professed objective of reaching back for cultural roots. Christian and westernised, its disciples were, in effect, reaching back for what was no longer there. There was a celebration of convenient symbols and trophies from the past – the external *bric à brac* that could easily be appealed to – but not the *essence* of the past, its systems of thought, which had been discarded for ever. Where they hoped to assert their African-ness by praise poems for the mask or in

50

verse sung to African instrumental accompaniment, Soyinka has worked with the essence itself. He has never renounced it; his appeal to it is spontaneous and natural. Nor is this mere lip service, for he is imaginatively engaged with a tradition that still happens to be alive. He is the only West African poet who, in this philosophical sense, can be said to do so. Hence his complete lack of nostalgia, his lack of that melancholy recollection of a dying world that marks so much West African verse. One cannot wax nostalgic about current affairs. With Soyinka there is no problem of authenticity.

This is not to say that he rejects the modern world with its new insights and its expanding scientific knowledge. His education in Nigeria and England has enabled him to absorb much that is modern; he is learned in the modern disciplines, and his style itself – recognisably modern – is evidence of absorption and adaptation. A modern grafting has been performed on a vigorous traditional plant. Or, to state it in his own way, he has achieved 'the ideal fusion – to preserve the original uniqueness and yet absorb another essence'. It means that Soyinka's work can be both strongly local and excitingly universal.

In the midst of a debate on its precise meaning, one can still suggest that where other religious and philosophical systems have rapidly withered before the advance of Christianity in Africa, Ifa, despite the assertions of some Christian spokesmen, still potently insists its cosmology and its values on the Yoruba people. There is no comparison, for example, between the current strength of Ifa among the Yoruba and the strength of traditional religion among, say, the Ibo of Nigeria or the Luo and Kikuyu of Kenya. Fela Sowande, himself a Christian, speaks of the 'silent shrines and deserted temples scattered all over Yorubaland'; but he is prepared to make the following firm prediction about his people's ancestral religion:

Ifa will not die, because Ifa cannot die; it cannot die, because it is the Africanised Ageless Wisdom, and like the Phoenix, it will always arise from its own ashes, fresh, young, invigorated, dynamic, instinct with new life and new vitality, to run another course. Every nation has its own equivalent of this Ageless Wisdom, for there is but one Source, and it is for this reason that the gods and goddesses of one Pantheon can be properly and usefully correlated with the gods and goddesses of another Pantheon ... But with reference to Yoruba Traditional Religion, we must recognize from the start that this Religion is but one single aspect of a System embracing all of Yoruba Traditional life ... [5]

There is an attractive human-ness about Ifa, for its gods lived among men, and usually shared man's foibles. It also offers a convincing reading of the universe, especially in its insistence on a divine balance of forces, which, as a rule, ensures harmony, but which results in chaos when the balance is disturbed. Ifa has not only survived; it has become modernised. Such is its flexibility that Sango, the god of thunder and lightning, has, with perfect ease, become also the god of electricity. Ogun, a god of prodigious power and responsibility, the deity associated with iron and metals generally, with war, exploration, artisans, and creativity, is now also the god of the roads and the god of workers. He would preside as naturally over Ibadan's Department of Metallurgy as Jeremy Bentham over the London School of Economics. There is, then, in Ifa, besides its human-ness, an open-ness and flexibility which have allowed it to survive into the modern world. It also enjoys what Sowande calls 'a Diversified Unity, and not a Unified Diversity likely to come apart at the seams'.

These may be some of the reasons why, as Jahn points out, Ifa has been exported into the West Indies and South America more successfully than any other African religion. From Haiti to Brazil vestiges are still found, and especially in Voodoo. Ogun and Obatala are almost as well known in these parts as they are in West Africa. This, then, is the system within which Soyinka works. There are two central tenets, however, which he uses in particular, and which can often be felt to underlie his poetic argument. One is the idea of reincarnation, an important belief in Ifa. The second, an idea closely associated with the first, is the cyclical nature of existence – of life and death following one another interminably *in saecula saeculorum*. Life is always on the brink of death; death, for its part, is forever on the brink of life.

Much of Soyinka's verse cannot fully be understood without some knowledge of the Yoruba background. 'Death in the Dawn' is a simple example. It *can* be read at a certain level of comprehension without the background knowledge; but it emerges as a subtler piece of writing when some of its local allusions are appreciated. Here it is:

> Traveller, you must set out
> At dawn. And wipe your feet upon
> The dog-nose wetness of earth.
>
> *
>
> Let sunrise quench your lamps, and watch
> Faint brush pricklings in the sky light
> Cottoned feet to break the early earthworm
> On the hoe. Now shadows stretch with sap
> Not twilight's death and sad prostration
>
> *

This soft kindling, soft receding breeds
Racing joys and apprehensions for
A naked day, burdened hulks retract,
Stoop to the mist in faceless throng
To wake the silent markets – swift, mute
Processions on grey byways . . .

*

On this
Counterpane, it was –
Sudden winter at the death
Of dawn's lone trumpeter, cascades
Of white feather-flakes, but it proved
A futile rite. Propitiation sped
Grimly on, before.

*

The right foot for joy, the left, dread
And the mother prayed, Child
May you never walk
When the road waits, famished.
Traveller you must set forth
At dawn

*

I promise marvels of the holy hour
Presages as the white cock's flapped
Perverse impalement – as who would dare
The wrathful wings of man's Progression . . .

*

But such another Wraith! Brother,
Silenced in the startled hug of
Your invention – is this mocked grimace
This closed contortion – I?[52]

The main events of the poem are explained in Soyinka's kind prefatory note: *Driving to Lagos one morning a white cockerel flew out of the dusk* [the use of 'dusk' here instead of 'dawn' is significant of the poet's cast of mind] *and smashed itself against my windscreen. A mile further I came across a motor accident and a freshly dead man in the smash.* The idea of a cock as a sacrificial offering, for divination as well as propitiation, is accessible enough. Nor is it hard to imagine that the words 'right foot for joy, the left, dread' have a local Yoruba reference. But the lines 'May you never walk/When the road waits, famished' have only a superficial meaning for the reader who is unaware that Soyinka is saying that it is Ogun, the *god* of the road, not simply the road itself, that waits famished; he is hungry for food, whatever its form, whether humans slain by accident, or dogs deliberately killed by his taxi-driving devotees. Then there is an allusion which even the most sensitive reader might miss. It occurs at that point in the poem where Soyinka reaches the crash scene and grows briefly cynical over the idea of human progress. He asks, 'is this mocked grimace/This closed contortion – I?' The point about the poet's humanity being mirrored in this ghastly scene, and the withering reflection this casts on the idea of human progress, is easily taken. But the word 'mock' here is loaded with an allusion that links this final scene with the incident of the cock impalement earlier in the poem. For, curiously enough, the Yoruba have an idiomatic saying 'to kill a cock in someone's mouth', which means, precisely, to mock. The cock killed on the poet's windscreen, killed almost in his mouth, presaged in a mocking way the disaster he was soon to encounter on the road. A slight point, perhaps, but it gives the verse a richer texture of meanings, a more tightly-knit organisation, than it might otherwise be allowed. It is a point that would be inaccessible without a modicum of knowledge of the poet's Yoruba background.

A similar case is the poem 'Season':

> Rust is ripeness, rust,
> And the wilted corn-plume;
> Pollen is mating-time when swallows
> Weave a dance
> Of feathered arrows
> Thread corn-stalks in winged
> Streaks of light. And, we loved to hear
> Spliced phrases of the wind, to hear
> Rasps in the field, where corn-leaves
> Pierce like bamboo slivers.
>
> *
>
> Now, garnerers we
> Awaiting rust on tassels, draw
> Long shadows from the dusk, wreathe
> Dry thatch in wood-smoke. Laden stalks
> Ride the germ's decay – we await
> The promise of the rust.[53]

Ostensibly a poem of the harvest season, an African ode to autumn that even a western reader can appreciate, the verse explores the human situation through nature reference. We men are like harvesters waiting for the fruit of life to mature (to rust), so that we can gather it in and move on to death, which is the fruit, the 'promise', of life at its most mature.

There is a good deal of compression here which, again, a sensitive outsider might detect. The sudden change of tense which comes with the verb 'we loved', for example, skilfully hints at a whole graph of life, the curving line from childhood to old age. What might be missed without some background knowledge is the depth of meaning given to that innocent opening phrase 'Rust is ripeness', a meaning which sends sap to the very roots of the piece. At one level of course the meaning is obvious enough: ripeness stands cheek by jowl with decay, which is what rust is; and the colour of rust on fruit is often a sign of ripeness. But the words are loaded more heavily than this; there are other resonances which make this essentially a Yoruba poem. Behind the piece, one suspects, stands Ogun. Now, Ogun's season is the harvest and the rains. The season which gives the poem its title is *his* season. It needs only a reminder that Ogun is also the god of iron and metal to germinate the idea that Ogun's life-giving rain at work on his own metal (used in any case for the garnering), produces, quite simply, rust, in the literal sense of the word. Ogun is at once the god of creativity and (via his metal weaponry) the god of death. In harvest time, the life, the fruit he has brought to ripeness, is already (as rust) dissolving into death.

The poem 'Abiku' also contains allusions to Yoruba life which are alien to the outside reader. The topic itself is essentially a Yoruba one, for Abiku is the spirit child who dies and keeps returning to plague its mother. J. P. Clark, an Ijaw, has written a poem on the same subject; but the belief belongs to Yoruba tradition not to the Ijaw. The references to branding on the child a tell-tale mark, to squirrel teeth cracking the riddle of the palm, and god's swollen foot (meaning the foot of a tree), are likewise Yoruba references and are often hard to follow. But what clearly emerge as central ideas in the poem are the cyclical nature of creation and the notion of reincarnation, both of which are fundamental tenets of Ifa. Significantly, the child says that it will return as the 'Suppliant snake coiled on the doorstep', and that its mother's will be 'the killing cry'. This is a parallel reference to the tail-devouring snake found in the poem 'Idanre' – used there as insignia for Ogun, who wears this kind of decoration round his neck as a symbol of the doom of eternal repetition. The final stanza contains ideas which were also basic to the poem 'Season':

> The ripest fruit was saddest;
> Where I crept, the warmth was cloying.
> In silence of webs, Abiku moans, shaping
> Mounds from the yolk.[54]

'The ripest fruit was saddest' is a restatement of the idea that life, at its fullest, is closest to death. Abiku is ready for death and ready for rebirth; the cycle must go on. The child moans, 'shaping/Mounds from the yolk', that is, building burial mounds from the sap of life.

'Idanre', Soyinka's account of Ogun's creation pilgrimage to the earth, is, to date, by far his most extensive and ambitious poem. Firmly based in the traditional Ifa system and containing within itself those main lines of thought that have marked Soyinka's verse throughout his career, this is a darkly powerful piece of work that in parts has a strong flavour of the mythopoeic about it. It is a difficult poem whose genesis Soyinka himself can best describe:

Idanre was born of two separate halves of the same experience. The first was a visit to the rockhills of that name, a god-suffused grazing of primal giants and mastodons, petrified through some strange history, suckled by mists and clouds. Three years later and some two hundred miles away, a rainstorm rived apart the intervening years and space, leaving a sediment of disquiet which linked me to lingering, unresolved sensations of my first climb up Idanre. I abandoned my work – it was middle of the night – and walked. Idanre is the record of that walk through wet woods on the outskirts of Molete, a pilgrimage to Idanre in company of presences such as dilate the head and erase known worlds. We returned at dawn, the sun was rising just below the hut where we had sheltered on the outward journey. The palm wine girl still waited, the only other human being awake in the vast prescient night, yet an eternal presence whose charity had earthed me from the sublimating essence of the night.

There was a final, postscript image. The rainstorm was the first of the season, yet it had the breath of harvest from the first thunderclap. And as the sun rose over a tarmac hill, the year's harvest followed it in extravagant procession, rich, glorious, sensuous with life.

I took my leave of her, my companions had vanished, I returned home wet from overladen boughs, brittle as the herald lightning to a storm. By nightfall that same day, Idanre was completed.[55]

Ogun is the rather satanic hero of the poem. Since he is 'the septuple one', the god who carries seven gourds with him into battle, it is not unfitting that the poem should be divided into seven sections. The first is deluge . . , a scene of violent primeval activity, where, in a raging storm and Cimmerian darkness torn only by lightning flashes, earth is in the process of creation. Ogun and Sango are at work, the one hurling his lightning about the sky, the other pouring on the rain of creation and running Sango to earth:[56]

Gone, and except for horseman briefly
Thawed, lit in deep cloud mirrors, lost
The skymen of Void's regenerate Wastes
Striding vast across
My still inchoate earth

*

The flaming corkscrew etches sharp affinities
(No dream, no vision, no delirium of the dissolute)
When roaring vats of an unstoppered heaven deluge
Earth in fevered distillations, potent with
The fire of the axe-handed one

*

And greys are violent now, laced with
Whiteburns, tremulous in fire tracings
On detonating peaks. Ogun is still on such
Combatant angles, poised to a fresh descent
Fiery axe-heads fly about his feet.

In the fury of this storm, the first of the actual season (Ogun's season) in Nigeria, and, for the poet's purpose, seen as the first storm of creation, Ogun is beginning his pilgrimage to earth. He is the god of the creative essence – the rain he brings promises new life. He is also of course the god of war who tempers his promise of life abundant with the threat of death. It is a sort of bloody conferring of life and death together. The threat of destruction is hinted at in the 'Cowls of ashes' that 'sweep about' Ogun's face, where ashes are meant as a token for death and dissolution. The hint is there; but the section ends on a note of rich promise, of anticipation of halcyon days ahead (p. 62):

> And no one speaks of secrets in this land
> Only, that the skin be bared to welcome rain
> And earth prepare, that seeds may swell
> And roots take flesh within her, and men
> Wake naked into harvest-tide.

This is deliciously sensuous writing spoilt only by the clever way in which our attention is drawn to the use of 'Wake' at the start of the last line. Sensuousness yields abruptly to word play, as Soyinka teases us with the though that 'Wade naked into harvest-tide' might have been a more appropriate, certainly a more sensuous, choice.

There is violence in the first section; but it is violence fraught with the promise of life. In the second section, ... *and after*, the promise, in keeping with the strangely dual nature of Ogun, is not completely fulfilled; or at least, it is fulfilled and then instantly blighted. The threat of doom hangs over a scene that appeared to be growing increasingly 'blissful'. We thus find stanzas celebrating the joy of Ogun's coming balanced, inevitably, by stanzas insisting on the bloody side of his mission. The wine girl, for example, who, Soyinka tells us, is a representational fusion of Sango and Ogun, first appears in a scene of relaxed, sunny happiness (p. 63):

> Calm, beyond interpreting, she sat and in her grace
> Shared wine with us. The quiet of the night
> Shawled us together, secure she was in knowledge
> Of that night's benediction. Ogun smiled his peace
> Upon her, and we rose.

But this rich serenity is shattered in an instant when, in the very next stanza, the girl appears as the dead victim of a hideous car smash. The lovely wine girl becomes 'a greying skull/On blooded highways', her lone face filled with sadness. Only moments before, Ogun, as the god of creation and of the harvest, had smiled his peace upon her; now, as the god of the road, as the god of war, he greedily slaughters her. But the mood changes again, and the fourth stanza of the section re-establishes an atmosphere of peace and plenty (pp. 63–4):

> Harvest night, and time to walk with fruit
> Between your lips, on psalming feet. We walked
> Silently across a haze of corn, and Ogun
> Teased his ears with tassels, his footprints
> Future furrows for the giant root
> His head was lost among palm towers
> And power pylons.

After a delightful inset of Ogun lying on high tension wires, slung in a hammock, and letting Sango's electricity flow over his shoulders, the mood darkens once more as the god's association with the highways is developed – that constant theme in Soyinka's work that reaches its culmination in his play *The Road*. Ogun's greed is emphasised. He is 'a demanding god' and the roads provide abundant meat for his diet. But again, using that curious idea of life *in* death and death *in* life, the poet suggests that this very slaughter, caused and demanded by the god, is in a way conducive to creativeness and new growth, those other aspects of the deity's nature and function. Hence the weird fusion of decay and fertility in the following description of a car hulk rotting by the roadside (p. 65):

> The weeds grow sinuous through gaunt corrosions
> Skeletons of speed, earth mounds raised towards
> Their seeming exhumation; growth is greener where
> Rich blood has spilt; brain and marrow make
> Fat manure with sheep's excrement

After some fine surrealistic writing, in which the poet describes some childhood fantasies, the section ends with Ogun bringing order to the world. He makes harmony out of dissonance, imposes a pattern on chaos, teaches the whole of creation to dance and sing (p. 68):

> He reached a large hand to tension wires
> And plucked a string: earth was a surreal bowl
> Of sounds and mystic timbres, his fingers
> Drew warring elements to a union of being
>
> *
>
> And taught the veins to dance, of earth of rock
> Of tree, sky, of fire and rain, of flesh of man
> And woman. Ogun is the god that ventures first
> His path one loop of time, one iron coil
> Earth's broken rings were healed

Ogun's path, then, his pilgrimage to earth, is an annual event, 'one loop of time'. The same point is made more firmly in the third section, *pilgrimage*. The journey Ogun is making is both his first pilgrimage and the annual pilgrimage he has been making ever since. This is how the Yoruba account for the seasons, and for the strange flow of human existence which is marked by waves of joy and waves of sadness, waves of plenty and waves of drought, waves of life and waves of death – all following, one after another, in an endless cyclical motion. Ogun explains it himself (p. 69):

> *This road have I trodden in a time beyond*
> *Memory of fallen leaves, beyond*
> *Thread of fossil on the slate, yet I must*
> *This way again. Let all wait the circulation*
> *Of time's acrobat, who pray*
>
> *
>
> *For dissolution: the chronicle abides in clay texts*
> *And fossil textures.*

After section four, which describes Ogun and the gods settling down to an earthly existence, we reach section five, *the battle*. As its name suggests, it is given over to the bloodier side of Ogun's life on earth. As the poet explains, Ogun, having reluctantly been made king of Ira, gets drunk while leading his men into battle. Instead of destroying the enemy, he turns on his own warriors and wreaks appalling carnage among them. His men shout to try and bring him to his senses; but all to no avail (p. 75):

> This blade he forged, its progress
> Never falters, rivulets on it so swift
> The blood forgets to clot

*

59

> There are falling ears of corn
> And ripe melons tumble from the heads
> Of noisy women, crying
>
> *
>
> Lust-blind god, gore-drunk Hunter
> Monster deity, you destroy your men!
>
> *
>
> He strides sweat encrusted
> Bristles on risen tendons
> Porcupine and barbed. Again he turns
> Into his men, a butcher's axe
> Rises and sinks

He is called a murderer, a cannibal; but the cries fall on deaf ears. 'His being incarnate', says the poet, 'Bathes in carnage, anoints godhead/In Carnage.' To the cries for help, Esu, the troublesome god of fate, who also happens to be present, will not listen either. The 'little prince of games sat/On his head, and he was deaf to identifying/Cries.' The fate of Ogun's men was a cruel one (p. 78):

> And they were cast adrift, without
> Direction for new prayers, their cry
> For partial succour brought a total hand
> That smothered life on crimson plains
> With too much answering

Eventually, the drunken god grows sober; he realises his mistake: 'Passion slowly yielded to remorse'. But it was (p. 80):

> Too late for joy, the Hunter stayed his hand
> The chute of truth opened from red furnaces
> And Ogun stayed his hand
>
> *
>
> Truth, a late dawn,
>
> *
>
> Life, the two-cowrie change of the dealer
> In trinkets lay about him in broken threads
> Oh the squirrel ran up an *iroko* tree
> And the hunter's chase
> Was ended.

Aside from its mythic basis, its attempt to explain a universal pattern, this section clearly has a contemporary relevance. The actual seems hinted at in that line deliberately set apart for display – 'Truth, a late dawn' – and also in two earlier lines of the section, lines that are bitter and assertive: 'Post mortem is for quacks and chroniclers/Who failed at divination.' At moments like these, the main narrative seems to make way for brief private comment on the contemporary scene.

Section six, *recessional,* is an important stage in the poem's development, and one in which the more personal statement, the conclusions drawn from the night's experience, are emphasised. It recounts the return journey, the poet coming home from his night spent in the woods and rain. The night is ending; so, too, its furious cataclysmic upheavals. Dawn approaches. One central reflection seems to emerge from the night's events. While the previous sections of the poem have been insisting on the cyclic pattern of Ogun's pilgrimage, its eternal inevitability, Soyinka now seems to ask: Are we, in fact, slaves to this pattern? Is it really so inevitable? Can it, indeed, be broken? In a sense, the Yoruba system within which Soyinka is working, itself provides one answer. For, as Soyinka reminds us, the Yoruba believe that Atunda, slave to the first deity, 'Either from pique or revolutionary ideas ... rolled a rock down on his unsuspecting master, smashing him to bits, and creating the multiple godhead.' The significance of this is that Atunda's action created diversity. Hence Ogun, though a monstrously powerful god, is, after all, only one god among many; his annual visitation, and the mixed blessings associated with it, represents but one pattern, though, of course, an important one. But Atunda brings a promise of diversity, variety of patterns; and he is praised heartily for it. The section becomes not only a celebration of diversity, but a vigorous plea for it. It is only a short step now to an *apologia* for the artist's independence, for the importance of uniqueness, of individuality. There is a plea for boldness, new directions, unfettered private growth and exploration – a plea, above all, for freedom in a myriad forms.

Incredibly, we find that Ogun, who seems to be all things to all men, can help here: is he not a bold innovating character himself? Is he not, after all, the god of adventurers and explorers? The 'self-devouring snake' pattern which he imposes can perhaps be modified. The ring which is its symbol can have a kink beaten into it (pp. 82–3):

> You who have borne the first separation, bide you
> Severed still; he who guards the Creative Flint
> Walks, purged spirit, contemptuous of womb-yearnings
> He shall teach us to ignite our several kilns
> And glory in each bronzed emergence.
>
> *
>
> All hail Saint Atunda, First revolutionary
> Grand iconoclast at genesis – and the rest in logic
> Zeus, Osiris, Jahweh, Christ in trifoliate

61

Pact with creation, and the wisdom of Orunmila, Ifa
Divining eyes, multiform
*

Evolution of the self-devouring snake to spatials
New in symbol, banked loop of the 'Mobius Strip'
And interlock of re-creative rings, one surface
Yet full comb of angles, uni-plane, yet sensuous with
Complexities of mind and motion.

The 'Mobius Strip' Soyinka explains as follows (pp. 87–8):

A mathe-magical ring, infinite in self-recreation into independent
but linked rings and therefore the freest conceivable (to me)
symbol of human or divine (e.g. Yoruba, Olympian) relationships.
A symbol of optimism also, as it gives the illusion of a 'kink' in the
circle and a possible centrifugal escape from the eternal cycle of
karmas that has become the evil history of man. Only an illusion
but a poetic one, for the Mobius strip is a very simple figure of
aesthetic and scientific truths and contradictions. In this sense, it
is the symbol of Ogun in particular, and an evolution from the
tail-devouring snake which he sometimes hangs around his neck
and symbolizes the doom of repetition.

Soyinka, then, is advocating what Fela Sowande described as a characteristic of Ifa itself, namely, a 'Diversified Unity', a many in one, the
multiform in the uniform. Within the pattern, the individual must fly
free; he must, even like Ogun and Atunda, show the spirit of adventure,
assert his uniqueness, his importance. As Soyinka puts it (pp. 81–2):

It will be time enough, and space, when we are dead
To be a spoonful of the protoplasmic broth
Cold in wind-tunnels, lava flow of nether worlds
Deaf to thunder blind to light, comatose
In one omni-sentient cauldron
*

Time enough to abdicate to astral tidiness
The all in one, superior annihilation of the poet's
Diversity – oh how his words condemn him, who declared
A fragrance in the stars, plunged to the mind's abyss
In contemplation of a desert well
*

Rather, may we celebrate the stray electron, defiant
Of patterns, celebrate the splitting of the gods
Canonisation of the strong hand of a slave who set
The rock in revolution – and the Boulder cannot
Up the hill in time's unwind.

The emphasis in section seven, *harvest,* returns to the promise of peace and plenty. Parts here read like a magnificent fulfilment of J. P. Clark's poem 'The Year's First Rain', which ended with an image of the earth 'Swollen already with the life to break at day'. Ogun withdraws into the forests, there is 'A dawn of bright processions', and then (p. 85):

> The first fruits rose from subterranean hoards
> First in our vision, corn sheaves rose over hill
> Long before the bearers, domes of eggs and flesh
> Of palm fruit, red, oil black, froth flew in sun bubbles
> Burst over throngs of golden gourds.

This is writing of a rare sensuous quality, unequalled by any other West African poet. Soyinka is describing the promise fulfilled, the promise heralded by the storm and the bloodshed. Reflecting on his country's sad contemporary history, which has parallelled Ogun's bloody pilgrimage, he laments that it is this and 'the brief sun-led promise of earth's forgiveness' that are awaited to round out, to complete, the cycle. Yet even in this final section, Ogun's dual nature as creator and killer, and the doom of repetition that he symbolises, are insisted on; for the closing stanza of this dark poem states that the golden harvest is already, in its egregious ripeness, moving towards decay, towards 'resorption in His alloy essence'. The cycle must go on.

The poem, then, with its dark backcloth and its epic resonances, provides convincing testimony not only to Soyinka's stature as a poet, but also to his ability to work within the traditional Ifa system. That there was something both timely and timeless about its inspiration is suggested in Soyinka's Preface (pp. 57–8):

> *Idanre* lost its mystification early enough. As events gathered pace and unreason around me I recognised it as part of a pattern of awareness which began when I wrote *A Dance of the Forests.* In detail, in the human context of my society, *Idanre* has made abundant sense. (The town of Idanre itself was the first to cut its bridge, its only link with the rest of the region during the uprising of October '65.) And since then, the bloody origin of Ogun's pilgrimage has been, in true cyclic manner most bloodily re-enacted.

Prodigals

Some Nigerian poets, most notably Michael Echeruo and Christopher Okigbo, do not seem as anxious as Soyinka and Okara to fashion their art wherever possible from traditional African material; yet their work is of major importance, and, in Okigbo's case, highly influential.

63

When Dr Echeruo delivered a lecture at Nsukka in 1966 called 'Traditional and Borrowed Elements in Nigerian Poetry' (it was later printed in *Nigeria Magazine,* No. 89) he established himself as one of the best literary critics in modern Africa. It was a skilful performance, tackling a difficult topic with incisiveness and tough intellectual independence. An exercise in the kind of scholarship that is kicking away the row of little boxes that have long stood before the house of criticism, it brought to a discussion of African verse insights gained from Eliot and Pound, from Tennyson, Arnold, and Vergil. It became, too, a statement of Echeruo's own artistic creed, and this was important, for though he was represented in Moore and Beier's anthology by only one piece, 'Sophia', Echeruo is now a poet of substance; a collection of his verse called *Mortality* was published in 1968. When, after quoting in his lecture the line 'Fate is a fully determined thing' from the close of an Old English poem, Echeruo remarks that modern European and Nigerian poetry have chosen to avoid so obvious a moral statement, 'preferring, for the most part, to fuse setting and reflecting into one poetic moment', he is talking about a preferred personal practice as well as indicating a development in European and African verse. Setting and reflection are certainly fused in this way in his poem 'Prologue', where Echeruo plays games with the familiar European cliches about darkness and light in Africa. The scene consists of early converts to Christianity gathered round their new church (p. 41):

> They turned their glances
> to the high roof;
> anxious with grimaces
> on their obvious faces;
> waiting for the Angelus
> and candlelights
> in the stagnant summer heat.
>
> *
>
> Some sang aloud:
> 'Save us, O save us
> from the jitters
> of our prime.'
> And some others:
> 'Hail! Alleluia!
> The doctors are gone;
> our sores shall fester
> in our hands till dawn,
> and the light of the sun
> shall shine us whole.'

We could hear other noises
from the juke-box.

*

The celebrants turned pale
with the dimmed lights;
and then commenced the apocalypse
of a sordid generation.

Setting and reflection are also fused in 'Ure Igne', where, in the midst of a normal scene at Sunday Mass, we are given the poet's private response to, amongst others, the curious celibate-sexual tension that the Catholic Church creates in her African followers, and to the idea of a man coming before others as a representative of God – as Father O'Brien does in the poem (p. 43):

Arrested
in the heart of a moment of reflection,
soul searches oracles for solace,
for gestures, ritual, communion,
for the logos.

*

Nnenna from the choirstand
soul-sings for young O'Brien naming apostles,
Petri et Pauli, while sacred fingers
consecrated and friendly
carry the chalice with devotion,
pleading *non sum dignus*
for her and those others
(*nobis quoque peccatoribus*)
while praying for the Fire.

*

Young pliant daughter of Christ
from the school of the Holy Rosary
sings at the choir to the Father
the god-written canticles of Solomon
to call down the Lord God
for O'Brien.

*

*If I met you outside, I would kiss you
and none would despise me.
I would lead you and bring you
into the house of my mother,
into the house of her that conceived me.*

The triangular conflict between the poet, Nnenna of the choir, and

O'Brien (an Orwellian echo as well as a convenient label for Irish Missionary Catholicism?), is skilfully worked out against a background of Christian liturgy and remembered African tradition, while a vein of rich ambiguity flows through the piece from the 'oracles' of the opening lines to 'a covenant of peace' at the close.

A fusion of setting and reflection is also found in 'The Signature', in 'Rain', and in 'Daedalus', which the author calls a poetic manifesto and a personal definition of African poetry. It ends (p. 51):

> Some stand today before the warped memory
> Of a silent people;
> And spin out fine the thousand profundities
> Of my as-it-were good people.

It is all part of what Echeruo calls the task of 'suppressing the over-explicit nature of traditional reflective poetry and of encouraging a more subtle complication of narration, reflection, and resolution'. The fusion he calls for is hard to manage, and he takes J. P. Clark to task precisely because he feels it is absent from a poem like 'Olumo Rock', where the rock is 'only an occasion for some reflection', and then not on the wider subject of nature but on the poet himself.

Echeruo complained at Nsukka about an 'oracular pose' that he found in much African verse, and he seemed to link this with the danger inherent in lyric writing of descending to cheap self-dramatisation. Significantly, there is not much 'I' poetry in Echeruo's collection, and where it occurs one is often unsure whether the voice belongs to the poet or to a *persona*. Anxious to avoid striking a pose, the poet chooses a plain diction and, on the whole, a calm delivery. The poems are apt to proceed in a straightforward, logical manner, Echeruo choosing to reach his objectives through argument and tone rather than through ornate language and sheer dramatic effect. He stands, in this respect, close to the practice of the South African poet Dennis Brutus. Echeruo has admitted a regard for the work of an unpublished friend, Kalu Uka, who 'conceives of his poems as philosophical statements, as propositions for truth', and who seeks to find the meaning of life 'not only by recalling the processes of life, but, primarily, by speculation on the significance of those processes'. This approach appeals strongly to Echeruo:

> In this respect, there is considerable affinity of interest between his idea of the poetic subject and that which has sustained some of my own poems. In 'Sophia', for example, I sought to represent the many faces of life, love and knowledge, all symbolized in the pregnant name of Sophia. The poem was meant to be a philosophical argument, no more.

'Man and God Distinguished' is in the same vein as 'Sophia'. The poet was reflecting on the paradox of man's splendour and his inconsequence, and used the idea of religion and God as a way into his subject. It begins (p. 42):

> Man sees the stars
> and turns aside
> suspicious of such tidings
> on a perilous midnight.
>
> *
>
> Man turns his face
> from the terrors of incense
> for the tigers are howling
> when Man means to go home
> on a star-spangled midnight.

This, says the poet, 'is not a consolation piece, nor a call for a return to Christianity. It is an attempt at statement.'

In Echeruo's view, Christopher Okigbo's verse is perhaps the most important landmark in the development of Nigerian poetry, and the Nsukka lecture gradually turns into an eloquent eulogy of this now deceased Ibo poet. Directly referring to Okigbo's method, he declares that we do not see the maturing of lyric talent in modern Nigerian verse until 'we move from the poetry of song and dance to that of "logistics"'. Echeruo defines two kinds of imagination, one belonging to the 'natural' poet, the other to poets of a more distinctly 'literary' mould. Both Okigbo and himself belong in the latter group. 'The indebtedness of a poet who is "literary" will', says Echeruo, 'appear there on the page, explicit.' It is another way of saying that some African poets, and particularly he and Okigbo, see themselves artistically as citizens of the world, the inheritors of a universal tradition of art and letters and not just as the recipients of an indigenous legacy. Hence Okigbo can rejoice in his catholicity and in his reforging of material from as much of the world of art as he can explore. Okigbo did not want African verse to be shackled within its own respected traditions. Hence his plea for freedom to venture where he would and his Shelleyian vision of the significance of verse. He once said that African literature 'is simply literature written in Africa' and that it is 'absurd to imagine it is a particular type, with solid traits that are particularly African, particular values associated with African civilisation'. This is neither scorn of his fellow writers nor a rejection of roots, but rather a bid for artistic freedom. A writer will naturally go to his own environment for material; but he must be at liberty to go elsewhere, too, especially if he is a modern scholar inheriting a world culture. Thus in Okigbo as in Eliot, the dead poets from different civilisations are briefly reborn, and monuments to their memory are carefully placed in the author's own artistic garden, which of course must inevitably be an African one. Are the images and thoughts from Pound, Eliot or Vergil, which are so obvious in Okigbo's verse, out of place in the art of a society where village oral performances in verse and song and tale consist in the recalling and refashioning of work from a myriad bards among the dead? Traditional Nigerian poetry, as Echeruo remarks, has not been concerned with the idea of poetry as pure pattern, which is one description of the Okigbo attitude; but neither has it shunned the steady accretion of richness which is implied in Okigbo's whole poetic effort.

But Gerald Moore is quite correct when he argues in *The Chosen Tongue* that poets like Okigbo largely ignore the technical devices of African traitional verse and 'make use of metrical, stanzaic and rhyming devices offered by the new language'. Okigbo, he says, 'uses the type of broken melody perfected by T. S. Eliot to evoke the reproachful sadness of abandoned shrines and rotting images, symbols which quite naturally carry the whole weight of an African tradition which has always concentrated the expression of its values upon them'. Okigbo's 'fractured and haunting lines', he says, 'mark a formal break with African poetic tradition, but they exploit the resources of English in a manner which matches exactly the shattered, undying gods they celebrate'. He cites the following lines from 'Limits' as evidence (p. 143):

> And the gods lie in state
> And the gods lie in state
> > without the long drum.
> >
> > *
>
> And the gods lie unsung
> And the gods lie
> > veiled only with mould,
> Behind the shrinehouse.
>
> *
>
> Gods grow out,
> > abandoned;
> And so do they ...

But a formal break with African poetic tradition is not a rejection of roots. Okigbo has not lost faith in Africa and neither has Echeruo, whose statement on the mixed elements in Okigbo's writing could well be applied largely to his own:

Okigbo's poetry is a poetry of the responses to pattern and organization. His poetry is also the poetry of an African, a native.

Its significance derives from these two elements. On the one hand, a very strong traditional feeling ... a feeling for the subject of Africa; on the other, an 'individual' poet who loves to write, not as an African, but as a 'prodigal' ...

The civil war brought Okigbo's career to a tragic and untimely close. But his influence lives on and his achievements stand acknowledged. *Busara,* Vol. II, No. 3 (1969) published the following 'In Memoriam' by Benedict Ogutu, a Luo poet from Kenya:

> Now I know –
> The pen is fallen and broken
> It is time for poets to die.
> Now I know –
> The muse MUST speak to men.
> It seems you were a warrior
> Venturing between peril and
> Peace stealthily stealing in.
> Now I know –
> From waters
> Of beginning
> Silence
> Has
> Limits.

To appreciate the full extent to which West African verse in English has achieved maturity and independence it is necessary only to compare the poetry of Equiano or Osadebay with, say, Okigbo's

> I have listened in cornfields
>   among the windplayers
> I have listened to the wind leaning
>   over its loveliest fragment.
>   ('Heavensgate')

or Soyinka's

> Rust is ripeness, rust
> And the wilted corn-plume;
>   ('Season')

or Okara's

> The snowflakes sail gently
> down from the misty eye of the sky
> and fall lightly lightly on the
> winter-weary elms.
>   ('The Snowflakes Sail Gently Down')

or Echeruo's

> I spat on the world from between my gums,

Shouted at the moon from between my lungs,
Hooted at the chirrupy mermaid of the dusk . . .
('Outsider')

There is a spirit of freedom abroad. Poets have found their own voices. They are no longer slavishly imitative, or imitate only when they have good artistic reasons for doing so. The age of colonial romanticism is dead. Some poets, like Okara and Aig-Imoukhuede, still seem aware of the problem of authenticity; others, however, such as Okigbo and Echeruo, seem scarcely aware of its existence. Echeruo in his Nsukka lecture complained of a lack of good lyric verse among the moderns. Yet surely his own 'Come, Come Spring' and 'The Singers', not to mention the achievements of Okara, have made good this omission. He also lamented the absence of any work approaching the epic. Now, with Soyinka's *Idanre*, even that lofty requirement has been satisfied.

3. *West African prose*

Appearance and reality

When a hitherto preliterate society acquires the use of the written word, one might expect that forms of literature based on prose will easily flower, since the ability to write prose is plainly coextensive with literacy itself. Those who can write, can write prose. The same line of thought might lead one to suspect that once literacy has been acquired, the art of simple reporting will soon be reached; and from there to a more creative use of the written word should be a relatively easy step. British literary history, however, provides evidence to the contrary. Looking back on the Anglo-Saxon period, to take the most vivid example, it is astonishing to discover how a civilisation with only a modicum of literacy produced in written form a substantial body of magnificent verse amidst so much consistently dull prose. The quality of *Beowulf* and the Elegies, doubtless the fruit of a highly developed tradition of craftsmanship, contrasts sharply with the honest prose of Alfred and a line of anonymous chroniclers. *The Conversion of Edwin* is remarkable largely because it represents a rare moment of glory in Anglo-Saxon prose.

Why did prose lag so seriously behind verse in Anglo-Saxon England? Some might argue that the national genius was simply poetic rather than prosaic, as perhaps the Italian genius has been. Whatever the reason, it does seem certain that the Germanic people's oral traditions had long contained a cherished and carefully cultivated art of poesy, so that in a literate age scribes were able to commit to writing the mature fruits of an ancient artistic heritage.

The modern African experience, despite initial appearances, has not been much different. There is, indeed, an enormous amount of prose writing coming out of anglophone West Africa (and Africans can no longer complain of publishing difficulties); but even a superficial scrutiny establishes that the bulk of it is poor in quality and merely satisfies an anthropological fad for Africa that the western world is currently enjoying. West Africans by the score are telling a fascinated public (mainly overseas) about their indigenous way of life, and, doubtless proceeding on the common assumption that we all have at

71

least one piece of fiction in us, are calling their efforts 'novels'. Criticism, unfortunately, allows this term to cover writing which lies at both extremes on the scale of artistic merit, and a masterpiece of Dickens or Jane Austen must shelter beneath the same roof as an offering from Agatha Christie, Ian Fleming, or, in the present context, Flora Nwapa, Obi Egbuna, Elechi Amadi, John Munonye, and a host of others waiting for recognition. Much of the fare provided, though unworthy of critical consideration, is engaging enough: painstakingly illustrative of strange lives and societies, it offers western readers an inexpensive trip from secure, humdrum Europe to a world still felt to be dark and forbidding. Those with a taste in autobiography might be well satisfied; but scholars looking for signs of a developing Sterne or George Eliot will be disappointed. Certainly, in the anglophone states, this writing will bear no qualitative comparison with the much smaller output of West African verse and drama. Unlike the development it has undergone in the hands of French Africans like Beti, Laye, and Oyono, here it is a form in its infancy – weak and faltering, largely uncertain of itself, and lacking (or showing in embryonic form only) most of the skills that make prose fiction artistically arresting. One suspects that Soyinka was particularly alluding to prose when he wrote in his article 'The Writer in an African State' (*Transition*, No. 31, p. 12):

> Publishers hovered like benevolent vultures on the still foetus of the African Muse. At a given signal they tore off bits and pieces, fanned up with powerful wings delusions of significance in commonness and banality. The average published writer in the first few years of the post-colonial era was the most celebrated skin of inconsequence ever to obscure the true flesh of the African dilemma.

It is not irrelevant to call to mind the Anglo-Saxon experience; for, again in West Africa, while there is evidence enough that verse has enjoyed a long history in the oral traditions, the same is not true of prose forms. True, Africa has always loved its tales and a good raconteur practises an immensely popular art. But oral tales and tall stories about the gods do not necessarily become good novels when they appear in print, if they become novels at all. The world of myth and fantasy, explored by Tutuola, holds little attraction for the majority of West African prose writers, who prefer to work with the more tangible substance of the contemporary scene and tackle the special problems their society is facing. Realism rather than fantasy is what they would choose. Hence they can derive little strength from their oral traditions, beyond perhaps the confidence to tell an engaging tale and tell it well. Facing their oral heritage they are singularly less fortunate than the poets.

A point needing emphasis is that we are dealing here with a funda-mental change in the use of language. To persuade with the written word is a basically different art from persuading with the spoken word and the leap from oral tradition to the 'Gutenberg Galaxy' bristles with problems for those who would study the process in detail. It represents an area ripe for intensive study. At a superficial level, Croll's essays on Ciceronianism and the Baroque suggest one line of approach.[1] Croll suggests that the Ciceronian school had cultivated and taught essen-tially oratorical arts, the effective manipulation of language as it is spoken and heard. He suspects that the rise of the anti-Ciceronian movement and the age of Baroque coincided with a crucial shift in the political habits of Europe away from the orator's scaffold into the seclusion of the statesman's private study.[2] A cultivation of the powers of the written, as opposed to the spoken, word began; hence the rise of the essay form, of Montaigne and Bacon, of the splendid prose of Taylor, Browne, and Hooker. That it was (despite the worthy efforts of Gascoigne, Grange, and Deloney) nearly a century later before real fiction as we know it began, after Defoe, Addison, and Steele had turned their attention to the workaday scene, suggests how long an apprenticeship English prose served before it became a vehicle for good fiction. If the process was so slow in England, there is no reason why it should be notably rapid in West Africa, where literacy is only a new arrival.

This is not to deny that the prose fiction scene in West Africa is one of ferment, and, in the case of a few writers, one of real promise. Furious activity and current ease of publication are creating an atmos-phere of stimulation which encourages literary talent to come forward and test itself. Nor is fiction writing confined to a particular social group. On the contrary, it is pouring forth from all ranks of society and at every level of literacy – from university dons down to humble doormen and half-educated schoolboys; from Achebe and Soyinka down to Tutuola and the Onitsha authors of such pamphlets as *Beware of Harlots and Many Friends, Why Boys Never Trust Money-Monger Girls, Drunkards Believe Bar as Heaven,* and *About the Husband and Wife Who Hate Themselves.* Themes, too, range from powerful recreations of pre-colonial society down to frankly impudent novelettes, and tracts offering moral guidance in an increasingly wicked world. Audiences are growing. At home, according to Achebe's testimony, a large section of the educated have become readers of West Africa's own writers, while even those with but the thinnest veneer of literacy find instructive entertainment in the cheap pamphlets of the Onitsha school. This latter group, as we shall see, has its own significance. Nowhere in the world outside Onitsha Market can ambitious schoolboys so readily achieve publication of their first faltering literary efforts; and in Nigeria such youthful writers are encouraging the growth of a distinctly urban or picaresque style of fiction which reflects their posture in the current struggle between the two cultures. They are part, however, of a scene whose predominant characteristic is dynamism rather than achievement. A problem of exclusion arises: this study attempts to focus on what seem to be the most promising and significant areas of prose writing.

Novels and stories

BORGES: Novels haven't impressed me as much as stories . . . Anyway, the novel is a form that may pass, doubtless will pass; but I don't think the story will.

MORENO: *Why not?*

BORGES: It's so much older . . . And also, even if there were a stop to writing stories, there wouldn't be to telling them. I don't think that novels could go on being re-told, do you? Take the *Quijote* as an example of a great novel. The *Quijote* can be read, and it can be re-read a number of times. But I don't know if you could relate it orally. If you just tried to tell about it, you'd sound rather foolish . . . Nowadays the novelist is considered superior to those writing in other forms, just as it was believed at one time that the writer of epic poetry was superior, or the author of a five-act drama . . .

(Cesar Fernandez Moreno, 'Weary of Labyrinths', An Interview with Jorge Luis Borges, *Encounter* (April 1969), p. 13.)

This South American dialogue, with its quietly voiced truths about the story and the novel – the antiquity of the one form, the youth of the other, the oral nature of the one, the essentially written nature of the other – has a timely relevance for modern Africa. It can be used to caution the growing throngs of critics who are heaping adulation on the African novel. From one end of the continent to the other, the African novel is being cried up. From book reviews, radio reviews, and the pages of scholarly journals, the cry has gone forth. The candles are lit; the ritual is begun; heads are bowed; holy water is sprinkled; the worshippers kneel in reverence. In universities across the world, the sacred word has been preached. Wise heads nod together; grave discussion proceeds. All this for a handful of good written fiction, and for a small group of successful novelists. Poets are mentioned; dramatists are acknowledged; but it is the novelist who is feted; it is at his shrine that the faithful gather.

What are the reasons for this? The power of the printed word? The assimilation of western literary tastes? One cannot be sure. But what can be affirmed is that the novel, as it is known in the West, precisely because it is a written form, has no history whatever in Africa. The continent has had its own fictive tradition; but it has been the tradition of the story, narrated orally. This, and not the novel form as we know it, has been the medium through which Africa down the centuries has bared its soul, taught its sons, and entertained itself. While the novelist, whatever his talent, is sought out for scrutiny, and usually for acclaim, the story-teller rots in neglect. Yet he belongs to an infinitely more numerous body than the novelist; his craft is more ancient; his fruits richer and unspeakably more abundant. Above all, his function and practice have been, and remain, more intimately bound up with African social life.

The novel, then, has no history in Africa. It is a literary import (of developing significance perhaps) from Europe; and its appearance provides evidence for those Africans who argue that their new writing is but a minor appendage to the mainstream of European literature. No doubt it can become a successful transplant (though works like Okara's *The Voice* suggest rejection symptoms). No doubt it can, in the words of Dr J. E. Stewart, be described as 'something that can be Africanised precisely because it is so malleable, so much the loose, baggy hold-all of the arts'.[3] But even if one accepts this, and also Dr Stewart's further point, that the novel 'does not impose a Westernness', the fact remains that this is a form that has grown up in the West; it is not, in its nature, an African form.

The oral story, then, has been Africa's dominant form. As Borges points out, a piece of the length and complexity of a novel could never be related by word of mouth. In Africa's oral past, and present, texts as long as *Things Fall Apart* or *The Interpreters* are not normally found. Africa has been brought up on much shorter narratives; epics like *Sundiata* being special, occasional, excepions, belonging more to the category of historical texts, and in any case of fairly short length. The *griot* who can commit *Sundiata* to memory is a rare professional; but even he, with his prodigious memory and his consummate skill with mnemonic devices, would find the complicated turns of plot, the minutiae of physical and scenic description, of even a short novel, an impossible burden. The novel, thus, unlike the story, is not a fact of the African past.

Important results stem from this. The African child, for instance, is faced in school with a written literary form imposed on him by an alien system of education. He may acquire a taste for the novel; but his home life, his society's history – in a word, his culture – predispose him naturally to the story. It also means that, for the moment, the African reader is a short distance performer. And curiously enough, so, too, are many of the writers. Notice the brevity of many of their texts, whether they are traditionalists like Tutuola or moderns like Soyinka and Clark.

The natural descendant of the oral story is the short written narrative. Let us, for convenience, call it the short story. It lies, alas, in the shadow of the novel; yet it has already emerged in a quality and an abundance which make it more exciting, more promising, than the novel. Many African writers (includng poets, novelists, and dramatists) have naturally worked in this form and answered the pull of their home tradition. Do we need evidence for this? Turn to the pages of *Black Orpheus, Zuka, Penpoint, Busara, Darlite*; turn to *Présence Africaine, Transition,* and *Nigeria Magazine.* Examine Cook's *Origin East Africa,* Mphahlele's *Modern African Writing,* Edwards' *Through African Eyes,* Segun's *Reflections,* Ogot's *Land Without Thunder,* Kibera and Kahiga's *Potent Ash,* Diop's *Les Contes d'amadou,* Dadié's *Le Pagne Noir,* Whiteley's *A Selection of African Prose,* La Guma's *A Walk in the Night,* Rive's *Modern African Prose,* Mphahlele's *In Corner B,* and Denny's *Pan African Short Stories.* The objection might be raised that the short story is being used as journey work, as a stepping-stone to more extended performances. But this does not explain why established novelists still persist in writing short stories. It does not explain why even aspiring dramatists like Christina Ama Ata Aidoo have turned their hand to this form. What seems beyond dispute is that the written story is the natural outgrowth of native tradition.

Let us look more closely at the details of this phenomenon. Established writers in the West, East, and South of Africa seem to have written short stories. Achebe wrote *The Sacrificial Egg and Other stories*; he contributed 'Uncle Ben's Choice' to *Black Orpheus,* No. 19, 'The Voter' to *Black Orpheus,* No. 17; he wrote 'Akueke' for *Reflections.* Nkem Nwankwo wrote 'The Gambler' for *Black Orpheus,* No. 9, 'His Mother' for *Nigeria Magazine,* No. 80, 'The Man Who Lost' for *Nigeria Magazine,* No. 84. James Ngugi, East Africa's best known novelist, has written many short stories, including four in the Makerere collection *Origin East Africa.* T. M. Aluko, author of *One Man, One Wife* and *One Man, One Matchet,* first attracted attention when his short stories won a prize offered by the British Council. Peter Abrahams, in addition to his novels, has written a collection of short stories, *Dark Testament.* His countryman, Alex La Guma, has written 'At the Portagees', 'Blankets', 'A glass of Wine', 'Tattoo Marks and

Nails', and 'Slipper Satin', all for *Black Orpheus,* and 'A Matter of Honour' for *New African.* Christina Ama Ata Aidoo, whose collection of short stories *No Sweetness Here* was published in Kenya, offered 'In the Cutting of a Drink' to *Pan African Short Stories,* and 'The Message' to Mphahlele's *African Writing Today.* Finally, to halt a list that could flow on indefinitely, Gabriel Okara wrote 'The Crooks' for *Black Orpheus,* No. 8.

The pull of tradition can even be felt when writers are not, ostensibly, offering the short story at all. Take the works of Tutuola or Fagunwa. What are they, if not a string of short narratives skilfully bonded into one longer tale? Examine Conton's *The African* and find a novel that is really a short story that missed its way, the fine polish and organisation of the opening chapters rapidly disappearing as the author's pen carries him into distances for which he has neither the training nor the energy. Notice how short is *The Voice,* a piece which stands in close proximity to the short narrative of tradition. Ekwensi is the most startling example of all. *People of the City, The Leopard's Claw, Iska, Beautiful Feathers, Burning Grass,* and *Jagua Nana* – they are alike in their impressive openings and their rapid descent into staleness, banality, or sheer lack of creative energy; and this because Ekwensi's talent is not for the novel, but for the short story. His novels have attracted the reviewers, but for sheer control, organisation, and sustained quality of writing, they compare most unfavourably with short stories like 'Ritual Murder', 'Lokotown', 'A Stranger from Lagos', or 'Glittering City'. Ekwensi, and writers like him, are exhibiting, unconsciously, the pull of their indigenous tradition. The sooner they appreciate this (as Abioseh Nicol has done), the sooner they will produce work of a consistently high quality. Even now, though the critical comment in print would not suggest it, there is no novelist in Nigeria (not even Achebe himself) whose creative flair and command of prose are superior to those of Abioseh Nicol, the Sierra Leonean who has devoted himself entirely to the short story.

Discussion of African prose-fiction has tended to avoid the inconvenient facts of African tradition, especially when praise is being lavished on the novelists. There are still only a few good novels from Africa; there are still only a few novelists who seem destined for international stature. Africa, indeed, could yet be one area of the world where the quiet remark of Luis Borges, that 'the novel is a form that may pass, doubtless will pass', is given powerful substance.

Obiajunwa Wali, the Nigerian critic who never fails to be controversial, adds useful material to the present discussion in an article called 'The Individual and the Novel in Africa', which appeared in *Transition,* in 1965. Focusing his attention on three books – Laye's *The Radiance of The King,* Achebe's *No Longer at Ease,* and Okara's *The Voice* – he demonstrates the loneliness and frustration of the central figures in each work; and he affirms that these are facts which arise from their essential apartness from traditional African society. They are men who wish to be free agents, individuals who refuse to fit into the traditional mould. The point is relevant. For, as Wali observes (with some minor inaccuracy as to period), the western novel has emerged precisely as a literary form that reflects individualism; and often, indeed, outright rebellion against established society. The central figures of the earliest novels were usually men and women who, in a sense, stood apart – hence their names could legitimately be given to the book's title: *Tom Jones, Moll Flanders, Robinson Crusoe, Clarissa, Pamela,* and so on. Certainly good novels have portrayed their protagonists accepting and working within the pattern of their society (the work of Jane Austen is a case in point); but even here the tendency has been to choose a figure who has strength and independence enough to distinguish him from his fellows, so that an in-depth exploration of character (the main concern of the 'pure' novel) becomes worthwhile. The modern African novelist, seeking to imitate western fiction, runs up against a social system whose watchword has always been conformity; which has, indeed, demanded conformity in the interests of social cohesion, and even of survival. Rebels have not thrived in traditional African society. With urbanisation, however, and the gradual breakdown of rural life, loneliness and rebellion are emerging. Conditions are growing easier for the novelist. Hence the frequent choice of a hero who has been wrenched from his traditional background by economic necessity, or, like the author, by an overseas scholarship.

Let Wali restate the crux of the matter. Of the three heroes his essay discusses, he has this to say:

In a real sense, the chief obstruction to the three characters is the community with its tyranny and incomprehensibility, the community where the individual does not exist in his own right but is compelled to lose his identity for the sake of social cohesion. In a certain technical sense then, we say that the character in traditional African society does not exist, yet the African novelist in order to make his craft possible is forced to hammer out characters from this social block which is amorphous in many ways. Failure of communication in a work of art may be regarded as a technical artistic failure, but the failure we are describing here does not fall into this category, but is due mainly to the nature of the material at the disposal of the novelist. The rise of the

European novel in the 19th century is not an accident, but owes its growth to the liberation of the individual which the industrial revolution, in addition to other contemporary social forces of the period, made possible ... The greatest challenge for the African novelist then is the question of character in so far as character lies at the centre of the traditional form of the novel, and in so far as the African writer, looking for themes and settings distinctively African, becomes involved in traditional African society.[4]

There is a further point. The modern novel, partly because it is a written form, unlike the oral narrative, is not addressed to the group mind; it is addressed to the individual in the privacy of his mind and study; and it comes from the pen of someone who is giving his own intensely private reading of life. The traditional artist has invariably offered a *shared* view; indeed it has been his function to insist on a shared view, and to communicate it in as lively and memorable a way as he can. Where the modern novelist is contributing to a *debate,* the oral artist expected only conformity.

Some Nigerian short stories

Although many of her writers have produced short stories, Nigeria's contribution to this particular form cannot yet be described as a rich one. Certainly, one does not always feel that men like Okara, Nzekwu, Owoyele, and Ekwensi are attempting to work within the form as classically defined by Poe in his review of Hawthorne's *Twice-Told Tales*; yet neither do they appear to be creating a new African mould for the form. There is not always in their writing a concern for economy and compression; a realisation that language here must be made to work almost as hard as it does in verse, if the overall impact of the story is to be a powerful one. On the contrary, there is much flat spiritless writing in evidence and a looseness of structure that undoubtedly is inherited from oral practice.

For the most part, the Nigerian stories retain the didactic nature of the oral tales. Evil does not triumph over good; crime still does not pay. Criminal activity is of course more sophisticated and urban settings are increasingly popular. But the tricks and sudden reversals of the old order, those devices that bring the narrative to a neat resolution, are still in favour. There is no reason why the traditional beast allegories should not be worked into the modern stories, but writers, alas, seem to have dispensed with them. Africa has thrown aside that convention which guaranteed polite obliqueness, that ensured harmony by not pointing fingers too directly.

Okara's 'The Crooks' is a straightforward piece, told chronologically like so many of the stories, and with rather too strong an element of predictability.[5] The Okara feeling for balance and symmetry, however, is strongly present, even in the basic situation itself, which is, simply, city cunning versus rustic cunning. Okonkwo and Okeke arrive in Lagos, ostensibly to buy a lorry. They are met by a city spiv who tries, with others, to cheat them of the purchase money; only to lose £100 in the attempt. The contrast between the rustics and the spiv is neatly done. Okara describes the former as follows:

> Their hair was all brown with dust. The clothes they had on were dirty and torn. Their bare feet were as dirty and brown as their hair.

There are other slight strokes which emphasise their appearance as innocents abroad in a strange crowded city. 'They walked one behind the other as if they were picking their way in the forest.' At the noise of car horns as traffic streams over Carter Bridge, they are 'startled over and over again'. They gape at the lagoon and at all the traffic.

> The spiv who tries to cheat them is the precise opposite. He is seen cycling leisurely along on a brand new green bicycle from the Idumota end of the bridge. His shirt and trousers were a dazzling white, and his two-tone black and white shoes were spotless. Tilted over his forehead was a white cork helmet.

His fellow thugs, when they appear at night, are 'dressed in heavily emroidered velvet *agbadas* and slippers'. When they are introduced to the scruffy rustics, the latter look awed and begin fidgeting. The illusion is thrown away, however, when Okara, writing of the dishonest host, says, 'They were the greenest things he'd ever come across, he thought!' Those last two words spoil the whole effect of expectation. We now expect the reversal that comes as the climax. The spivs, to gain the rustics' confidence, let them win £100 at cards. But Okonkwo and Okeke are equally smart. They fly in the middle of the night and take the train home, counting their easy money; their haversack, thought by the spivs to have contained £750, is now empty of its 'stones and old rags'. The formal neatness is complete as they laugh to one another about their success: 'They'll never learn,' said Okonkwo as he wiped his face. 'They are as green as green peas, the whole batch of them'! The ending makes their earlier appearance, showing fright and awe, beautifully ironic. Morally, there is a nice balance of blame: both sides are crooks – the title, presumably, was never meant only to refer to the Lagos rogues. Both town and country can produce them. The fact that the townees are worsted in this encounter, and that both we and Okara enjoy their misfortune, does not hide an implied comment that the conventional view of rustic innocence and urban depravity is absurdly simplistic. No milieu has a monopoly on dishonesty. Stylistically, this is not written in the experimental Africanised English which Okara uses in *The Voice*. Instead, there is some clever, and humorous, use of pidgin, as the spiv tries to come down to the rustics' level and ingratiate himself with them.

There is more crime in David Owoyele's 'The Will of Allah'; and again it is shown not to pay – though not with quite the same subtle ambivalence that we find in Okara's piece. There is a suitably gloomy atmosphere and spareness of detail that provide a useful backcloth to a story that ends in tragedy. There is also some engaging humour – the kind which is always possible when crooks work together, with their motives of greed, and their proverbial absence of honour. Sule and Dogo are burglars with long prison records; and they are, tonight, 'on duty' as they put it. There is a long section of unconvincing dialogue between Sule and innumerable judges he has faced – dialogue where the writing grows slack, where space is simply being filled. But a comic point about Sule is made when Owoyele remarks:

> Sule was a deeply religious man, according to his lights. His religion forbade being dogmatic or prophetic about the future, about anything. His fear of Allah was quite genuine. It was his firm conviction that Allah left the question of a means of livelihood for each man to decide for himself. Allah, he was sure, gives some people more than they need so that others with too little could help themselves to some of it.

Dogo, Sule's partner in crime, is not religious and not especially enamoured of Sule. They work together but are suspicious of each other. This is what leads to their downfall. When Sule breaks into a house, Dogo waits outside and receives a large gourd through a window. He carries it off to the bank of a stream. A scene reminiscent of Chaucer's *Pardoner's Tale* ensues. Dogo feels Sule need not share equally the contents of the gourd. He thrusts his hand in, expecting to find money, only to be bitten by a cobra; it is a snake-charmer's gourd! Now deciding that he *will* indeed share the loot equally with his partner, he lets Sule thrust his hand in, too, with the inevitable consequence:

> They were silent for a long time, glaring at each other. 'As you always insisted. we should go fifty-fifty in everything,' said Dogo casually. Quietly, almost inaudibly. Sule started speaking. He called Dogo every name known to obscenity.

The closing scene in which the dying men, while cursing each other, laugh at the irony of it all – that fate should have at last turned the tables on them, that vice has demanded its final punishment – is powerfully

81

done. It is a pity that some slack middle passages dissipate the tension of this moral story. It is an even greater pity that since this piece appeared in *Reflections* (1962). nothing further has appeared from Owoyele's pen.

There is little of interest to detain us in Onuora Nzekwu's 'The Death of a Game'.[6] Its emphasis is all on events; character portrayal is not at a premium. In parts it is badly written. As Jane Austen might have said, there is 'too much of right and left', too much inert detail. Nor does its plot. an account of events leading up to the disappearance of a traditional game from Ibo life, offer much interest.

The opening sentence, 'Izualor looked around the oval-shaped village square', is not exactly a happy one, though one might let it pass without too much protest. But when Nzekwu writes:

In it one village was pitched against the remaining six. every Saturday between November and March each year. The village whose turn it was, represented by three *otu-iche* masqueraders.

one simply has to protest that the last unit of writing in the quotation, offered as a sentence, is not a sentence at all. For flat, lifeless writing, the following passage would be hard to equal:

As Patrick watched, a small wooden drum was sounded. It was a signal that the masqueraders were ready to start. An attendant followed it up with shouts of 'Olue o!' 'Olue o!' Immediately. things began to sort themselves out. The masqueraders were alone with their attendants in the centre of the square. They formed a triangle with sides about forty feet long and were busy throwing unripe oranges as hard as stones at the athletes, who stood in twos and threes all round them but well out of reach. teasing and taunting them. A group of boys with bags of oranges slung across their shoulders ensured a steady flow of missiles for the use of the masqueraders.

In slow procession. one dull detail dies quietly on the page after another. The scene is not vividly evoked. One wonders whether it was really worth evoking at all. Such writing might pass for a sociological essay submitted to *Nigeria Magazine* – an explanation of how one strand of traditional life passed out of existence. But for the short story something very different is needed: Nzekwu does not provide it. One of its few moments of interest comes when it includes a song, an ingredient not normally associated with the modern short story. but a common feature of the oral stories. The athletes here sing:

'Ado come together let's brave the odds
Me mme ho-ho!

Ado come together let's brave the odds
Mme mme ho-ho!
Mme mme ho-ho! We're braving it well
Mme mme ho-ho!'

It is the only breath of life in a very dull story. There is no interest in character; none in setting; none in emotional effect. It dies as quietly as it began.

'Akueke' and 'The Voter', two short stories by Chinua Achebe, are more impressive performances. Achebe's style is closely knit. There is a concentration, an economy of language found nowhere in the Nzekwu piece. Briefly, and effectively, the opening sentence of 'Akueke' sets the scene and establishes the conflict at the heart of the story. 'Akueke lay on her sick bed on one side of the wall of enmity that had suddenly risen between her and her brothers.'[7] Akueke is ill, apparently mortally so: it seems to be a punishment for rejecting so many suitors. The sickness is the swelling disease; and to allow her to die in the house would be an abomination to Ani, the earth. Disaster might befall all the nine villages of Umuofia should such a thing be allowed to happen. Her brothers, who love her, have an agonising choice to make. Tradition wins and Akueke is carried to the bad bush to die. But her grandfather collects her and takes her home (she has always been his favourite): later he makes her appear like Hermione before her terrified brothers.

The choice of subject is simple but appealing; it generates emotion, sympathy, and tension. The problem of choice is worked in; so, too, the old versus young conflict. which is won here by the wily grandfather. When Akueke marries, *he* will get the bride price because now she is legally his daughter. Add to this neat reversal a middle passage of reminiscence that is perfectly natural for a person mortally sick and an artistic complication of the hackneyed chronological narrative, and you have the ingredients of a well-wrought short story. The reminiscence also serves the further purpose of filling out Akueke's character a little more, and preparing us for the saving intervention of her doting grandfather.

'The Voter' has a more modern theme, politics, a subject which has increasingly caught Achebe's attention and was finally thought to deserve a whole novel, *A Man of the People*.[8] There are several thematic strands woven into the tissue of this story. One is the conventional conflict between the old and the new; but it is an imaginative exploitation of the conventional in so far as Achebe pits old foxiness against the new political foxiness which he loathes. There is a sneaking sympathy for tradition here. revealed especially in the author's scarcely suppressed guffaw at the discovery of the power of the ballot box as an

83

answer to the power of the politician. If the elected member can get rich so quickly, then surely the means of electing him must be worth a certain amount of cash too:

> The villagers had had five years in which to see how quickly and plentifully politics brought wealth, chieftaincy titles, doctorate degrees and other honours . . . Anyhow, these honours had come so readily to the man they had given their votes to free of charge five years ago that they were now ready to think again.

Behind Achebe's sympathy for the voters in their dealings with the despised politicians, the subtle point is also being made that the voters in fact *are prepared to be bribed,* that they are abusing democracy, that they are fostering corruption. That they will get as much for their vote as they can, may, in the circumstances, be comically understandable; but it is not to be admired.

There is implied criticism, too, in Achebe's comment that the village of Umuofia 'already belonged *en masse* to the People's Alliance Party': tribalism, unthinking conformity, and the herd instinct are under attack. The people are not satisfied with Chief the Honourable Marcus Ibe's performance, but they will vote for him anyway, though now only at a certain price. Of course, Ibe himself is also the object of Achebe's satire; he is drawn as a thoroughly second-rate man with low morals and a strong taste for opulence. He is, nevertheless, a brilliant opportunist:

> . . . only the other day Marcus Ibe was a not too successful Mission-school teacher. Then politics had come to their village and he had wisely joined up, some say just in time to avoid imminent dismissal arising from a female teacher's pregnancy. Today he was Chief the Honourable; he had two long cars and had just built himself the biggest house anyone had seen in those parts. But let it be said that none of these successes had gone to Marcus's head – as they well might. He remained a man of the people. Whenever he could he left the good things of the capital and returned to his village which had neither running water nor electricity. He knew the source of his good fortune . . .

Rufus, his political organiser, is criticised too. Although he enjoys the honour of being one of the few youths who have not left the village and trekked into the towns, he gladly engages in bribery on behalf of Ibe; and when the opposition's creature offers him five pounds for *his* vote, his reaction is instantaneous:

> No words were wasted. He placed five pounds on the floor before Roof and said, 'We want your vote'. Roof got up from his chair, went to the outside door, closed it carefully and returned to his chair.

At the sight of so much money, his principles buckle at once. His situation, however, with a foot in both camps, becomes fraught with strain; and the story reaches its climax with Roof tearing his ballot in half and voting for both parties – keeping, of course, the five pounds! The piece, which is clearly a preliminary exercise for *A Man of the People* (notice the ironic use of this phrase in connection with Ibe above), firmly makes its point: we are shown a society in miniature miserably corrupt from top to bottom. It might have gained further strength, however, had Achebe chosen to attack on a narrower front; if, for instance, the burden of the story had been focused on Roof's dilemma.

There is nothing, so far, in the short stories from Nigeria to compare with the work of Abioseh Nicol from Sierra Leone. Take, for example, the opening section of Nicol's story 'Love's own Tears':[9]

> 'Bosom! Bosom! Bosom!
> Take me into thy Bosom, Lord,
> take me quickly!'

The little black boy paused in awe outside as he listened to his grandmother dying inside the wooden-frame house with the shutters now let down. It was hot. The heat shimmered over the tin roofs of the African city and settled in a thin blue haze over the surrounding mountains. He bounced his ball slowly; he knew granny was dying – that was an established fact – he had heard his mother saying so over the fence to the neighbours next door. He knew also that it was something ordinary, because although the old woman yelled at the top of her voice, no one paid exceptional attention apart from giving her a little water now and again, and sometimes patting her gently where she said it hurt most. On the other hand, he felt something eventful was going to take place from the snatches of whispered conversation he had overheard; the steady but concerted buzz of activity; and the fact that no one paid much attention to his normal misdemeanours. Only once had he been shoo-ed out of the way. He had gone inside on some pretext and had asked his mother what was a bosom. She had paused. 'Granny's dying', she said. 'Granny's being taken into the bosom of her Lord. There are such a lot of things I've got to do,' she continued with an abstracted air. 'I've got to get some white silk material for her shroud from the new Indian shop near the railway station; and also white gloves and white stockings. Then I've got to find someone to turn round all the looking-glasses with their faces to the wall. This one in the parlour is too heavy for me to turn round since my operation. But what in heaven's name am I doing standing about and talking when there is so much to do and what are you doing here? Didn't I tell you to stay outside? In fact, find your hat and you'll go and stay with our Aunt Jemima until everything is over.' He was bitterly disappointed, but only momentarily as his father had come along and pleaded indulgently for him. 'Let him stay, the little rascal,' he said. 'He's growing up. It is time he started to know the facts of life,' and standing behind his mother's back he sent a little wink down to him. He ran outside reprieved and started bouncing his ball again slowly. The little girl from next door looked in to play. 'What's the matter with your granny,' she asked, 'she's been shouting all day. I asked my Mama,' she continued, 'but she slapped me and said not to humbug her.'

'Granny's dying, that's what it is,' he replied importantly, 'Granny's being taken into the bosom of her Lord. Catch!'

There is no need to draw detailed comparisons between this and the Nigerian stories we have examined. The difference announces itself. There are qualities here which place Nicol in the very forefront of African short story writers. It all looks so simple, so utterly natural; as though Nicol is casually taking a slice of real life and offering it to us in all its workaday detail, all its blending of the tragic and the absurd. Yet the style that allows this effect must possess the translucence of crystal; and the sensibility behind the style must be one of marvellous richness and iron control. Notice how much is packed into this opening section. There is the Freetown setting, with its backcloth of mountains; the activity about the house; the child at play; the neighbours over the fence; the shimmering heat of the day; and, behind all this, two central facts: the fact of death, universal, inescapable, of the utmost moment for all, yet commonplace, ordinary, a topic for over-the-fence chats; and then the developing consciousness of a small boy really ignorant about death, yet vaguely aware that something important is about to happen. Death is linked, rather comically, with 'white gloves and white stockings', and with superstition. There is a hint that this particular death will lighten someone's burden. And death, so massive in its significance, is set alongside play; hence the slowly bouncing ball (suggesting almost the minutes ticking away as well as the awed thoughtfulness of its owner). Hence also that final climactic comment which pulls together in brilliant fusion the main elements of this whole section: 'Granny's being taken into the bosom of her Lord. Catch!' These closing words – dare one say it? – display the simplicity of great art.

Nigeria may not have West Africa's best short story writer, but in Cyprian Ekwensi she has the most prolific. If West Africa wanted the libretto for a twentieth-century *Beggar's Opera*, there is little doubt that Cyprian Ekwensi would be asked to write it, for his work shows him to be particularly well equipped for the task. Despite minor excursions into the area of rural and traditional Africa (*Burning Grass*, published in 1962, is the most notable example), he is above all an urban writer: it is city life that he loves and mirrors best. One might go even further and call him West Africa's first picaresque author, for he excels in the depiction of the criminal side of city life; and a random selection of his characters reads like a roll-call for West Africa's underworld. Pimps, forgers, burglars, prostitutes crowd into his pages, bearing impossible names like Charlie the Coin-Diver, Fussy Joe, Nancy of the Grand Palm Hotel, and First Trumpet.

Beier gave the best clue to an understanding of Ekwensi's writing when he concluded his article on the Onitsha School with a brief remark that Ekwensi began his career there in 1947 with a pamphlet called *When Love Whispers*.[10] This is important for there are two dominant characteristics of the Onitsha writings (apart from their illiteracy) and Ekwensi has inherited both. They are a fascination for the modern western way of life associated with the cities, and a concern solemnly to warn the young and innocent of the dangers which the modern age holds out for them. The list of Onitsha titles is evidence enough: for every *Rosemary and the Taxi Driver* there is a *Beware of Harlots and Many Friends*; for every *How to Get a Lady in Love* there is a *What is life?* (*dedicated to Moral Regeneration*). Ekwensi's major attempts at the novel form – *People of the City* and *Jagua Nana* – both have urban settings, and the epigraph to the opening chapter of the former reads, significantly, 'How the city attracts all types and how the unwary must suffer from ignorance of its ways'. It states clearly enough Ekwensi's general field of interest. He loves the crude, sprawling, cities that are developing in West Africa; like the great cities of England in the late eighteenth and early nineteenth centuries, they are bursting at the seams under the ever-increasing pressure of uncontrolled urbanisation. They are westernised cities, and hold a strong fascination for Ekwensi. (It is worth recording that unlike so many of his fellow writers, he lived for several years in England and read pharmacy, not literature, for his degree.) He is not a man of cultural tensions – his writing seldom betrays an inner struggle or conflict – and he appears to have undergone a painless cultural change and landed safely ashore in a new westernised Africa. Meanwhile, he can point out for the rustics from up-country (or the Eastern Greens as he calls it in *People of the City*) the fatal attractions of big city life, with its bars, nightclubs, and underworld. A familiar theme that ran through Elizabethan and

Restoration drama and into the fiction of Defoe, Richardson, Fielding, and Cleland, reappears in a West African setting; and what London meant for Moll, Joseph Andrews, Tom, Clarissa, and Fanny, Lagos and Accra mean to a variety of Ekwensi's characters – all born in the countryside and all lured by various temptations into the city.

Ekwensi is better known as a novelist than as a short story writer, but he has achieved only minor significance with the novel form, as an examination of his two main efforts will show. *People of the City* was first published in 1954. The blurb writer for the 1963 edition noted that when the book first appeared 'it was immediately acclaimed as the first major novel in English by a West African to be widely read throughout the English-speaking world'. He went on to say that 'Despite the added reputation Ekwensi . . . achieved with his later novels, *People of the City* remains a work of much greater significance in the development of modern African writing.' This is ambivalent comment. The writer is trying to have it both ways, to say that the work is one of substance and yet hint that better things have followed. One must ask whether *People of the City* is in fact a major novel and what significant influence it has exerted on the development of modern African writing. On the first question critical scrutiny reveals this to be a very minor novel; and as for the second, it is very hard indeed to trace any clearly defined influences which this book has had on the development of African prose in English.

One wonders indeed if the blurb writer has actually read the text. Is it true to say, as he does, that this novel 'tells the story of a young crime reporter and dance-band leader . . . who comes to see that what he can do for the developing country in which he lives is more important than the considerable and varied personal pleasures he can find in the hectic life of the city'? Is this the central theme of *People of the City*? If so, then the information must have come from sources other than the text. And do we really see Sango Amusa, the hero, emerging at the close as a man determined to become a self-sacrificing patriot, keen to lead a life of spartan virtue? Hardly. Perhaps the blurb writer was thinking about this quotation from the closing chapter (p. 155):

'Yes. We want a new life, new opportunities . . . We want to live there [the Gold Coast] for some time – but only for some time! We have our homeland here and must come back when we can answer your father's challenge! When we have *done* something, *become* something!'

The drift of these remarks is personal and individual rather than social, selfish rather than altruistic: the challenge which Sango felt his father-in-law offered was to become 'somebody', to be important, to succeed

88

materially. The context suggests that Sango's interpretation of what this implies is material rather than spiritual. He is unlikely to become a Nigerian Gandhi.

The technical ineptness of a writer at the start of his career is evident in *People of the City*. Take the central question of character. There is nothing here like the tremendous focus we get in *Jagua Nana,* a later work, on one cardinal figure around whom all turns, who gives the book its peculiar tone, its atmosphere, its morality; in a word, a character who creates the world of the book. Ekwensi was not ready for that kind of portrayal in 1954. Instead he offers a string of portraits, some scarcely more than labelled blanks, who have a superficial appeal but pass before us so quickly that we have no time to get acquainted. Even in Sango's portrait there is much that is either confusing or unconvincing. The casual relationships he is supposed to have with a series of loose city girls are more often than not mentioned but not shown.

Even the Aina affair is badly handled. Aina first appears as an attractive girl more sinned against than sinning; a girl whom Sango ungallantly refuses to help when she is arrested on a theft charge. There is a prison sentence from which she emerges coarse and brutalised. At all events Sango's relationship with her is a lifeless spasmodic affair. Yet Ekwensi tells us (p.148) that eventually the hero 'vowed that he would end once and for all this evil relationship with the temptress who always awakened the meanest traits in him'. This is sheer melodrama, hollow and overstrained. Where are we shown this deadly love affair with a *femme fatale*? There is no basis in the text for Ekwensi's comment.

And what of Bayo, one of the lesser characters? How well does the reader get to know him? Hardly at all until his convenient fascination for the Lebanese girl Suad, a relationship which, once established, Ekwensi is uncertain how to develop. And Suad herself. What does she look like? What are we told of her cast of mind, her mannerisms, her love for Bayo, her interests, her tone of voice, her particular turn of phrase, or anything at all that makes her at once alive and memorable? Unfortunately, very little. And the same deficiencies are found in other portraits from *People of the City*.

One might try and defend Ekwensi here by arguing that he is merely in the position of Sango who made a practice of going to sit in a barbers' shop. 'It was always restful and anyone who sat there saw the city unroll before his eyes, a cinema show that never ended, that no producer could ever capture – the very soul of man' (p.151). The quotation tells a good deal about Ekwensi and his art, but as an excuse it is inadequate. Life in the city *is* shallow and unstable; but at least one

might have expected to learn something more about the deeper reactions of the main figures to it.

The town-country clash is present in *People of the City*. It represents
the larger continental debate that Ekwensi never adequately articulates.
Rustic innocence is contrasted with city vice, and the countryside
exerts a strong emotional pull on those who have left it for the city.
When Elina comes to town, she comes as a symbol of rural purity.
Conversely, when Sango visits her convent in the Eastern Greens, he
seems to be soiling the place with his city dirt. He is aware of this, and at
one point drops on his knees in a piece of absurdity unequalled since
Richardson wrote *Pamela* (p.78):

> Sango, confronted with pictures of the Madonna and Child, the
> Sacred Heart of Jesus radiating mercy to sinners like himself, saw
> no hope of his own salvation. He knelt down suddenly and made
> the sign of the cross.
>
> At that moment he vowed to spend the rest of his life doing
> good. . .

Jagua Nana (1961), with a similar urban setting, is a much better
book, despite Judith Gleason's comment in *This Africa* that *People of
the City* is Ekwensi's most exciting piece to date. Jagua, the fashionable
city whore, possesses two contrasting sides to her character. On the one
hand, she is a free-flowing soul, with a warm heart and a basic
innocence. She weeps easily, is quick to help friends, and feels anguish
over the death of her father and Freddie. She has a natural yearning for
children of her own, and weeps for days after her baby's early death.
She frequently invokes the name of God, though she has neither
attended church for years nor said formal prayers. On the other hand,
Ekwensi shows early on that there is much that is contrived and
artificial about Jagua. The bared shoulder, the make-up, the mincing
gait, the luminescent bra – she knows how to display her wares
professionally. She is a mistress of the meretricious arts, which are
geared of course to the pursuit of gold. This, above all, is what so often
seems to matter most with Jagua; this, plus the reassurance she needs
from young males that she is not really so old as she knows herself to be.
'I done old', she sighs in the opening pages, 'Sometimes I tink say
Freddie he run from me because I done old. God 'ave mercy!' And
this becomes a refrain heard time and again as the story unfolds. Her
philosophy is hedonism. The trouble with the world, she says, is that
'people take life too serious' . . . 'You die, you're dead . . . It's over.
You've left nothing, not a mark.'

From the moment she walks out of the British Council lecture, with
Freddie at her heels, she is the dominant party in this somewhat

improbable relationship. She is the active, he the passive, partner. She takes him to the *Tropicana*. She gets him up to dance. She even takes him to bed.

The main figures here – Freddie, Uncle Namme, Ma Nancy, and of course Jagua herself – are more convincingly drawn than the ciphers of *People of the City*, though, Jagua apart, they do not match the portraits of writers like Achebe, Mongo Beti, or Oyono. But by now Ekwensi is a better novelist. There is, in particular, a more skilful handling of voice as the author seeks to individualise his characters by exploiting a range of speech styles. He nicely captures the cadence of West African pidgin and there are memorable exchanges between Jagua and Ma Nancy in this idiom. At one point in the Bagana scenes, notable for their moments of appalling banality, Ma Nancy blames Jagua for the capture of her daughter by the Krinameh people, Uncle Namme's rivals across the river. 'Ma Nancy shouted. "De ol' witch woman mus' hang. Bloody harlot!" ' To which a penitent Jagua replies, 'Uncle Namme, ah never dream of dat. We only quarrellin' an' I follow de gal to teach am sense. And den–.' It is effective dialogue, in marked contrast to the mixed style of Uncle Namme, who cannot decide whether to speak middle class English, colloquial American, or pure pidgin. Of Nancy's predicament he says (pp.65–6):

'They will torture her. They will kill her. Is too late now. And she's my guest: such a good dancer! . . . I say there! Go at once! Beat the war drums! . . . Be patient. Ma Nancy. I know how you're feeling. Nancy's a fine gal. D.V. nothing will happen to her. We all love her. The whole of Bagana.'

This rings as hollow as a drum: but it is still evidence of Ekwensi's attempt to capture the true sound of conversational English as he hears it in Nigeria and exploit a varied range of spoken style.

Elsewhere, in the letter-writer's scene, one of several finely drawn insets in this book. Ekwensi shows that he has a sharp eye and ear for the sort of stylistic errors peculiar to West Africans writing English. It is not easy to plan for bad writing of the kind that goes into Jagua's letter to Freddie, but Ekwensi does the job with skill. Mistakes of tense and idiom follow one another in a piece of romantic nonsense built from cliches (p.49):

My Darling Freddie,

I remembered the very day you left me for England. I was charmed by your beautiful face which took me to a land of dream at the very night; you know where hearts agree there joy will be, your love attracted me: my heart and soul were aflame, the love in you cannot be abolished by any human creature except God the

Almighty. I last night dreamt of your beautiful and your smiling face which seems to me like vision.

Look, dear one, I am specially moved by feelings from heart to heart to love you always dearly and I hope you will have some love for me through your long stay in that cold firmament the United Kingdom.

I will be always loving you and adoring you with all my heart till you return. There's nothing lives longer than love, which sends perfect happiness to the soul, therefore, will you summon your beautiful strength and body to me as I am dreaming on my side. God's ways are mysterious, nobody knows Him or His contemplation on the end. Therefore let us live lonely and happily as you know, you are a nobleman and charming among your fellows, don't you see God creates you apart of them?

With its built-in mirth, its second-hand feelings, and its strong echoes of Onitsha, this is Ekwensi at his best and he crowns the exercise with an ironic remark that a part of Jagua 'had gone into that envelope and was now on its way out to Freddie'!

Jagua at the letter-writer's, Jagua at her toilet, Jagua seducing Chief Ofubara, Jagua at the riverside – these are high moments in the book. Jagua as an instrument of peace, however, or Jagua talking about national unity or Pan-Africanism, is less successful. There is a definite development in Ekwensi's craft as a novelist, but *Jagua Nana*, despite its strengths, is an uneven performance.

After his attempts at the full length novel, Ekwensi will probably settle down to the short story form. The extended and multiple characterisation necessary for the former are too much for him. His writing usually begins well, and he is a master of the introductory detailed picture. In Mphahlele's Preface to *Reflections*, praise was given in particular to the 'intensity of detail' with which Ekwensi opens his short story 'Gone to Mecca', a quality which, according to Mphahlele, 'helps the reader to visualise his characters, the drama in which they are involved, and the setting'.[11] Here it is:

Allah Be Praised! That Mallam Abdul's Maker had spared his life to celebrate yet another Sallah day. In itself this was a great thing and he was grateful. He yawned and turned over in his bed, lingering a few moments longer before getting up.

He took his kettle and went to the back-yard where he washed his sleepy face, feet and hands. It was not until he had gargled the lukewarm water and spouted it into the drain, murmuring 'Al-ham-didil-lahi', that he felt the first full surge of wakefulness. 'Madellah!' he murmured.

He went up and from his window saw the dryness in the air. The thatch on the rooftops had been bleached out of recognition by the pitiless sun.

Seeing the hawks already circling the sky, no doubt watching the bins for ram entrails, Abdul remembered that he had seen neither his money, nor the rams for the festival. And yesterday had been the last day on which the Alhaji had promised to settle his outstanding debt.

Such detail, such engagement with the 'minute-by-minute experience', is by no means common in West African prose.[12] *Jagua Nana* too, has an auspicious beginning, with a minutely detailed picture of the courtesan at her toilet. The opening scene of *Burning Grass* receives similar careful treatment, and exhibits a measure of the sensuous quality for which Ekwensi's style has rightly been praised (pp.1–2):

The old man sat still, tolling his chaplet. The trees were skeletons bleached in the sun – barren, with peeling skins bruised by decades of thirst and hunger. He sat with his son in the dry atmosphere of Northern Nigeria and on the grass beside him lay his bow and quiverful of arrows steeped in poison. The somnolence in the air crackled. Gusts of heat rose from the earth and shimmered upwards to an intense blue sky that hurt the eyes. He could smell the smoke fumes and he knew they were burning the grass. He and his son lifted their eyes and took in the undulating hills, the rivulets and rocks. And it was lonely. But they were nomads, wandering cattlemen, and loneliness was their drink. So they rested under the dorowa tree not talking, the son leaning on a stick the way fowls stand on one leg on a thirsty day.[12]

In a different vein, but with equal detail, here is the opening of *People of the City*; it calls up a milieu and theme that Ekwensi likes most (p.3):

Most girls in the famous West African city (which shall be nameless) knew the address Twenty Molomo Street, for there lived a most colourful and eligible young bachelor, by name Amusa Sango.

In addition to being crime reporter for the *West African Sensation,* Sango in his spare time led a dance band that played the *calypsos* and the *konkomas* in the only way that delighted the hearts of the city women. Husbands who lived near the All Language Club knew with deep irritation how their wives would, on hearing Sango's music, drop their knitting or sewing and wiggle their hips, shoulders and breasts, sighing with the nostalgia of musty nights years ago, when lovers' eyes were warm on their faces.

But the thoroughness and psychological plausibility evinced by these opening scenes are rarely repeated after the early pages, and Ekwensi's writing rapidly descends to the banal. In a way, despite his gift for introductory detail, he illustrates once more one of the basic facts about West African anglophone prose, namely that it does not, as a rule, distinguish itself over long distances.

Lokotown and Other Stories is a collection of short stories that seems to suggest a more settled and confident manner than is evident in the novels.[13] The titles contained in the volume aptly reflect Ekwensi's forte: 'A Stranger from Lagos', 'Spider's Web', 'Fashion Girl', 'Glittering City', and of course 'Lokotown' itself. The title story is important for introducing into West African literature the first picture of new industrial man and his working community (p. 1):

> Lokotown had become as much a part of Ajayi as his oil-stained overalls. At seven in the morning he instinctively listened for the scream of the siren. This was the time when the men in smudgy clothes trooped to work, the street lights were still peering through the dew and the city was turning on its side, trying to wake up.

The point of the story, however, is largely moral. Ajayi and Nwuke work the same train out of Lagos and share the same mistress, Konni, a highly successful whore-cum-seamstress, who has given up marriage and four children to seek her fortune in the city. The story is constructed to show how both men are cured of their infatuation for Konni and how they learn to realise that she is simply an insatiable parasite bleeding dry the honest hard-working folk of Lokotown. Konni receives her due, which includes a severe beating (West African society is as harsh on the fair sex as was eighteenth-century society in England) and finally commits suicide. Her lovers return to the secure domesticity of life with good traditional non-westernised consorts. Ajayi 'had never doubted that Bintu was good and beautiful, but she was not westernised, and she did not catch his imagination. Sometimes he hated her. He did not see why she did not wear the new fashions and high-heeled shoes. Why was she so simple?' She was far too 'slow' to appreciate smoking and drinking. She had never heard of clubs like The Midnight Oil, and before her marriage had 'slept on a mattress spread on the floor, with her younger brothers and sisters in the same room'. But whereas Konni meant ruin, Bintu meant peace and a stable home.

As we have already observed, the clash between the cultures is most visible in West Africa's cities; but there is little sense of conflict in Ekwensi's writing. Situations that finer sensibilities would portray as being fraught with tension betray scarcely any tension at all. In 'The Glittering City', for instance, he tells us how Essi, a 'young, provincial' girl, arrives for the first time in Lagos – a traumatic moment for any young rural African, one that must shock and overwhelm. Ekwensi's account, however, is superficial, and yet it is certainly a typical specimen of his work (p.107):

> The girl standing on the railway platform turned as Fussy Joe approached. He saw her face and decided: young, provincial, eighteen or nineteen at the most, tall for her age, elegant, a knockout. She had the fair skin that went with most beautiful Nigerian girls, a clear skin that spoke of fresh fish from the waters of the River Niger and palm oil from the plantations. Her eyes with their keen and inquiring look gave her away as a stranger in the city.

With the possible exception of his story 'Ritual Murder', Ekwensi seldom probes deeper than this. There is little or no suggestion of an inner life, no inward turbulence of mind and soul. It is a reminder that, although Ekwensi has a certain talent for the short story, his literary skills and interests often seem to be those of the journalist. And this is directly related to the question of style; for to describe the externals of African city life, its vice, its frauds, its glittering seductions, any western style will suffice and the style of the journalist perhaps best of all. To record powerfully the inner movement of African minds, however, at a time of doubt, contradictions, and ironies – this would require an altogether different viewpoint and technique. It helps to explain Ekwensi's apparent satisfaction with his style, which, in an anthology of Commonwealth short stories, would scarcely, apart from its occasional use of pidgin, be distinguishable from that of writers in the white Commonwealth. Unlike Okara and Achebe, Ekwensi has made no attempt to shape for himself a recognisably 'African' style; and though he is heir to the ancestral artist's moral concern, and his ability to tell an engaging story, he is the most westernised of the modern generation of Nigerian prose writers in point of style. We shall return to Ekwensi in our discussion of juvenile literature.

A vernacular novelist

We can find a useful contrast to Ekwensi's western-ness by briefly considering D. O. Fagunwa, whose work lies close to the West African oral tradition because he uses the Yoruba language and indigenous themes. He is worth examining because his writing displays some of the imaginative strength which the oral tradition has kept alive and to which even those Africans using the metropolitan language are heirs.

For our knowledge of Fagunwa, however, those of us who do not read Yoruba must rely on the critical work of Ulli Beier, so long a champion of Yoruba culture and of West African writing in general.[14] (There is also available, however, Soyinka's translation of *Ogboju Ode Ninu Igbo Irunmale,* under the English title *Forest of a Thousand Daemons*.) Beier tells us that, despite Fagunwa's choice of the vernacular, which has effectively denied him an international readership, the novelist has built up a large African audience, which includes schoolchildren, adults, and even 'illiterate grandparents', to whom the newly literate children read aloud.

Fagunwa's books are close to oral traditions for they have the familiar characteristics of a 'fairy tale atmosphere', a simple plot, and an abiding concern with pointing a moral. Beier notes, however, that though Fagunwa is close to oral sources, he is not entirely in the oral tradition, because he is using the written, rather than the spoken, word. Fagunwa attempts to create afresh, while working in the broad confines of the traditional pattern, a point discussed by Beier in his comments on the author's book *Igbo Olodumare*:

> Fagunwa's plot is a rambling, somewhat disorganised fairy tale. It is a succession of adventures, loosely strung together. There are elements of traditional Yoruba stories in his books, but Fagunwa does not draw as heavily on Yoruba folklore as Tutuola. Most of the stories are invented, many of them are also taken from European tradition. The true Yoruba flavour of Fagunwa's work lies not in the material he used, but in the language, in the manner and tone of his story-telling. These are the elements to which the average Yoruba reader responds with delight: for Fagunwa has the humour, the rhetoric, the word play, the bizarre imagery that Yorubas like and appreciate in their language. He impresses the reader with his knowledge of classical Yoruba . . . and he is as knowledgeable in proverbial expressions as an old oracle priest. Yet he is not content with that: he uses the language creatively and inventively, constantly adding to the traditional stock of imagery and enriching the language.[15]

Retaining a feature which was vital in the oral tradition, Fagunwa's language is extremely visual. Beier quotes him as saying of a man in love, 'love spread across his face like palm wine overflowing a calabash', of a quarrel, that it sticks in the throat like a fish-bone, and defining a lion as a man 'who has blood in his belly but spits white saliva'. In a land where the rhetorical arts are still cultivated, it is not surprising to find Fagunwa delighting his readers with the following interrogation, which takes place when the hero of *Igbo Olodumare* meets a spirit in the bush:

> Who are you? What are you? What are you worth? What are you up to? What will you become? What are you seeking? What do you want? What are you looking at? What are you seeing? What are you thinking? What is wrong with you? Where are you coming from? Where are you going? Where are you living? Where are you walking? Answer me, child of man, answer me in one word.[16]

The hilarious final imperative should not obscure the delightful object of this verbal exercise, which in the vernacular, an essentially tonal language, carries a tremendous charge of excitement. Beier remarks that Fagunwa 'is a master of rhetoric, who can make repetitions and variations swing in a mounting rhythm, like Yoruba drumming'. Fagunwa illustrates, too, a familiar African way of personifying *anything* when the occasion suits, a device which can always be relied on to give flesh and blood life to phenomena otherwise abstract and rather dull. The following passage, for instance, derives a certain charm and liveliness from the use of this ancestral device:

> And the epileptics were cured by my father, and those who suffered from guinea worm were cured likewise, and thousands of lepers became healthy people in our house. And my father punished small-pox, and attacked malnutrition; he spoilt the reputation of rheumatism, and turned stomach pain into a pauper; and headache became a helpless child, and backache was speechless; cough went into hiding and pneumonia fled; the tiny itching worms kept dead silent and fever was lost in thought; dysentry bent its head, the sore wept and the stomach ulcer was disgusted; the rash wrinkled its brow and the cold cried for help.[17]

Such writing suggests clearly enough something of the vitality inherent in the Yoruba literary forms upon which English-speaking writers like Tutuola can draw. The following portrait of Death is a further example:

> His eyes are as big as a food bowl, round like moons and red like fire; and they are rolling about like ripe fruit dangling in the wind. The teeth in his mouth look like lion's fangs, and they are bright red, for it is not yam he likes, nor bananas nor *okra,* nor bitter leaf; he likes nothing but human flesh.[18]

The oral tradition as it appears in a developed, written, form has its own strengths to offer the African prose writer, particularly if he is using the vernacular, but even when he is using English, as we shall see in our discussion of Tutuola and Achebe. One of these strengths is its markedly poetic nature, a point once alluded to by L. S. Senghor when he wrote:

> The prose story also has the grace of rhythm. In Africa, there is no fundamental difference between prose and poetry. Poetry is only prose with a more pronounced, more regular rhythm and in practice can be recognised because it is accompanied by a percussion instrument. The same sentence can be turned into a poem by accentuating the rhythm and so expressing the tension of being . . .[19]

Senghor believes that in the distant past every story was strongly rhythmical; every story, that is, was a poem. Prose recitals in modern Africa are still rhythmical but not markedly so. They are different from European modes in several ways:

> First of all, there is no economy of dramatic interest, or rather the economy is not achieved, as it is in modern European storytelling, by avoiding repetition. On the contrary, dramatic interest arises from repetition . . . repetition of a fact, an action, a song, of words, which form a leitmotiv.[20]

Tutuola: a writer without problems

Faced with the curious phenomenon of Amos Tutuola, literary criticism is not sure how to proceed. Rush for Frazer? Call on Frye? Take down Campbell? Concentrate on the bad grammar? Hunt for signs of pidgin? Or simply, as his Nigerian colleagues are said to do, ignore him and walk by? The difficulty is real, for Tutuola is Africa's magnificent exception; he is the unselfconscious eccentric who refuses to fit neatly into traditional categories, a writer who ruins the comfort of the easy generalisation. He is constantly called a novelist, yet his works are patently not novels. He is grouped with a generation of writers who include Soyinka, Achebe, Clark and Okara, and yet he is altogether unlike them. He is regarded (quite rightly) as a traditional artist, and yet, until the appearance of *Ajaiyi and His Inherited Poverty* in 1967 (a didactic piece using many Yoruba proverbs), he showed the traditional artist's interest in neither proverb nor didacticism. 'No thinking African can escape the pain of the wound in our soul' asserted Achebe; and yet here is one who can. 'All African writers face the problem of identity' has been the burden of a good deal of comment in this study; yet here is an African writer who apparently does not.

This eccentricity is worth examining more closely. Perhaps it stems ultimately from an unselfconsciousness that marks both the man and his work; for although Tutuola is a loyal Yoruba, he appears to lack an

98

awareness of cultural, national, and racial affinities. Certainly, one could never imagine him carrying a banner for negritude. He seems, in a sense, linguistically unaware, too, for one feels that he wrote in English quite by chance, almost, perhaps, as a passing whim. While Soyinka reviles the politicians and Achebe seeks 'to expose and attack injustice', while poets are accused of gun-running and dramatists are jailed for agitation, Tutuola has quietly gone about the business of enjoying the private life of his imagination and occasionally has allowed us to share in it. While his tribal loyalties are alive – one reason why he wrote was a fear that Yoruba myths would be forgotten – the great cultural issues and their labels mean nothing to him. Pan-Africanism, the African Personality, African Socialism, negritude, these are as dead for him as Colonialism itself. If Achebe and Soyinka want to write in order to change the world, Tutuola has other reasons, less dramatic but no less valid. 'I wrote', he says, 'for my own pleasure without thinking of publishing what I wrote. Also, I had nothing else to do in the evenings.'[21] The words, as significant as they are humble, establish that here is a writer who is in no way 'committed', as most West African writers have been committed, to the colonial struggle and its aftermath, to African rehabilitation and so on – indeed a writer initially unaware of an audience. It means that his work is literature in the service of itself, not in the service of political and social causes; not, even, in the service of entertainment.

An outline of Tutuola's eccentricities does not help much towards an understanding of his work. Fortunately, more orthodox signs are evident. For instance, although he does not share the traditional artists' love of didacticism – their proverbs and moralising are rarely found in his work – he does share their unselfconsciousness and general manner of procedure. And with the Yoruba oral artists of course, he shares a common imaginative world, shaped by the ancestral Yoruba mythology and religion. Of those writers who use English as their medium of expression, he is the closest to oral sources, and this is one reason why he is not writing what we could ordinarily call modern fiction; as our introductory remarks on African prose have suggested, the oral legacy is of little help to those who would write in the tradition of the western novel. There is precious little memorable character drawing in Tutuola's work: the burden is placed on incident, minute description, and atmosphere.

Tutuola's art, then, lives close to the indigenous tradition. 'What many critics did rightly seize upon is the intensely oral quality of Tutuola's writing', Gerald Moore wrote in 1962. 'On every page of the *Drinkard,* we can hear a warm human voice speaking. The lovely rhythms of Tutuola's English are rhythms of speech'.[22] Let us examine a typical passage from the *Drinkard:*

> When it was early in the morning of the next day, I had no palm-wine to drink at all, and throughout that day I felt not so happy as before; I was seriously sat down in my parlour, but when it was the third day that I had no palm-wine at all, all my friends did not come to my house again, they left me there alone, because there was no palm-wine for them to drink.[23]

The rhythm is halting – though scarcely lovely – and suggests the movement of an oral recital. There is, too, the constant repetition of salient details (we are told twice in a few lines why his friends deserted him), which seems to indicate that the narrator is struggling to keep the situation clear before him and so give a faithful account. These features – a halting rhythm and repetition – are hallmarks of the Tutuola style, and are frequently joined by broken grammar and slack-jointed syntax.

An example of Tutuola's debt to indigenous story-telling occurs in *My Life in the Bush of Ghosts,* where the author applies the device of constant repetition to intensify the effect he is striving for. The passage, which is pure Tutuola, is taken from 'My First Wedding Day in the Bush of Ghosts', an episode in which the hero is baptized, 'with fire and hot water', by the Devil himself:

> After the baptism, then the same Rev. Devil preached again for a few minutes, while 'Traitor' read the lesson. All the members of this church were 'evil-doers'. They sang the song of evils with evils' melodious tune, then 'Judas' closed the service.
>
> Even 'Evil of evils' who was the ruler of all the evils and who was always seeking evils about, evil-joking, evil-walking, evil-playing, evil-laughing, evil-talking, evil-dressing, evil-moving, worshipping, evils in the church of evils and living in the evil-house with his evil family, everything he does is evil, attended the service too, but he was late before he arrived and when he shook hands with me on that day, I was shocked as if I touch a 'live electric wire' . . .[24]

Tutuola is using a traditional rhetorical device mentioned by Senghor and witnessed in Fagunwa; and he is applying it here to an original creation, a macabre child of his own bizarre Yoruba imagination. As we shall see, however, it is a device which he uses with less literary skill than Gabriel Okara.

Another illustration of Tutuola's proximity to indigenous traditions is cited by Jahn. He argues most interestingly that *Drinkard's* creator shows signs of what Bantu philosophy calls 'Kuntu', namely a modal force seen as a force acting independently. Laughing, for instance, is an action that somebody performs; but Tutuola can separate in his imagination performer and action, and give the latter an identity of its own. The following passage shows how it can be done:

So as he mercilessly stabbed us with that stick, we felt pain and talked out, but at the same time that the whole of them heard our voice, they laughed at us if bombs explode, and we knew 'Laugh' personally on that night, because as every one of them stopped laughing at us, 'Laugh' did not stop for two hours. As 'Laugh' was laughing at us on that night, my wife and myself forgot our pains and laughed with him, because he was laughing with curious voices that we never heard before in our life. We did not know the time that we fell into his laugh, but we were only laughing at 'Laugh's' laugh and nobody who heard him when laughing would not laugh, so if somebody continue to laugh with 'Laugh' himself, he or she would die or faint at once for long laughing, because laugh was his profession and he was feeding on it. Then they began to beg 'Laugh' to stop, but he could not.[25]

More clearly than either *The Palm-wine Drinkard* or *My Life in the Bush of Ghosts*, *Feather Women of the Jungle* serves to show Tutuola's indebtedness to tradition, for it is a prose account of an oral performance in the traditional manner. Standing behind the mask of his *persona*, Tutuola introduces himself as follows (p. 11):

When I was seventy-six years old, the chief of my village died. But as I was the oldest man in the village that time, therefore, I was chosen by the rest people in my village to be their new chief.

The villagers are keen to hear a life-story which has ended in power and wealth, so one night they are invited to the chief's quarters:

All sat in front of my house. The women sat in the left of the circle while the men sat in the right and I sat on my usual old high armchair a little distance in front of them. Then I supplied each of the people with a keg of palm-wine, and the biggest keg was in front of me.

The scene is carefully set. It is the dry season with a full moon – ideal conditions for story-telling. It is all very theatrical and a reminder of the close relationship that exists in Africa between this kind of 'oral' performance and drama. The narrator's seat, a 'high' armchair, is the stage. The open space before the house is the auditorium, and it is filled with an audience. And there is the magic atmosphere of theatre, the tingling anticipation of the curtain going up; so much so that the people 'could not drink their palm-wine so much'. And then the performance begins – 'the entertainment of the first night' – for the whole story requires several sittings, more even than the Greeks were able to endure:

Now, my people, I am very glad indeed that you are anxious to hear the story of my past adventures, and I will start to tell you the story as from this night. But I advise every one of you to pay attention so that you may be able to sort out the useful senses which, I believe, will be useful to you in future.

I was very clever and fast enough when I was about fifteen years of age to know which was bad and good, which was to be done or not to be done. But this time I just began to experience difficulties, hardships, punishments, etc., but I had not yet experienced the difficulties, hardships, punishments, risk, dangers, etc., of the adventures.

This is all good traditional stuff – an old man spinning fantastic autobiographical tales and warning his audience to heed the moral of his words. Yet the didactic element is not so strongly present as critics have presumed. The tradition in which Tutuola belongs is, of course, a highly moralising one. But on reading Tutuola one feels that the writing is not deliberately and primarily didactic; the impulse behind it is not in essence a moral one. Tutuola is more interested in the story-telling itself; moral seeds which are a natural part of the material with which he deals are left to grow if they will. This is because Tutuola – despite the artifice in a book like *Feather Woman* – is not addressing a local audience. Writing an 'oral' account is a different exercise from the oral performance itself. And as he once said, he was writing to amuse *himself*.

Significantly, the tales of *Feather Woman* are obliquely didactic. For example, the feats of courage might be seen to prove that the narrator-chief is worthy of his leadership; that he has won his position through prowess as well as age. Also, it might be argued that the work is didactic in the sense that the horrific encounters in Tutuola's fantasy world are tokens of the hardships faced in real life, with the magic protection normally provided for the hero suggesting that in the real world we should always go well-armed. These horrors are worse than life as we know it, and, therefore, paradoxically, provide reassurance. Things, we feel, cannot be as bad as all that. It is rather like the Greek effort at catharsis. Finally, a man must prove himself in the fire of experience; and here is another qualification for the chief's place at the head of his people.

Yet, having said this, and admitting that behind, say, *Simbi and the Satyr of the Dark Jungle* there is the buried message that young girls must obey their parents, the impression remains strong that Tutuola is not basically a moralist. It is the joys of story and imagination that he relishes most.

The moral argument aside, *Feather Woman of the Jungle* reveals further evidence of Tutuola's traditionalism and eccentricity. The book appeared in 1962, just two years after Nigeria's Independence. Yet one finds here no trace of the euphoria surrounding that great historic moment. Nor is there a single reference to colonialism or to the new African political order that is succeeding it. There is a reference to the white man; but it is couched in mytho-magical rather than socio-historic terms. He is said to have come down from heaven to the sacred city of Ife where his footsteps can still be seen on the rocks. The name Nigeria which Europeans gave to Tutuola's country is mentioned only twice, and in one instance it seems to have been inserted by an editor anxious to be helpful to overseas readers. Nigeria as a whole does not interest Tutuola. Instead, it is his home area of Abeokuta – both town and province – which means most to him. There is detailed historical information about the Egba inhabitants of the town. He provides a 'Biography of my Town in Brief', telling of its eighteenth-century founding, the type of houses built, the shape of the compounds, shrines, women's dress, means of communication with cowries, and entertainment with 'fables, folk-lores, proverbs, riddles, etc.' And then the final poignant remark: 'All these things are still existing but are gradually dying.' The journeys of *Feather Woman* begin in Abeokuta and references to other towns visited *en route* are made in relation to this starting point. Tutuola is also at pains to describe Yoruba gods. In the sixth journey, during a visit to Ife, we meet Sango the god of thunder and lightning and his wife Oya in a sort of updated TV interview. Tutuola then is not only traditional but (which is to say the same thing) tribal too.

It has never been disputed that Tutuola derives his material from unwritten indigenous sources. Wauthier actually quotes Tutuola himself as saying, 'it seemed necessary to write down the tales of my country since they will soon all be forgotten', and it is Beier's opinion that Tutuola draws more heavily on Yoruba foklore than even Fagunwa, the vernacular novelist. An important question, then, is not so much the extent to which Tutuola has used existing oral tales – he has on his own admission used them a good deal – but how far and how successfully he has recreated them. Doubtless an authoritative answer will eventually be forthcoming from Yoruba literary scholars. In the meantime, it is a revealing exercise to take one example of a borrowing and examine the transformation it undergoes on its journey through Tutuola's imagination. The 'Complete Gentleman' episode from *The Palm-Wine Drinkard* provides useful material. This strange tale is not an original creation by Tutuola, for a version of it can be found in A. B. Ellis' *The Yoruba-Speaking Peoples of the Slave Coast of West Africa,* published as long ago as 1894. Ellis, a Lieutenant Colonel who served in West Africa with the First Battalion West India Regiment, says that the story is an *alo* or tale told by a Yoruba *akpalo kpatita,* 'one who makes a trade of telling fables, a performer who gathers an audience around him, cries out, "My *alo* is about so-and-so", and then proceeds with his tale'. Ellis does not quote an exact source, but offers the tale in question as though he had transcribed and translated it from an oral performance. It runs as follows (pp. 267–8):

My *alo* is about a woman named Adun.

Adun was very beautiful, and all the men wanted her. They were always entreating her, but she always refused.

One market-day a person borrowed legs from one, arms from another, and a body from a third. He joined all together, and went to the market. He wanted Adun, and he would have her.

His appearance pleased Adun, and they talked together. Although he belonged to a distant country, she consented to go with him. She took him to the house and showed him to her mothers. Her mothers said, 'Very well, go with him.'

They went. On the road, the master of the legs took away the legs, the master of the arms took away the arms, and the master of the body took away the body. Nothing was left but the head. And the head went on, while Adun, nearly dead with fear, could not run away.

They arrived at the house of the head.

Next morning, before he went to work in his plantation, the head said to Tortoise, 'If Adun tries to run away, sound the horn to warn me.'

The head had scarcely gone out of sight when Adun took her bundle, and began to run away.

Then Tortoise sounded the horn. 'Head, head,' he cried, 'Adun is going. She has tied up her calabashes, she has gathered her dishes.'

This is almost the end of the tale. The head catches Adun repeatedly but in the end, after consulting a *babalawo,* she escapes by stuffing Tortoise's horn with *ekuru* cake. When he tries to sound the alarm the cake falls into his mouth and prevents the alarm being sounded in time.

Tutuola's version of the story is more modern and extensive. Compared with Ellis' version, Tutuola's account in *The Palm-Wine Drinkard* is much more ambitious, covering thirteen pages: it is long enough to be divided into sections bearing such subheadings as THE

DESCRIPTION OF THE CURIOUS CREATURE, 'DO NOT FOLLOW UNKNOWN MAN'S BEAUTY', 'RETURN THE HIRED PARTS OF BODY TO THE OWNERS; OR HIRED PARTS OF THE COMPLETE GENTLEMAN'S BODY TO BE RETURNED', 'A FULL-BODIED GENTLEMAN REDUCED TO HEAD', 'THE FATHER OF GODS SHOULD FIND OUT WHEREABOUTS THE DAUGHTER OF THE HEAD OF THE TOWN WAS', 'THE LADY WAS NOT TO BE BLAMED FOR FOLLOWING THE SKULL AS A COMPLETE GENTLEMAN', 'INVESTIGATION TO THE SKULL'S FAMILY'S HOUSE', and 'THE INVESTIGATOR'S WONDERFUL WORK IN THE SKULL'S FAMILY'S HOUSE'.

Around the bones of the basic myth as we find it in Ellis' version, Tutuola wraps a rich covering often of a most precise nature (outlandish guesswork, offered as precise, diligently recorded information to serve the cause of realism, is a standard feature of Tutuola's writing). Thus, the market at which the girl was abducted 'was fixed for every 5th day' and always closed by '4 o'clock in the evening'. Moreover, it was attended not only by people from the surrounding villages but also by 'spirits and curious creatures from various bushes and forests'. The maiden, we learn, is a petty trader, and is clearly something of a modern miss, too, for she has refused to marry a man chosen by her father and he has 'left her to herself'. Where the earlier version briefly says of the curious creature that, 'His appearance pleased Adun', Tutuola contrives to fashion an absorbing case of a *femme fatale* in reverse. The young lady is so fascinated by the vision that *she* makes the approach, leaves her goods in the market and blindly follows, even after being told to return home. Tutuola tries to explain the magical attraction of this strange man and gives us one of those detailed descriptions of which he is so fond. The man was tall but stout, and expensively dressed, a 'beautiful "complete" gentleman', who would have cost two thousand pounds if he had been 'an article or animal for sale'. Indeed, writes Tutuola, in a nice blend of ancestral and modern elements, if he 'went to a battle field, surely, enemy would not kill or capture him and if bombers saw him in a town which was to be bombed, they would not throw bombs on his presence, and if they did throw it, the bomb itself would not explode until this gentleman would leave that town, because of his beauty'.[26]

At every point, Tutuola expands and elaborates on the earlier version. To the dismantling of the complete gentleman, the central element common to both stories, he gives special treatment; for, instead of a rather sudden, but flat, revelation occurring in the girl's mind, she is seen steadily to move from a fascinated obsession to amazement, fear, and revulsion. And this arises directly from the dismantling process itself which is horrifying in its detail. Instead of returning 'borrowed' legs, arms and body, Tutuola's gentleman is more modern and complex: he returns, with the appropriate 'rentage money', a whole list of 'hired' parts: left foot, right foot, belly, ribs, chest, arms, and neck, until he reaches the gruesome business of returning 'the skin and flesh which covered the head', leaving the lady in company with a skull. Even the language adds to the effect of horror, exerting an appropriate physical effect on the reader as Tutuola describes how with each limb the creature 'pulled it out'. Other deliberate brushstrokes increase the terror of the girl's experience. For instance, with both feet surrendered, the creature begins 'to crawl along on the ground'; later, with only head, neck and arms remaining, it 'could not crawl as before but only went jumping on as a bull-frog'. Reduced to a bare skull, it developed a terrible voice with a humming sound which could be heard two miles away.

Tutuola's detailed expansion and complication of the original fable testify to his skill as a painstaking story-teller with a highly developed sense of the macabre and a Defoe-like concern with detail whose effect is to make us feel that events really did happen in that way. A more important indication of Tutuola's imaginative power, however, is the manner in which he allows Drinkard to make this story his own. An *alo* current among the Yoruba for generations becomes one of Drinkard's own exploits; a fable previously narrated in the third person becomes an 'I'-narrated heroic monomyth, the property and experience of Drinkard himself. Indeed, the whole point of the tale's inclusion in the book is to depict Drinkard as its hero. One of his many trials in the other world, it is refashioned largely to display the hero's bravery and magic. The episode is artistically introduced and rounded off, and so remains a complete adventure in itself; but Tutuola skilfully weaves it into the texture of the book as a whole, for the story is told, and the rescue carried out, only in exchange for information which Drinkard needs in his search for his tapster – which is the central quest uniting the different phases of the book. The complete gentleman episode thus becomes a subordinate but important stage of a larger adventure. It is independent, a story in its own right, yet Tutuola fuses it with the whole by having Drinkard narrate it as *his* adventure, and also by having him marry the rescued girl and take her off to be the heroine of his journey to the land of the dead.

The whole episode can thus be seen as a clear example of Tutuola's imagination selecting indigenous material, expanding and refashioning its components, and, with terrific assertiveness, offering it as the true experience of his hero. The whole performance is rather like the decorative 'double' of a Baroque sonata in which the player adds his own ornaments to the composer's melodic scheme. Or, again in musical phrase, it is an especially brilliant variation on an original Yoruba theme. J. P. Clark uses the same legend, less successfully, as the basis for his play *The Masquerade*.

As we have suggested, Tutuola's imaginative life is firmly rooted in the soil of Yoruba culture – a heritage he shares with Fagunwa and Soyinka. Hence his love of the macabre, of which the encounter with Death in *The Palm-Wine Drinkard* provides a memorable example. Sent to fetch Death from his house, in exchange for information on his tapster's whereabouts, Drinkard blithely sets forth to capture him, for, in a style of personification more convincing than anything we have in mediaeval literature, Drinkard genuinely regards Death as a human being like himself. As indeed he is, for he owns a fine tropical house in the forest, with a verandah, European style; and when Drinkard arrives, he is working in his garden – as any or every man might be doing. When Death calls out 'Is that man still alive or dead?' and Drinkard replies, 'I am still alive and I am not a dead man', a struggle ensues. But they are evenly matched and, on a truce being called, Death leads his enemy to the verandah, shakes hands in perfectly normal African manner, and ushers him into the house. It is at this point that Tutuola's Yoruba imagination begins to extend itself: the workaday normality of death, its solid ordinariness, are compounded now with all the age-old horror and mystery which our species has felt in face of it:

He took me around his house and his yam garden too, he showed me the skeleton bones of human-beings which he had killed since a century ago and showed me many other things also, but there I saw that he was using skeleton bones of human-beings as fuel woods and skull heads of human-beings as his basins, plates and tumblers etc.

Nobody was living near or with him there, he was living lonely, even bush animals and birds were very far away from his house. So when I wanted to sleep at night, he gave me a wide black cover cloth and then gave me a separate room to sleep inside, but when I entered the room, I met a bed which was made with bones of human-beings; but as this bed was terrible to look at or to sleep on it, I slept under it instead, because I knew his trick already. Even as this bed was very terrible, I was unable to sleep under as I lied down there because of fear of the bones of human-beings, but I lied down there awoke. To my surprise was that when it was about two o'clock in the mid-night, there I saw somebody enter into the room cautiously with a heavy club in his hands, he came nearer to the bed on which he had told me to sleep, then he clubbed the bed with all his power, he clubbed the centre of the bed thrice and he returned cautiously, he thought that I slept on that bed and he thought also that he had killed me.[27]

But horror and comedy easily melt into each other in the Yoruba imagination. When morning comes, Drinkard badly shocks Death by going to his room and wishing him good day. And later, his confidence lapping a high-water mark, he digs a hole in the road nearby, spreads a net and soon has Death in captivity. Without delay, he rolls up the net and strides away, for all the world as though he is carrying a head-load of bananas to market. The sight of Drinkard staggering into town with Death on his head terrifies everyone. The old man, who had sent Drinkard on this errand, orders him to take Death back where he belongs; whereupon weary Drinkard flings down his load and Death escapes. 'The whole people in that town ran away for their lives', remarks Drinkard, and then, casually pushing his story back into the mists of time and turning it into a 'creation' myth, he concludes, 'So that since the day that I had brought Death out from his house, he has no permanent place to dwell or stay, and we are hearing his name about in the world.' The claim is enormous, but it is made as though it were an item of domestic trivia. The narrative is a grotesque piece of fantasy; but we are asked to accept it as bedrock fact. Such is the confidence and the power of Tutuola's typically Yoruba imagination.

The modern African writer faces the problem of marrying his own traditions with those of Europe. This point has been made often enough. Tutuola, however, seems to have faced no such problem; or at least his blissful unconsciousness of artistic issues has enabled him effortlessly to solve a problem he was never aware of facing. He wrote out of himself and let the consequences look after themselves. On examination, the consequences reflect a sensibility and imagination solidly African, and exhibit only a modest quantity of western influence, this being confined to the material objects which European contact has introduced into West Africa. This often gives the writing a bird's nest texture – substantially built of one material with a scattering of alien feathers woven in for convenience. Such is the impression given by Tutuola's account of White Mother's habitation in the *Drinkard*; it is a sort of African Garden of Eden replete with dance halls, 'techni-colours', 'a photographer', walls decorated with 'about one million' pound notes, and an assortment of other items from the West. They do not shake the indigenous foundations of the writing. Nor do the many similar references Tutuola includes elsewhere, such as the 'high-heeled shoes which resembled aluminium in colour', the 'white and black deads' who are 'living in the Deads' town', the farms 'as flat as a football field', the creatures whose bodies are 'as cold as ice and hairy and sharp as sand-paper', or the 'half-bodied baby . . . talking with a lower voice like a telephone'. They are an integral part of the seamless coat that is Tutuola's style.

Sometimes, however, despite its narrative and imaginative strengths, Tutuola's style descends into sheer obscurity and confusion. No amount of imaginative power or narrative skill can compensate for writing which fails to communicate its meaning. The events at Lost or Gain Valley in *My Life in the Bush of Ghosts* are a case in point.

After carefully examining this episode several times, one suspects that Tutuola is saying something like this: Having crossed a river, the hero and his wife proceeded for four miles until they came to a ravine which was crossed by a single plank. A notice in ghosts' language told all travellers to strip, leave their clothes, and cross the plank singly. They crossed and waited for travellers crossing in the other direction who, of course, had to deposit their clothes, too. The Loss or Gain idea involved the quality of the clothes one picked up at either side.

Tutuola's account, mainly because of his limited vocabulary, succeeds only in obscuring these details. The confusion begins when Tutuola calls the ravine a 'valley' and then says it is crossed by a 'slender stick', when of course he means a tree-trunk or plank. The picture of a stick bridging a valley is hard, though not impossible, to imagine; but when Tutuola goes on to say that to cross the valley he and his wife have to 'climb' the stick, the scene begins to blur. We tell ourselves, however, that one side of the valley must be higher than the other, with the hero on the lower side. But this refocused picture blurs again when Tutuola, explaining about the disrobing, says that those travelling from the opposite direction (i.e. from what we must assume to be the higher side) have to undress before they *'climb'* the plank too. The author here has signally failed in his efforts to set the scene clearly. Interestingly, the same problem occurs in Bunyan's *Pilgrim's Progress,* where Christian climbs out of the Slough of Despond by a ladder!

The logic of events around the notice-board is equally hard to fathom: 'we saw a notice-board on which all these warnings are written in the ghosts' language as follows: – "Put all the clothes on your body with loads down here before climbing this valley." And I did not understand it. But as this slender stick was so slender, so we tried all our best to climb it with clothes on our bodies and failed before we understood what is written on the board . . .'[28] It is unsatisfactory enough to tell us what the notice said and then claim that he did not understand it. To then state that he and his wife tried hard to climb the stick, fully dressed, *precisely because it was so slender,* defeats the imagination. And who provides the interpretation of the notice? Presumably his wife, who, as a ghostess, speaks the language; but Tutuola does not say so. And if, as we can reasonably suppose, she did provide the interpretation, why did she fail to provide it before the absurd attempt to climb the stick because it was so slender? In a Carlylean essay entitled 'Tutuola, Son of Zinjanthropus', published in *Busara,* in 1968, Taban lo Liyong, East Africa's most controversial critic, cited the following authorities in a defence of Tutuola's work as a whole: Nietzche, Pound, Ionesco, Antonioni, Emile Brontë, Barth, McLuhan, Freud, Lewis Carroll, Shakespeare, Ben Jonson, David (and Goliath), Ovid, Hitler, Kant, Schopenhauer, Emerson, Thoreau, Gandhi, Gogol, Beethoven, Dryden, St John the Baptist, Robert Burns, Aristotle, Field Marshal Okello, Kipchoge Keino, and Max Müller – to name but a few. It must be insisted, however, that not even the combined assistance of these luminaries could save the above episode from condemnation. This is thoroughly bad writing and it is the business of criticism to say so.

And yet, behind the faults of grammar and syntax, and despite the handicap of a woefully limited vocabulary, a vigorous imagination is at work, boldly striding through the forests of myth and fantasy, and driving the narrative onward as one fantastic, yet imaginatively 'true', event succeeds another. It is, surely, this overwhelming sense of a rich and creative imagination at work that marks the special quality of Tutuola's art, and which provides the reason for our taking him seriously. And this is why Tutuola was so warmly received by Dylan Thomas, a man who was perfectly equipped to recognise imaginative power when he saw it.

There is another point. Excitement is growing in Africa over the extent to which myths, tales, and legends are shared by different peoples of the continent. The Luo and Kikuyu of Kenya and the Acholi of Uganda have tales and myths almost identical to the stories of Tutuola. The legend behind the Complete Gentleman episode is one example. Versions of it occur not only throughout West Africa, but in East Africa as well. The *femme fatale* stories are even more widespread. Examine Luo oral literature, for example, and find the tale of Lwanda Magere, a hero who marries a lovely Dalila, who finds the source of his strength (it lies in his shadow) and betrays him to her own people. The *femme fatale* idea is alive even in *current* Luo rumours about a demon girl who appears by the roadside and lures men to their doom. It means that Tutuola can be understood and appreciated by Africans far beyond the borders of Yorubaland.

More remarkable are the shared archetypes, which Jung described as primordial images formed by repeated experience in the lives of our ancestors, inherited in the collective unconscious of the human race, and often expressed in myths and dreams as well as in literature. As Mark Abrams has pointed out, when a literary artist uses an archetype he expects it to evoke a profound emotional response in the reader or listener because it resonates with an image already existing in the unconscious mind. Basic archetypes like the death-rebirth idea, and the journey beneath the sea, are frequently found in African tales and the writings of Tutuola are no exception. A terrifying example of an archetypal situation shows man in a corner with death staring him in the face. Typically, the victim is in a tree with his enemies below trying to reach him. This is how it appears in *Feather Woman of the Jungle,* where the 'hideous night woman' and her axe-swinging assistants have the hero trapped up a tree. At the critical moment, however, when it seems that he must be torn to pieces, the hero thinks of a way out (pp. 57–8):

Then with perplexity, I stood up right on top of the tree and I hopelessly called with the topmost of my voice: 'My dogs! My dogs! My dogs! The Cutter, the Sweeper, the Swallower! Let all of you come to this forest now!'

An identical situation is found in a Luo story called 'The Four Sons'.[29] But what is truly astonishing here is that the situation is repeated right down to calling the dogs by their names. The villain at the foot of the tree is Opul the Hyena who is furiously hacking away at the trunk. When the gentle Dove who has been helping the hero grows tired, the dogs have to be called. They arrive and are urged on to the kill:

White one, catch him!

Black one, eat him!

Grey one, swallow him!

Brown one, kill him!

Spotted one, finish him!

The situation of course finds parallels even outside Africa. When the distinguished film director Ingmar Bergman was choosing archetypal material for his piece *The Seventh Seal* this was precisely a situation he selected. The forest scene in which Death cuts down a tree with his victim vainly protesting in the branches above is one of the most nerve-stretching of the film. Tutuola then is giving vent to material that has its roots deep in the human psyche.

Yet for all this, Tutuola remains in isolation. As the first writer of West African monomyths in English, he stands as a pioneer without followers, a master without apprentices. It makes the innovator's lot seem an unhappy one. The enthusiastic declaration by Parrinder in 1954 that here was 'a beginning of a new type of Afro-English litera-ture' has been followed by a frosty and gloomy silence among the ranks of Tutuola's fellow African writers.[30] Is it true, then, that Tutuola represents a literary cul-de-sac? Does his isolation really mean that unlike, say, Kyd or Fielding, he is not creating a form that can be handed on? These are perhaps early days to give a confident answer. One point, however, does seem clear enough. Poets and playwrights can draw on the artistic capital amassed by their ancestors and do well; but, should the prose writer choose to do so, the strength and inspira-tion he will receive will equip him for precisely the 'fabulous' writing at which Tutuola excels – but not for a genre we could call modern fiction.

In a way, it is easy to understand why a younger generation have not imitated Tutuola. Better educated, they are not only far from sharing the unselfconsciousness of the traditional artist, but are acutely aware of the outside world and the great issues which beset it. It is this 'real' world, not the world of myth and fantasy, that concerns them, and just now they feel, so to speak, on stage before it. They are a generation of problem-solvers. 'Reality, the ever present fertile reality' is what Wole Soyinka keeps his attention on; and when he calls on fellow writers to act as 'the voice of vision' in their own time, he is clearly not using the word 'vision' with quite the same meaning which European critics have in mind when they apply it to Tutuola.[31]

There are probably psychological reasons, too, for Tutuola's isola-tion and lack of followers, and there is evidence enough that Africa's psychological problems are acute. It might not go wide of the mark to suggest that he is ignored by other Africans because he has committed the grave sin of ungrammatically describing their inner lives for readers in the western world – a western world where respect for a clinically clean, ghost-free, inner life holds sway. He has opened a window onto a part of the African soul which for the moment most of his westernised compatriots prefer to keep hidden. Everyone, Okara would say, 'has locked up his inside'. How else can we explain African bitterness against Fabers for publishing his work? How else can we explain the attitude of a country which gives its first international writer the exalted post of a storekeeper at a radio station? How else can we interpret recent reports that Tutuola in translation, that is, in the vernaculars, has become very popular?[32] Enjoy him in the protective secrecy of the vernacular, but heaven forbid that he should appear in an international language!

Perhaps when the urge to reflect the passing scene and to cure Africa's ills subsides, when prose writers can contemplate their inner lives with more calm and surrender, Tutuola's star will rise and the forces which shaped his work will be more freely acknowledged and harnessed.

'The Voice': Okara's prose experiment

For West Africa's younger generation of writers Tutuola's work does not provide an example of how they can realistically explore the contemporary scene. It was perhaps an awareness of this that stimulated Gabriel Okara to try to provide an alternative. Acting on his basic artistic aim of putting into the whirlpool of literature the African point of view, of putting across how at least an Ijaw African thinks, he decided to create a piece of experimental prose which would stand midway between the traditional form offered by Tutuola and outright imitation of western models; a work which mirrored and explored contemporary issues while remaining essentially African in style and point of view. The result was *The Voice*. A trial chapter appeared in *Black Orpheus*, No. 10, and the full text was published in 1964.

The Voice is an unusual document. The work of a practising poet, and the result of the same transliterative device which Okara uses in his poetry, it seems to partake of the nature of both prose and verse, and further reminds us of Senghor's insistence on the basic similarities of the two forms as they exist in Africa. It takes its origin from mid-twentieth-century actuality, yet its landscape is dark and hazy, as though glimpsed in a nightmare; it is symbolic in a way that recalls allegory, and its theme is at once contemporary and timeless. Okara told the novelist Andrew Salkey that the book is a struggle between the forces of darkness and light; and this is certainly the impression it conveys. Heavily moral in tone, it rings with the familiar Okara sincerity; and it has, too, those same qualities of moral concern which are so marked in the poems, and which Wole Soyinka seemed to have in mind when he stated that 'The artist has always functioned in African society as the record of mores and experience of his society *and* as the voice of vision in his own time.'[33] Literally translated, the hero's name means 'the voice', and we can take it here to signify the voice of prophecy and wisdom; or perhaps, as some would have it, the voice of negritude.

But Okolo is a composite character who can be seen either as a particular individual or as representative thinking man; even, perhaps, as the artist in society. His formal education complete, he returns home like a prophet emerging from the desert with a vision of how his nearly independent society can be splendidly reborn. He finds, however, that

113

village society has become morally and spiritually bankrupt; it has lost its ancient human values and replaced them with a hideous species of materialism learnt from the white man. It has sold its soul for a fistful of gold – and an offence briefly tilted at in the poem 'The Snowflakes Sail Gently Down' (where Okara refers to 'abandoned roots' and suns 'frowned' on because 'they reached not the brightness of gold') becomes a target for extended attack: 'Man has no more shadow, trees have no more shadow. Nothing has any more meaning but the shadow-devouring trinity of gold, iron, concrete . . .'

While dramatising a struggle between light and dark, between past and present, *The Voice* uses the quest motif, a device reminiscent of Tutuola's work, but different here in that Okolo is in search of nothing so tangible as a dead tapster; he is, in fact, in search of *it* – an embarrassingly absurd token for some such large idea as goodness, truth, faith, or the basic meaning of life. The book opens with a clear statement of Okolo's isolation, rendered in the Ijaw-based style that results from transliteration (pp. 9–10):

Some of the townsmen said Okolo's eyes were not right, his head was not correct. This they said was the result of his knowing too much book, walking too much in the bush, and others said it was due to his staying too long alone by the river.

So the town of Amatu talked and whispered; so the world talked and whispered. Okolo had no chest, they said. His chest was not strong and he had no shadow. Everything in this world that spoiled a man's name they said of him, all because he dared to search for *it*. He was in search of *it* with all his inside and with all his shadow.

Okolo started his search when he came out of school and returned home to his people. When he returned home to his people, words of the coming thing, rumours of the coming thing, were in the air flying like birds, swimming like fishes in the river. But Okolo did not join them in their joy because what was there was no longer there and things had no more roots.

Driven out of Amatu, his home town, and forbidden to return under pain of death, Okolo goes to Sologa, the big city across the river, and is horrified to find it infected with the same moral disease that infects the town. It seems as if the whole of contemporary society, rural and urban, is afflicted; for everyone appears to share the temporising judiciousness of a city white man who warns Okolo that if he wants to 'get anywhere', he must learn to shut his eyes to certain things, for 'truth and honesty . . . simply don't exist in real life'.

Meanwhile, Okolo seethes with inner conflict; among his fellow men, yet rejected by them and despising their values, he laments the passing of an order built on firmly spiritual foundations (p. 126):

Belief and faith in that something we looked up to in times of sorrow and joy have all been taken away and in its stead what do we have? Nothing but a dried pool with only dead wood and skeleton leaves. And when you question they fear a tornado is going to blow down the beautiful houses they have built without foundations.

Unable to decide which way to turn (there is even talk of the asylum as a way out of the dilemma), Okolo eventually chooses to go home, risk death, and fight for the cause as best he can. In a world dominated by a modern brand of materialism, he fights with traditional weapons handed on by a father who had always done 'the straight thing' and preserved his integrity, 'a sweet inside and clean as the eye of the sky'. He had wanted to give Okolo an education because of the changing world in which 'engine canoes and whiteman's houses have everybody's inside filled'. He had also given him the following advice (p. 126):

Argue with no one about whiteman's god and Woyengi, our goddess. What your inside tells you to believe, you believe, and always the straight thing do and the straight thing talk and your spoken words will have power and you will live in this world even when you are dead.

'Your spoken words will have power' brings into focus a subject that constantly recurs in this study, namely, the sanctity of the spoken word with all its magical and creative properties. The subject, of course, is suggested even in the book's title. 'Spoken words are living things', says Okolo, 'like cocoa-beans packed with life. And like the cocoa-beans they grow and give life.' Nor do they perish. 'Money may be lost forever but words, teaching words, are the same in any age.' It is by means of the spoken word that Okolo's message of salvation will be implanted in the minds and hearts of the people. It will 'remain there and grow like the corn blooming on the alluvial soil at the riverside'. It is this thought that lights up the gloom of Okolo's misery and assures him of ultimate victory over his enemies. As one of his neophytes puts it, 'Nobody withstands the power of the spoken word. Okolo has spoken. I will speak when the time is correct and others will follow and our spoken words will gather power like the power of a hurricane and Izongo will sway and fall like sugar cane.' Significantly, though the book has a tragic finale, there is no sense of Okolo having died in vain, for the closing dialogue of the book ends with the prophecy 'Your spoken words will not die'.

There is a familiar balance of forces in evidence here, the same ordering principle which Okara adopts in his verse, and it gives *The Voice* an impressive clarity of outline and organisation. Thus, the clash is between the forces of light and darkness, between tradition and modernity. In human terms, this involves two conflicting parties: town society led by Izongo and a small group led by Okolo, including his two closest friends – Ukule, a cripple, and Tuere, an alleged witch. Significantly, these two are also social outcasts, strong representatives of an old order which, at one point, is memorably symbolised in a picture of Tuere sitting with the cripple by a fire, talking and listening to the sound of drumming. The fire is low. 'It was not a proper fire be', writes Okara. 'It was like a leper's fire.' A warm, humane past is symbolised, a past with a concern for the unfortunate. But only broken remnants of it now remain, powerless and despised in the modern world. The new dispensation, vulgar and inhuman, is symbolised by Izongo, a chief who appears on the night of Okolo's death significantly dressed in European clothes, 'a black suit with brown shoes and on his head . . . a white pith helmet in the dark night'. Equally significant, he is drunk.

The book ends tragically, but also on a highly symbolic note. After a night of orgies, Okolo and Tuere, twin symbols of the past, are tied back to back in a canoe and sent to their destruction at the bottom of a whirlpool.

> Down they floated from one bank of the river to the other like debris, carried by the current. Then the canoe was drawn into a whirlpool. It spun round and round and was slowly drawn into the core and finally disappeared. And the water rolled over the top and the river flowed smoothly over it as if nothing had happened.[34]

The past has been submerged in the raging whirlpool of the present. But we have been told that Okolo's words 'will not die'. His physical death will provide the germ for a spiritual reawakening in society. Okara is offering us at the close of this highly poetic prose work something reminiscent of Shakespeare's sea change, or the drowned-poet idea so often found in Canadian literature; the artist sinking temporarily to undergo marvellous mutation and re-emerge in a new and rich guise. It firmly suggests, too, Okara's continuing basic concern not simply with the commonplace idea of old versus new, but also with the fascinating idea of an order that is becoming, a new Africa ready to emerge from the womb of time.

The Voice is a boldly experimental work, the most extensive of its kind yet undertaken in West Africa. But does it succeed? Reactions will differ, and so far the work has attracted its share of adverse comment.

Eldred Jones, in a passing reference to the book, asserted that the vernacular English is a failure.[35] This is too easy a dismissal. Certainly Okara's style creaks at times, and the doubled form of the verb 'to be' is an especially ugly feature; but occasionally it can rise to fine poetic effects. For example, the main verbs placed at the end of a sentence can give the prose a sense of cadence, peculiarly effective in a passage such as the following, describing the end of a day (p. 13):

> It was the day's ending and Okolo by a window stood. Okolo stood looking at the sun behind the tree tops falling. The river was flowing, reflecting the finishing sun, like a dying away memory. It was like an idol's face, no one knowing what is behind. Okolo at the palm trees looked. They were like women with hair hanging down, dancing possessed. Egrets, like white flower petals strung slackly across the river, swaying up and down, were returning home. And, on the river, canoes were crawling home with bent backs and tired hands, paddling. A girl with only a cloth tied around her waist and the half-ripe mango breasts, paddled, driving her paddle into the river with a sweet inside.

In an unpublished essay on *The Voice,* an American student in East Africa, Janice Shiarella, argued the essentially poetic nature of Okara's work, citing it as an example of a well wrought poetic novel. She rightly distinguished those effects which emerge naturally from the transliterative process and those which have been especially contrived for their poetic character. 'A line such as "hands clawed at him, a thousand hands, the hands of the world" is unlikely', she wrote, 'to be formed simply by the dictates of the Ijaw language', and with an image such as 'hurrying waves, waves hurrying with white caps as if to deliver a message', with its parallel structure, alliteration, and metaphor, 'we are sure that we are encountering the craft of a poet, not merely a minor peculiarity of a local language'. Rhythmic patterns, often reinforced by rhyme, might, she argued, emerge as a by-product of transliteration; but not entirely, for even when a sentence takes the natural English order, 'Okara is likely to construct through word choice a distinctly metered line'. She quotes the following examples:

> Do not ask the bottom of things, my friend.
> I want you and that is the end.
> One said 'go' and the other said 'stay' and
> Before he could decide on which to obey . . .
>
> *
>
> I have not reached house and hunger is holding me hard.
>
> *

The people were sleeping. He looked towards his left.
The people were sleeping. He looked towards his right.

Most importantly, in Mrs Shiarella's view, the style of Okara's prose construction 'reinforces the cyclical symbols which are the bases of his themes'. In the course of the book, she feels, 'a pattern of overlying symbols begins to emerge from which individual metaphors are taken'. She goes on to observe that the dominant symbol for Okolo is water, 'soft, cool, death-bearing, yet paradoxically regenerative'. Tuere's symbol is fire, vibrant, warm, yet also carrying the double image of life and death. The Chief and his spineless crew are symbolised by dry wood, swaying grass, and stone. Among the water images for Okolo, she notes that those of the river and whirlpool 'increase in tempo relentlessly as the end approaches, almost like waves coming faster and faster in anticipation of a storm, until at the final moment Okolo becomes one with them'.

As it flows along, echoing the vernacular, Okara's style reveals some basic features of Ijaw thinking. For the Ijaw, apparently, good and evil, truth and falsity, happiness and misery are neatly tidied under a limited number of antonymic pairings. 'Straight' and 'crooked' dispose of every variety of truth and untruth; 'sweet' and 'sour' represent all shades of happiness or misery. A man's inner life, whether it affects his heart, mind, or soul, is said to be lived simply in his 'inside', a ubiquitous word in this most introspective book, and one that also appears with great frequency in Okara's poems. Thoughts can fly in one's inside 'like frightened birds hither, thither, homeless . . .'; and, according to whether men are good, wicked, or happy, they have clean, ugly, or sweet insides. Okara renders the English saying 'Out of sight, out of mind' as 'when I do not see you, you will not be in my inside'. The sun is almost invariably 'the eye of the sky' or 'the eye of the day', and to live a year is to 'kill' it, one's past life being referred to in terms of 'dead years'. We might feel that an expression such as 'the forty to fifty years killed woman' sounds awkward, and even ambiguous; but it is the Ijaw way of describing a woman in her mid-forties. Where in English we habitually choose from a rich store of adverbs to emphasise a point (e.g. extremely good, very good, wonderfully good, marvellously good, etc.), the same kind of emphasis in Ijaw is usually achieved by means of simple repetition, as in 'black, black', 'slowly, slowly' and 'lightly, lightly'. In a somewhat modified form, we find Okara saying that 'the hut became dark with exceeding darkness', and 'It did not rain like rain. It rained more than raining.' He talks of 'silent more than silence', and 'bad more than badness'.

European readers might reasonably object that Ijaw appears to be a

118

limited tongue, and that by placing himself so fully within its prescriptions Okara is needlessly reducing his range of colour and expression. On the other hand, it seems clear that only by *accepting* the limitations of Ijaw and surrendering himself to its dictates can Okara hope to create the African style for which he is striving. And the results of his experiment are encouraging. We have already seen the merits in Okara's description of a day's ending, with its sense of things beginning to droop and drowse – a quality largely managed by placing key verbs near the close of the sentences. Elsewhere, Okara draws on the vernacular to achieve different effects. In the following passage, for instance, where Okolo first falls a victim of his people, Okara makes his style suggest rough and jerky movement; an effect, in the main, of repetition, a device to which we have frequently called attention and one that is common in all African oral traditions (p. 32):

> Then they put him down and dragged him past thatch houses that
> in the dark looked like pigs with their snouts in the ground; pushed
> and dragged him past mud walls with pitying eyes, pushed and
> dragged him past concrete walls with concrete eyes; pushed and
> dragged him along the waterside like soldier ants with their
> prisoner. They pushed and dragged him in panting silence,
> shuffling silence . . .

Repetition is evident, too, in the author's description of Okolo's first visit to the big city of Sologa. The key word here is 'eyes', and by the simple act of repeating it with different qualifications, Okara gives us not only a vivid sense of the hero's reaction to the clamour of the city, but at the same time a thumbnail sketch of collective humanity (p. 90):

> So Okolo walked in Sologa . . . passing frustrated eyes, ground-
> looking eyes, harlots' eyes, nothing-looking eyes, hot eyes, cold
> eyes, bruised eyes, despairing eyes, nothing-caring eyes, grabbing
> eyes, dust-filled eyes, aping eyes . . .
>
> Okolo walked passing eyes, walked passing eyes, walked
> passing eyes until hunger held him.

It is a brief passage; but it is a brief passage of creative writing in which Okara skilfully achieves the effects he is seeking, even to the extent of vetting a sense of weariness into the last two lines. Okara the poet is here, Okara the shrewd observer of mankind, Okara the man of moral vision. After the manner of Tutuola, he is using a common ancestral device; but he is using it with far greater skill than the Yoruba writer, with a keener sense of its potential effectiveness and versatility. It is a sign of Okara's finer literary craftsmanship.

A final illustration will serve to show the author's progress with his experiment. It is a single sentence which occurs near the beginning of

119

the book. Okara is saying that Okolo had once felt guilty that neither he nor his society had treated Tuere humanely when she was accused of witchcraft. He goes on to say (p. 20), 'But this feeling in his inside had slowly, slowly died with each dying year under the mysterious might of tradition.' Who would deny the quality of writing such as this? On first sight, it neither looks nor sounds peculiarly African. But careful scrutiny reveals it to be a felicitous combination of three familiar Ijaw elements: first there is the reference to 'inside'; then the emphatic duplication in 'slowly, slowly'; and finally the idea of the years 'dying' as they pass. There is, too, a fine sense of controlled movement here, of vowel harmony, rhythm, and alliteration. It is an elegant sentence built on vernacular foundations by the careful hand of a poet. Finally, it is one more sign of Okara's literary skill, and one more reason why his experiment with the vernacular must not be lightly dismissed.

In one sense, although a strongly African piece, *The Voice* is much closer to western norms than Tutuola's work. Unlike Drinkard, Okolo is a character who belongs to the modern world; he is a man of inner tensions and conflicts, an introvert suffering an unending depression. Certainly the work has its faults and we must constantly remind ourselves that Okara is offering it as an experiment. The emphasis on Okolo is too great; he looms so large in his humourless virtue (has not Okara even a buried sense of fun?) that he verges on the ludicrous. Perhaps he is meant to be a pathological introvert (and there *is* talk of an asylum); but pathological introverts, even those as moral, brave, and sensitive as Okolo, can make insufferably dull characters of fiction if their conduct is never marked by a laugh, or even a tearful smile. Okara can portray intensely, but psychological intensity is not matched here by psychological development; the difficult art of making plot and character interact is a skill which the author has yet to learn.

One might complain, too, about a certain vagueness in Okolo's position. It is a vagueness that usefully gives the book's themes a timeless quality; but what, one feels constantly obliged to ask, is Okolo trying to achieve? He is in search of *it* – a ludicrous token which the author should never have used. But is he simply anti-materialistic? a latter-day luddite? an arch-conservative? The vagueness is intentional but the book's moral purpose suffers marginally as a result.

Nevertheless, *The Voice* is an important attempt to solve a problem facing the development of West African prose. In so far as it steers a middle course between the realism of western fiction and the fantasy of traditional African modes such as we find in Tutuola, it appears to offer a satisfying synthesis – a prose form whose preservation of Tutuola's imaginative surrender, fused with a passionate concern to wrestle with the problems of the current scene, make it pregnant with the possibilities of development. It suggests a form that could be handed on. So far, however, Okara has suffered the fate of Tutuola. No followers have appeared. The example enshrined in this most important experiment has, for the moment, sunk out of sight. It remains to be seen if, like Okolo's message, it has sunk only to be splendidly reborn.

Chinua Achebe: the novelist as teacher

Chinua Achebe, an Ibo from Nigeria's Eastern Region, has made two major pronouncements on his aims and ideals as a novelist, and they provide an important clue to an understanding of his work. The first was made in 1964 at the Leeds Conference on Commonwealth Literature:

> Here, then, is an adequate revolution for me to espouse – to help my society regain its belief in itself and put away the complexes of the years of denigration and self-denigration. And it is essentially a question of education in the best sense of that word. Here, I think, my aims and the deepest aspirations of my society meet . . . I would be quite satisfied if my novels (especially the ones I set in the past) did no more than teach my readers that their past – with all its imperfections – was not one long night of savagery from which the first Europeans acting on God's behalf delivered them. Perhaps what I write is applied art as distinct from pure. But who cares? Art is important but so is education of the kind I have in mind.[36]

It was a blunt statement of his aims in a paper which he called 'The Novelist as Teacher'. The second pronouncement came two years later in 'The Black Writer's Burden', an article written for *Présence Africaine*.[37] It is a curious document that begins by re-emphasising, in more strident terms, some of the material from the Leeds paper. 'Without subscribing to the view that Africa gained nothing at all in her long encounter with Europe', he writes, 'one could still say, in all fairness, that she suffered many terrible and lasting misfortunes. In terms of human dignity and human relations the encounter was almost a complete disaster for the black races.' He goes on to attack the white man's 'gunholster culture' and the hypocrisy of its claims to Christianity and civilisation, warmly refers to negritude writers such as Senghor, Césaire and Diop, and throws in Zimbabwe, Nok culture, and the Ife bronzes as further support on the side of Africa. But all this is merely the preface for a plea to the black writer to forget the racial issue altogether and accept the first real challenge independent Africa has

121

offered him – namely, to 'expose and attack injustice' wherever it appears, but particularly in his own African society. He wants the freedom to criticise African societies without having anxiously to watch the effect which this might have on the black man's enemies. He criticises Mihajlov, the Yugoslav writer, who is reluctant to give joy to capitalism by castigating socialist societies. 'We must', writes Achebe, 'seek the freedom to express our thought and feeling, even against ourselves, without the anxiety that what we say might be taken in evidence against our race.' The feeling of forever standing before a tribunal must be discarded. 'We have stood in the dock too long pleading and protesting before ruffians and frauds masquerading as disinterested judges.'[38]

Thus, Achebe's declared aims are twofold: to teach his people, and to satirise them; or, as he puts it, 'to help my society regain its belief in itself' and 'to expose and attack injustice'. The first is part of his contribution to the task of giving back to Africa the pride and self-respect it lost during the years of colonialism, to repair 'the disaster brought upon the African psyche in the period of subjection to alien races'.[39] In this way, he takes his place alongside the band of historians, anthropologists, and political scientists who are hard at work on the massive task of African rehabilitation.

The second, the satirist's vocation, is in a sense loftier than the first, since it can transcend the bounds of temporary needs and exigencies; it also suggests an important role which the author has always been called upon to play. But Achebe's espousal of it arises directly out of West Africa's current predicament, in which the sins of the former conquerors are being cynically committed by the newly liberated. 'No more now the foreign hawks/On alien chickens prey – But we on us!' wrote the poet John Ekwere.[40] 'Triumphant putrefaction' is how Mabel Segun sees the new dispensation, 'Under a black, unsmiling sky'.[41] It is against a background as gloomy as this that Achebe has begun to sharpen the knife of satire. A satiric note is certainly heard in the first three novels; but while bearing this in mind, it is convenient here to take these works as representative of what we might call the author's more 'pedagogic' period and to see the fourth novel, A Man of the People, as the beginning of a phase pre-eminently satiric in nature.

Achebe's desire to teach raises a number of interesting points. It is generally agreed that African literary artists have always fulfilled this function in society, so that Achebe, ostensibly espousing a modern cause, is simply falling in line with tradition. Furthermore, teaching, by its nature, implies an audience. Achebe told the world at Leeds that he does have an audience; that it is large, and, in the main, indigenous.

122

Consisting mainly of young readers, still at school or college, this audience pays him the compliment of regarding him as its teacher.

But what really concerns us here are the implications which this holds for Achebe's style and method. Proudly African, and believing his 'pupils' should share his pride, Achebe is obviously concerned to portray with all the power at his command the beauty and rhythm of African life. What is more, since this is an indigenous audience, the most successful ways of appealing to its imagination and sensibility will be those that lie closest to indigenous modes and practice. Here the characteristics of traditional African literary art and the present need for good pedagogy meet; for a docile audience must be taught by lessons that have a strong central line and little sidetracking; hence, in the novelist's case, a narrative with one central figure and few digressions; a species of language that is clear and familiar, which stirs the emotions and drops anchors in the memory. The visual aids of the classroom must take a new form, appearing preferably as strong, clear images that quickly appeal and are easily retained. Aware of these necessities, Achebe developed his technique accordingly. His books *do* have a simple narrative line; their canvas *is* dominated by one central figure; imagery *is* clear and his style has the added virtues of lucidity and economy.

But one of the most useful devices which Achebe has employed to achieve his aim has been the African proverb. This, one suspects, is why the rich vein of proverbs and proverbial allusion that appears to be simply a happy *coup d'essai* in his first book, *Things Fall Apart* (1958), becomes an important feature of style in the two novels which follow: *No Longer at Ease* (1960) and *Arrow of God* (1964).

The reasons why Achebe uses the proverb are easily found, for the gnomic tradition, familiar in western literary history since Anglo-Saxon times, has occupied a central position in African life since time immemorial, and indeed has included precisely this didactic function with which Achebe is concerned. What is more, many scholars assert that the gnomic tradition, while either dead or moribund in the West, is still vitally alive in Africa. Doob observes that the Ibo store of proverbs is 'so profuse that often it is impossible to understand the full meaning of a conversation without knowing some of the more common ones'.[42] Among the Ashanti of Ghana, he adds, proverbs are so popular 'that they are used as a form of entertainment: contests are staged in which two men seek before a panel of judges to cite one proverb after the other'. The Yoruba of Western Nigeria are estimated to have forty thousand proverbs still in use. J. B. Christiansen has written on the role of proverbs in Fanti culture; Arnott has examined Fulani proverbs, and

Evans-Pritchard those of the Sudanese Nuer, while O. R. Dathorne has argued that proverbs form a type of oral literature in themselves. 'The proverb', says A. Adandé, a Yoruba from Dahomey, 'is conversation's horse; when discussion gets lost, you retrieve it with a proverb.'

But the proverb is also a fundamental ingredient in the intellectual traditions of African pre-literate societies; and, as Adandé points out, this fact should be firmly grasped by those who would understand African thinking: he is speaking of Dahomey, but his comments have a general significance:

> By their sheer ingenuity and aptness these proverbs bear witness to remarkable gifts of observation and a consciousness of moral duty. I believe that a study of these sayings is indispensable for those who wish to understand the souls of African people.[43]

The proverbial tradition, according to Marcel Jousse, 'is a practical, incarnate science, which stems from everyday actions; it is the ethnic regulation of these actions and their lasting codification'. This is not to say, however, that thinking based on the proverb must always remain bucolic or earthbound; on the contrary, says Jousse, it 'may rise to dizzy heights by means of simple human bilateralism, "just as the eagle soars towards the sun simply by beating his wings alternately" '.[44]

African proverbs, then, represent an astonishingly versatile device. They are guides to conduct, aids to instruction, rallying cries to tribal unity, and, in a continent where the rhetorical arts are yet vigorously in bloom, the weapons of debate and the buttresses of oratory. As a rule, the proverb reflects the basic details of rural African life and is frequently built around a central image of striking beauty, drawn from the people's long acquaintance with the forest and its teeming animal life. In a manner which recalls mediaeval practice, the African proverb likes to render the great abstractions of life, suffering, and death in familiar, workaday terms, and usually in the form of personification. It is perhaps too much to claim that a West African's life can be simply regarded as a movement from one proverb to the next; but the range of human experience covered by the proverb is certainly vast. No situation appears too unusual for it, no aspect of social behaviour lies beyond its reach.

In the society that Achebe's novels often portray, it is the tribal elders who are the great masters of the proverb and the most fervent believers in its power.[45] Enjoying the status of patriarchal sages, they see themselves as the guardians of the clan's cultural heritage, much of which has been handed down in the form of proverbs, and in a body of folk-tales allusions to which immediately acquire the stamp and tone of regular proverbs. This society does not regard the aged as a burden but rather as its venerable mentors who are expected to counsel and advise. Thus, in *Arrow of God,* when young men are keen to fight and risk destroying the clan, an old villager tries hard to restrain them with the powerfully blunt reminder that 'the language of young men is always *pull down and destroy*; but an old man speaks of conciliation'. The elders see their instruction of the young as a natural social function. Before Obi, in *No Longer At Ease*, sets off for England, on a scholarship provided by the Umuofia Progressive Union, one of them feels it his duty to warn him not to rush into the pleasures of the world too soon, 'like the young antelope who danced herself lame when the main dance was yet to come'; nor to marry a white woman, for thus he will be lost for ever to his people, like 'rain wasted in the forest'.[46] Versed in his clan's myths and tales, these are allusions whose meaning and force Obi readily understands. On the hero's triumphant return from overseas, with an Honours degree in English (regarded by the clansmen as a kind of modern day Golden Fleece), an illiterate elder, no doubt feeling challenged by so much erudition among the young, explains to him why he still feels competent to offer advice. He draws a meaningful distinction between wisdom and mere factual knowledge (p. 82):

> You are very young, a child of yesterday.
> You know book. But book stands by itself
> and experience stands by itself. So I am
> not afraid to talk to you.

It is not from books but from experience and from listening to old men that the young learn wisdom; such is the perpetual theme of the elders' pronouncements. 'The fly that has no one to advise follows the corpse into the grave' is a proverbial warning to those who might be foolish enough to ignore their help. In *No Longer at Ease,* a meeting of the Umuofia Progressive Union (Lagos Branch) offers a useful example of how the senior clansmen practise their pedagogic skills. The Union is shocked at the apparent unconcern with which Obi has greeted news of his mother's death; but an elder, rising and taking as his text the words 'This thing called blood. There is nothing like it', declares that he is not surprised at all, for in his lifetime Obi's father had been no better. Clearly it is a case of like father like son. This sage pronouncement greatly excites the Union President, who immediately seizes the opportunity to draw the moral for his audience and sanction it with as much proverbial force as he can readily muster (p.160):

> 'You see that,' said the President. 'A man may go to England,
> become a lawyer or a doctor, but it does not change his blood. It is
> like a bird that flies off the earth and lands on an ant-hill. It is still
> on the ground.'

125

More often than not, Achebe's proverbs are basically images with a didactic function, and can be used in the manner imagery is commonly used in literature, to bring into focus, and then sustain, themes the writer happens to be exploring. (When a series of proverbs is so used, however, they are a richer device than the rhyming image, for though their drift will necessarily remain constant, the 'pictures' they employ may well vary considerably.) The matter of clan solidarity is a case in point. Since Achebe is rehearsing the beauty of a traditional way of life and recording the anguish of its steady disintegration, this is an important concern in two of the first three books, especially when, as in *No Longer at Ease,* the clansmen are in Lagos, far from their homes in Iboland. In unity there is security and mutual aid in times of crisis. The clansman knows that 'He who has people is richer than he who has money', and the collective wisdom of the tribe, distilled from centuries of experience, has given him the saying 'when brothers fight to death a stranger inherits their father's estate'. Even the hero of *No Longer at Ease,* who, painfully caught between two worlds, has good reason to despise the heavy demands of tribal loyalty, can bring himself to preach the need for solidarity to brother members of the Umuofia Union. Though, in its context, perhaps faintly mocking in tone, Obi's performance on this occasion is eloquent enough, and an incidental reminder that the elders have taught their arts effectively (p.81):

Obi rose to his feet and thanked them for having such a useful meeting, for did not the Psalmist say that it was good for brethren to meet together in harmony? 'Our fathers also have a saying about the danger of living apart. They say it is the curse of the snake. If all snakes lived together in one place, who would approach them? But they live every one unto himself and so fall easy prey to man.'

More richly illustrated, however, is the strong sense of tragedy pervading the novels, which all recount the downfall of their central character – Okonkwo in *Things Fall Apart,* Obi in *No Longer at Ease,* and Ezeulu in *Arrow of God.* When the High Priest of Ulu is shocked into silence by the news of his son's death, which he believes is a punishment from his god, Achebe uses a proverbial comparison quite magnificent in its simplicity:

They say a man is like a funeral ram which must take whatever beating comes to it without opening its mouth; only the silent tremor of pain down its body tells of its suffering.[47]

A diligent if obstinate priest, Ezeulu cannot understand his fate; and his predicament is the more pitiful because he cannot explain it by resorting to tribal proverbs. Indeed, lying at the very heart of his grief, and

potent enough to drive him insane, is a conviction that some of the
fundamental precepts enshrined in the proverbs of the old dispensation
– especially those governing parents' duties to their children and a god's
relations with his priest – have been shockingly and brutally violated.
In his final *cri de coeur,* with its weirdly impressive conclusion, he
expresses amazement that his god could treat him so harshly. It is a
heavily proverbial piece of prose (with the climactic effect of a Mozart
symphonic coda) that demonstrates the truly original quality of
Achebe's work (p. 286):

> Why, he asked himself again and again, why had Ulu chosen to
> deal thus with him, to strike him down and cover him with mud?
> What was his offence? Had he not divined the god's will and
> obeyed it? When was it ever heard that a child was scalded by the
> piece of yam its own mother put in its palm? What man would
> send his son with a potsherd to bring fire from a neighbour's hut
> and then unleash rain on him? Who ever sent his son up the palm
> to gather nuts and then took an axe and felled the tree? But today
> such a thing had happened before the eyes of all. What could it
> point to but the collapse and ruin of all things? Then a god, finding
> himself powerless, might take to his heels and in one final,
> backward glance at his abandoned worshippers cry:
>> If the rat cannot flee fast enough
>> Let him make way for the tortoise!

Ironically, the closing chapter of the book explains Ezeulu's tragedy in
terms of two ancestral truths that he had somehow forgotten: 'that no
man however great was greater than his people; that no man ever won
judgement against his clan'.

In all three novels there are brave efforts to bear up beneath the
burdens of misfortune; and sometimes the hero will proceed by adopt-
ing an attitude of stoic realism, as Obi does when he tries to ease the
pain of his mother's death with the reflection, 'The most horrible sight
in the world cannot put out the eye' and then with an apparently
negating proverb, 'The death of a mother is not like a palm tree bearing
fruit at the end of its leaf, no matter how much we want to make it so.'[48]
In spite of this, however, the novels firmly insist on the inevitability of
human suffering whether man accepts it or not. This is how Moses, the
carpenter in *Arrow of God,* sees the idea, in an illustration that
effortlessly reduces an abstraction to solid, homely details: 'When
suffering knocks at your door and you say there is no seat left for him,
he tells you not to worry because he has brought his own stool.'[49] Nor
does one calamity rule out the likelihood of others to follow. Life is not
like that, Achebe's people say, for 'The very thing which kills Mother

Rat is always there to make sure that its young ones never open their eyes' and 'Even while people are talking about the man Rat bit to death, Lizard takes money to have his teeth filed.'[50] Life, then, is simply a continuum of misery, a *via dolorosa* offering few prospects of joy and refreshment. The most memorable witness to this pessimistic philosophy occurs in *No Longer at Ease* when Obi, disagreeing with an Englishman about the nature of tragedy and about Scobie's suicide in Graham Greene's *The Heart of the Matter,* quotes a remark from a village elder that has clearly won a place in the clan's anthology of powerful sayings (p. 39):

> It's much too simple. Tragedy isn't like that at all. I remember an old man in my village, a Christian convert, who suffered one calamity after another. He said life was like a bowl of wormwood which one sips a little at a time world without end. He understood the nature of tragedy . . . Real tragedy is never resolved. It goes on hopelessly for ever.

The protean nature of the proverb makes its precise function sometimes difficult to determine. It might be tentatively argued, for instance, that many of the sayings, besides having an obviously didactic purpose, are attempts, based on experience and observation, to tidy life's complexities to manageable proportions; to suggest, as though from experiment, the laws by which creation and human life proceed.[51] Suffering, perhaps, is easier to bear when it can be seen as part of a recognisable pattern of events. But whether imposing order on chaos, rallying the tribes to brotherhood, asserting ancestral truths or evoking the pathos of man's earthly estate, it is clear that proverbs are cherished by Achebe's people as tribal heirlooms, the treasure boxes of their cultural heritage. Through them traditions are received and handed on; and when they disappear or fall into disuse (as the novelist may well fear could happen) it is a sign that a particular tradition, or indeed a whole way of life, is passing away.

Certainly English history suggests that this is true. Sir Thomas Wyatt was prepared to make a firm assertion about the survival of at least two proverbs in his *Satires*:

> these proverbs yet do last.
> Reason hath set theim in so sure a place
> That length of yeres their force can never wast.[52]

It is hard to believe, however, that he would be quite so optimistic about the chances of the few proverbs current amongst the English today; for proverbial truth has made way for the more precisely defined truths of science, and men are apt to feel that the proverb's simplification is merely a substitute for further inquiry. As a result, the proverb rarely occupies an active place in our vocabularies, and thus plays little part in our literature either. It is unlikely that proverb-laden narratives will ever appear from the pens of Graham Greene, or C. P. Snow.

It comes as a shock, then, to find an author in the middle of the twentieth century assiduously cultivating the proverb as an element of style. English Literature has seen nothing quite like it since the Elizabethans.[53] And significantly its only modern equivalent is found among other writers from Africa; in, for example, the dramatic works of Obatunde Ijimere, and especially in fellow Nigerian Wole Soyinka.

The shape and rhythm of the proverbs, their richness and variety of imagery, add to the virtues of the prose, which is often dignified, measured, and poetic. Thus the adornments of a vast oral literature are carrying over into the writings of an author whose development Angus Wilson has called 'one of the few really hopeful things that have happened to the English novel in the past ten years'.

Achebe as satirist

Achebe's first three novels showed the author as teacher. His most recent book, *A Man of the People* (foreshadowed, as we have seen, by his short story 'The Voter'), represents the kind of writing which 'The Black Writer's Burden' manifesto led us to anticipate. The novelist is here in his new role as the scourge of villainy, the outraged *vox populi* crying out against oppression and injustice. From instructing his society to lashing it with satire; from portraying with a touching nostalgia the beauty of a vanishing world to savagely pillorying what is succeeding it – *A Man of the People* indeed marks a new departure. Achebe's former avowal of giving back to his people their self-respect has been set aside for an angry statement of their present sins; and a concern with the ills inflicted on an unwilling race by colonialism has made way for concern with the ills which that race has inflicted upon itself.

This novel, therefore, differs in aim and theme from those preceding it, though a satirical note was strongly sounded in *No Longer at Ease*. Equally important, it also marks a new departure in technique, for Achebe uses here for the first time (and probably in imitation of Mongo Beti) a *persona,* a mouthpiece or other-self, who can conveniently and independently narrate and comment on the events of the plot. This *persona,* a university graduate and schoolmaster, has become alienated from the common people; he inveighs against their fickleness, and, ironically, while showing moral weakness himself, reviles them for their spinelessness in face of oppression. His creator fills him with righteous indignation towards a hopelessly corrupt political élite and a cynical people who recognise evil yet will not revolt against it. Yet he is as much an object of satire as everyone else. As we have seen, it is Achebe's view that the novelist can and must influence his society; and by using the *persona* device he can safely point a finger at the warts and sores on the face of contemporary society. Readers are immediately aware that this *is* the present-day Nigerian scene, that these *are* the ugly facts of West African life.

Unfortunately, this in itself is not a guarantee of good fiction. It is the illusion of life that fascinates us in great literature, not real life itself. We have the mass media – radio, television, and, above all, journalism – to give a plain account of real life; but the work of fiction is different, it must create, not copy. 'But who cares?' Achebe says, and the reply must be, 'Literary criticism cares.' One of the main strengths in Achebe's first three novels lay in his dispassionate detachment and in a style which recalled Pater's remark that 'the true artist may be best recognised by his tact of omission'. He called up a world, stood away from it and left us to gaze on its details. Historically, of course, the use of a *persona* has normally guaranteed detachment, too, and writers as far apart as Swift, Conrad, Salinger, and Waterhouse have all used the device to devastating effect. But in Achebe's hands the technique is a failure. It is as if the burning zeal displayed in the pages of *Présence Africaine* was politically rather than artistically directed; with the result that one feels as if artistic detachment has been surrendered to political ends: there is no gap between the author's real and declared self. 'Perhaps what I write is applied art as distinct from pure. But who cares?'[54] Thus spoke Achebe in 1964; and, as one reads *A Man of the People,* those words keep echoing on like the last defiant cry of one approachng suicide. Righteous indignation with a corrupt political élite is well enough; but as a primary aim in writing it is more in line with the tradition of the political tract than with the tradition of fiction. This is indeed the contemporary scene which Achebe is mirroring; these are real people he is drawing; but they are the 'real' people of journalism rather than those whom great authors create. The book's title is ironic; but so, surely, is the comment printed on the book's jacket from *The Times Literary Supplement*: 'An essentially and admirably journalistic triumph of documentation. Nearly all the most telling and odious features of recent Nigerian life are here, intelligently observed.'

In his anxiety to solve the present problems of his society, even if it means writing 'applied art' instead of 'pure', Achebe's artistry declines alarmingly.[55] The teaching role suits him better; it has long roots in

African tradition and makes demands on those qualities for which Achebe is distinguished. The good lesson requires minute preparation and painstaking presentation; it requires the voice of persuasive reasonableness and a care for consistency, above all, perhaps, impartiality. These are demands to which Achebe is remarkably well equipped to rise. Newcomers to satire, however, are apt to feel that its only requirements are white hot zeal and a loud voice; neophytes are apt simply to cry destruction and smash idols. But those who would venture into a field honoured by the genius of Pope, Swift, and Sterne, had better display more qualities than noise and iconoclasm if they are to make their mark. Satire, one suspects, has not enjoyed a long history in Africa; and for Achebe the absence of this kind of strength at his back has been disastrous. The prose is uneven. Its unsteady rhythm might well be taken as reflecting the turbulence of a committed and indignant spirit; but the effect is not artistic since there is little feeling of restraint. Success at the Swiftian *saeva indignatio* requires, above all else, control; in the heat of his moral tirade this is precisely what Achebe has lost. Much has been made of the rather prophetic close to *A Man of the People:* 'But the Army obliged us by staging a coup at that point and locking up every member of the Government.' It sounds suspiciously as though Achebe is suggesting a solution. It is not, generally speaking, the job of art to provide answers; art which does so simply moves towards propaganda.

The first three novels were enough to establish Achebe's superiority over such fellow writers as Onuora Nzekwu, T. M. Aluko, Nkem Nwankwo, and Cyprian Ekwensi. Not only did the novels display the quality of his literary skill; they illustrated the successful way in which he, unlike many of his colleagues, had faced up to, and largely solved, the literary problem modern African writers must tackle: how to write, in the metropolitan language, recognisably modern literature, which reflects contemporary mores and problems, and yet retains a large measure of cultural authenticity. As we have seen, Achebe met this problem in part by using the proverbial idiom of his people – one of the most ancient and protean teaching devices which his continent had to offer. One hopes that he will, eventually, return to a style of writing that uses still further the resources of the indigenous tradition. Then the decline represented by *A Man of the People* will be remedied and the work of journalism left to the journalists themselves.

4. *Further prose: children, highlifers, and politicians*

Juvenile literature

In the rise of Nigerian literature in English, children's books have not been neglected; and it is an important fact that several established authors have felt drawn to make a contribution at this level. Nkem Nwankwo, author of *Danda,* one of the more amusing novels to come out of Nigeria, has written *Tales Out of School*; Onuora Nzekwu, well known for his *Blade Among the Boys* and *Wand of Noble Wood,* has collaborated with Michael Crowder to produce *Eze Goes to School*; the Yoruba poet Mabel Segun, famous for her piece 'Corruption', has written a delightful autobiography *My Father's Daughter*; Chinua Achebe has offered *Chike on the River*; and Cyprian Ekwensi, Nigeria's most prolific prose writer, has written such engaging pieces as *The Drummer Boy, An African Night's Entertainment,* and *The Passport of Mallam Ilia.*

It is as though Nigeria's literary men are accepting responsibility for the rehabilitation of a *whole* society and not merely for the adult segment of it. In the kind of cultural battle they are waging, no effective strategy could exclude the rising generation of schoolchildren, those vessels for the visionary optimism of the adult world who are always felt to carry the promise of a better tomorrow. Nigeria's writers, it seems, know the truth behind the dictum 'bend the twig when it is young'.

There is, too, a conviction throughout the continent that school is Africa's best friend. Everywhere, an academic holy war is being waged; and Nigeria's case is not untypical. As Tai Solarin wrote in 1961, 'The whole country is geared to the teeth to get its children educated. In this first year of our independence, the Western Region of Nigeria spent just over 43 per cent of its slim budget on education alone. As far as I know, no other country in the world has done that.'[1] As for the *kind* of education that should be fostered, there is a growing awareness of the folly of retaining those aspects of an inherited system which are, pedagogically, at best absurd, and at worst plainly harmful. The widespread colonial practice of proceeding from the unknown to

132

the known is one notorious example: approaching African history via European history; learning the rivers of Europe before the rivers of Africa; reading European literature and no African literature at all.

In the wild stampede for education at any price, many such malpractices are still allowed to flourish; but sensitive spirits, especially the men of letters, are beginning to pause and point out the pitfalls. To an audience once too impatient, or too conservative, to listen, they are firmly insisting that in matters of history, geography, sociology, and literature, Africa's students must, henceforth, work outwards from their home base. *They must move from the known to the unknown; the primacy and centrality of the African experience must now be accepted.* The importance of African humanities in all this, and especially perhaps African literature, cannot be overstated. A thorough grounding in the sciences will produce Africans who are, intellectually, citizens of the world; but inattention to that complex tissue of forces that have shaped the soul and moulded the landscape of an imagination, can only produce citizens who are, despite their education, culturally stateless persons.

In Nigerian schools, children were fed on a literary diet prepared (not always with care) from the library shelves of Europe. With political and cultural independence tending to travel hand in hand, this situation was unlikely to survive the waving off of colonial flags. When the repatriation of school syllabuses was advocated, it was quickly realised that there existed an acute shortage of suitable African texts. In Nigeria itself, the African Universities Press, Lagos, was set up precisely to meet this problem. As it proudly announced on the covers of its first publications, 'AUP is the first indigenous publishing house in independent Africa. The greater part of its output will be educational books chosen to answer the needs of Nigerian schools and colleges.'[2] In 1962, a translation of the Hausa document *A Chronicle of Abuja* was published; and then, in the same year, came the inception of a series called The African Reader's Library. It opened on a strongly local note with Cyprian Ekwensi's *An African Night's Entertainment,* soon to be followed by Nwankwo's *Tales Out of School,* Akinsemoyin's *Twilight and the Tortoise,* Nzekwu's *Eze Goes to School,* Onadipe's *The Adventures of Souza,* and Mabel Segun's *My Father's Daughter.* The growth has been rapid and is still accelerating.

Nigeria's children tend now to *read* literature rather than to *hear* it. *An African Night's Entertainment* struck a local note precisely because, though in written form, it stands close to the oral convention with which African children have been familiar. As the cover blurb puts it, with mystifying precision, this is a story for children 'from nine years old

133

upwards, based on a Nigerian folk-tale and told with great charm and spirit'. Ekwensi's Introduction deliberately evokes a traditional story-telling scene (p. 7):

'Put your money on this sheepskin,' said the old man, 'and if, by the time I finish my tale, there is one of you awake, that man shall claim everything we have collected.'

Young men, old men, children, women, they all put some money on the sheepskin beside the story teller. He waited till they had sat down. He himself settled comfortably on the *catifa* and smiled.

'It is a long tale of vengeance, adventure and love. We shall sit here until the moon pales and still it will not have been told. It is enough entertainment for a whole night'.

AN AFRICAN NIGHT'S ENTERTAINMENT.

When the end is reached and the moral announced ('One must not take it upon oneself to inflict vengeance'), the audience is still awake, so exciting have they found the old man's narration.

Between the opening scene and the denouement flows a violent and bloodstained tale. A version of the Sohrab and Rustum story, mixed with a good deal of faery and a generous helping of Ekwensi's criminal realism, is firmly pinned to the episodic framework of the picaresque. Alas, even in an African setting, it is hard to combine with complete success the realms of fantasy and realism. When, for instance, after magical journeys through monster-ridden forests and spell-casting orgies that send a man wandering bewitched through the land, a character suddenly steals a bicycle or catches a train to Lagos, then one suspects that matters have gone too far! The need to keep spinning out episodes appears to override considerations of form and probability.

And yet the plot is engaging enough. Mallam Shehu, a rich man with three wives, has no children. A dream is interpreted to mean that he might court and marry a fourth wife late in life and that she might bear him a child; but, since the woman will be already promised to another, Shehu should avoid a union which can only bring evil results. The Mallam's answer is simple: 'Will Allah indeed let me see a son of my own? . . . If so, I do not care how much I suffer after that!' He entices into marriage Zainobe, a neighbour's daughter betrothed to one Abu Baki; and the girl soon produces him a son called Kyauta, that is, 'Allah be thanked'. While Kyauta grows into a model Muslim youth, a friend of the poor and obedient to his parents, the furious Abu Baki roams the countryside seeking revenge. He visits Tutuolan towns where everyone has the gift of clairvoyance; he loses an eye and ear at the hands of brigands; he wanders in the Forest of Death, meeting pythons that change into hags, who in turn change into leopards. After multitudinous adventures, all undertaken in defiance of a sacred proscription of revenge, he finally succeeds in his quest. Magic sap obtained from a certain tree will cruelly harm Kyauta if it is rubbed into his skin, provided, at the same time, that a lock of the boy's hair is buried in a newly dug grave.

The magic works. Kyauta runs mad and begins a life of crime. It is here that Ekwensi's cherished world of criminality breaks in. The fairy atmosphere is shattered beyond recall when Kyauta steals money and a bicycle, goes drinking and whoring, and then, after joining a gang of smash-and-grab robbers in the best Chicago style, takes the train to Lagos; between which city and Accra he continually commutes on criminal expeditions. There is a delightfully contrived denouement. Tired of jailing Kyauta, the Lagos police banish him to a remote part of the North. Quite by chance, Shehu and his wife have also gone there, to escape the shame of their son's reputation. Unwittingly, Kyauta organises a raid on Shehu's home and kills his father in the course of it; but he is recognised and held by Zainobe. She reveals the truth about his situation, and, with the spell broken, he reverts to his former pious self. Full of remorse, he shares his inherited wealth with the local king, the blind, the lame, the lepers, and a mosque building fund; and then, in a curious breach of the tale's morality, he vows revenge on Abu Baki, hunts him down, and slashes off his head, before running amok for a whole year 'eating wild fruits, hunting game, sleeping in the rain and in the sun'.

An African Night's Entertainment was published as the first volume in AUP's African Reader's Library series. But Ekwensi had begun providing texts for African children two years earlier with his *The Drummer Boy* and *The Passport of Mallam Ilia*. *Passport,* like Ekwensi's other *juvenilia,* shows a neat sense of form, the plot, episodic and 'circular', moving out from a given starting point and returning there about eighty pages later. The episodic structure recalls European picaresque, but Ekwensi is using a structure commonly found in African oral practice too. The hero undertakes a journey which provides a peg upon which the author can hang any number of adventures requiring no organic relationship beyond the fact that they happen to one man. Often, as in the picaresque, lost identities are revealed by keepsakes or special marks on the body. All these features can be found in *The Passport of Mallam Ilia.*

The plot begins in the coach of a train travelling to Northern Nigeria, and takes us by way of the Mallam's life-story (recounted in the coach at the request of one Hassan) into the history of Hausaland before the British conquest, through the Hausa Wars of the early century, across to the Cameroons for the German campaigns of 1916, into the vast lands of French Equatorial Africa, over the Sahara to Mecca, down into East Africa for the Second World War, and, finally, back into the train coach. The events cohere because they are all part of one man's experience. But there is a further unifying factor, reminiscent of *An African Night's Entertainment,* in the shape of a revenge quest. A deadly feud has long been raging between Ilia and a certain Mallam Usuman, a huge devilish creature whom Ilia as a youth defeated in a fight for the hand of a Tuareg prince's daughter. The denouement, again, is tidy. Usuman, *mirabile dictu,* is on the train itself, working as a steward! There is a fight reminiscent of Western films on the gangway between the coaches, and Usuman hurtles to his doom. And now, for some curious reason deciding on suicide, Ilia takes poison. But before he dies, Hassan displays a parchment inscribed in Arabic proving that he is in fact Ilia's long-lost son, left behind in Mecca many years before. The dying man also learns that Hassan's mother, the faithful wife he also deserted in Mecca, is waiting at Jos, the next station on the line! He dies before the train pulls in, a strange, lonely figure, whom Ekwensi portrays through the cold details from his passport (p.11):

> It described him as Mallam Alhaji Ibrahim Ilia, a man five feet six inches tall, with no tribal marks on his face, a man born in 1882, and travelling to Mandara, Marua, and Fort Lamy for the purpose of trade. It was signed by the Resident at Kano, and dated May 1927.

Passport is a skilfully worked piece of fiction and Ilia's story engages our interest and our sympathy. For Nigerian schoolchildren it offers a fascinating journey from their own environment to exotic areas of the world beyond. The text, thus, fulfils the need to feed, exercise, and expand the imagination of African children with genuinely African material.

An unappreciated fact about Ekwensi is his ability to write authoritatively about all the main regions of Nigeria. Books like *Burning Grass, Jagua Nana,* and *The Passport of Mallam Ilia,* show that the semi-desert towns of the North, the dry dusty plains of Bauchi, are as familiar to him as the humid cities of the coastal fringe. *An African Night's Entertainment* and *The Passport of Mallam Ilia* are centred in the main on Northern Nigeria, and the heroes are Hausa Muslims. *The Drummer Boy,* however, published in 1960, has its setting in the South, mainly in Yorubaland, though Akin, its blind hero, wanders in true Ekwensian fashion as far as the Eastern Region to escape a pious plan to send him to school. We find once more a well-tried formula: a 'circular' plot (Akin *does* return and go to school) and an episodic structure. Nor is the familiar criminal ingredient omitted. There is arson here, forgery, murder, and organised robbery. A woman whose restaurant is burned down by the hirelings of a rejected lover, is later, in a midnight scene of scarifying horror, almost whipped to death by the same thugs disguised as masqueraders of the Yoruba god Oro. A European teacher, attempting to resist the thugs, is brutally slain. On the side of the angels are Joe, a nurse, Madam Bisi, the philanthropist eager to have Akin educated, Fletcher, the European founder of a boys' home on the Ogun River, and, of course, Akin himself, a sort of African St Francis who sees himself as an instrument of peace as he travels about playing his drum. He is a sensitively drawn figure, whose main delight in life is making others happy. He sings 'about the rich and the poor; the suffering and the happy', about 'love and death and good and evil'.

Appearing in Nigeria's year of Independence, the book, not surprisingly, shows a bias towards such morally glowing themes as social and personal reform. Typically, at the trial of the thugs, we find that their crime springs from social causes. Herbert, the youngest of the gang, took to 'forgery, burglary and arson' after being expelled from school. Escaping the sentence of his comrades, who are to be 'hanged by the neck until they [are] dead' (Nigerian schoolchildren are evidently a tough-minded breed), Herbert joins Akin at the Boys' Forest Home, where, after receiving six strokes daily for a whole week, he begins a programme aimed at his reform. The idea of regeneration, the promise of a new dawn, is strongly present in the closing stages of the tale. Akin's parents arrive. It seems they had abandoned him to a beggar's life, having carelessly allowed him to go blind after an accident.

The closing scene of *The Drummer Boy* would do justice to Hollywood – a not infrequent source of Ekwensi's inspiration. Akin is seen in the woods near the school, deliriously playing his drum, while around him 'like rats around the Pied Piper', dance the boys, 'the delinquents, the dangerous criminals, the thieves, the liars, the run-aways-from-home . . .' And then (pp. 80–1):

> . . . just at that moment, as if even Nature herself had been conquered, the evening sun came out in one last red glow. The entire sky was transformed into a dazzling arc of red so that the white clouds were tinged and they stood out against a red-blue sky. The trees stood out dark and silent, and all Nature seemed to focus its last effort in that red glow of Nigerian sunset.

Madam Bisi and Joe held hands. Ayike looked on, like a child lost in wonder. Akin had brought with him some form of magic, some strange enchantment and power, over Fletcher's Forest Home. She glanced at Fletcher. His eyes were misty. Bisi, too, was trying to conceal a tear, big and bold, that was quickly stealing down her cheek. She looked quickly away to the woods, where Akin the Drummer Boy was radiating happiness, in a manner to make everyone think only of doing good, of being good, and of living a clean life.

'God bless Akin,' she murmured.

At the close of this violent moral tale, Ekwensi reaches depths of sentimentality to which his writing has never elsewhere descended.

Although Mabel Segun's little book *My Father's Daughter* contains some idyllic reminiscences of a Nigerian childhood, in many ways the most stimulating work to appear in the African Reader's Library series is *Twilight and the Tortoise* by Kunle Akinsemoyin.[3] Only Beier and Gbadamosi's *Not Even God is Ripe Enough* can rival this collection of fourteen tales for charm, wit, and endless good humour. Akinsemoyin explains that his stories are among the best-loved tales in Nigeria. They can be heard at twilight, in any village, he says, when the children, having spent a tiring day helping in the fields, gather at the feet of the story-teller. In the growing silence, there descends the atmosphere of magic casements opening on to fairy landscapes, just as it descends on children awaiting a bedtime story the world over.

But when Akinsemoyin writes, 'In any Nigerian village at twilight, you might hear any of the stories in this book', he should not be taken too literally. For surely, it is, in part, the widespread knowledge that African children are now hearing *less* of the old tales that has caused an increasing amount of the oral heritage to be committed to the cold permanence of the printed word. Did not Tutuola himself offer this as one of his main reasons for writing? African children are reading their folk-tales in school rather than listening to them at home. Hence, indeed, Akinsemoyin's own collection. There is a further point. Despite the claim that these are stories popular all over Nigeria, the collection, in fact, concentrates on the southern half of the country, and especially on Yorubaland. Although Tortoise, the book's hero, is popular among the Ijaw, the Ibo, and the Efik, he is, above all, the darling of the Yoruba. He is not, for instance, popular in tales from the North, where he is replaced by Pozo the Spider.

The whole volume, then, celebrates the exploits of Mr Tortoise. The stories are told with clarity, a lively style, and unflagging ingenuity. Some exhibit the explanatory nature of the creation myth; some carry in their depths a hidden moral; but the point of others is sheer fun and nothing more. But why Tortoise? Why has this weird creature exercised so powerful a hold over the African, and especially the Yoruba, imagination?

In an environment where the behaviour of the animal world easily slips over into discussion of human behaviour, the Yoruba, down the centuries, have watched Tortoise's life-style with rapt attention and boundless admiration. Unlike the Chinese, who, according to Frazer, regard the tortoise as 'an animal of the very worst character', the Yoruba are more kindly disposed. Tortoise figures in many of their proverbs. *Ahun nre ajo, o gbe ile re dani,* they say, applauding a man's independence – 'The tortoise is going to a distant place and is carrying his house with him.' When a man struggles hard against adversity but conceals his efforts, the following proverb might be quoted: *Ajapa nmi, igba ehin re ni ko je ki a mo* – 'The tortoise is breathing, but its shell prevents people from seeing it.' A man confident that his enemies are powerless to harm him will assert: *Asa wo ahun titi, awodi wo ahun titi; kini idi baba asa on awodi le fi ahun se?* – 'The hawk looks at the tortoise for a long time, the kite looks at the tortoise for a long time; what can the eagle, more powerful than the hawk or kite, do to the tortoise?'[4]

In a world where disease and famine have always made life hazardous, here is a tiny animal with prodigious powers of survival. A living fossil resembling his ancestors of millions of years ago – who looks aged even from birth – this strange creature outlives all the old men and the vast majority of the beasts. He is a dwarf among giants whom he can both outwit and outlast. He is felt to be more of a thinker than other animals; indeed, he actually appears to think before he makes each move. He is believed to have an old man's wisdom, that uncanny knowledge of life which makes for survival in a hostile world. He is slow, yes, but he is sure. He is the solid rock that holds fast while the shallow currents of life sweep round him. When life for Tortoise becomes unbearable, he simply retreats into his house and moves on to quieter pastures. To a people who admire the power to survive amidst adversity, whose literature constantly preaches a stoic patience in face of misfortune, Tortoise is a natural hero. He is also a rather amiable fellow, enormously tough for his size, yet friendly and innocuous. He has no venom to spit, no claws with which to tear and maim; he survives, yet threatens no one else's survival. With his wisdom, his ability to ride the storm no matter how furious, and with his armour always in place, he is, in a word, all that common sense and applied intelligence can produce. From Tortoise, say the Yoruba, man has much to learn.

The tightly organised tales in Akinsemoyin's book, with their

139

humour, their imaginative turns of plot, and their neat resolutions, reflect, on the whole, Tortoise's intelligence, Tortoise as thinker. Often, when faced with a problem, he is seen thoughtfully scratching his head, or retiring to bed to think matters over quietly. The stories fall roughly into two groups: those in which Tortoise cleverly wins the day; and those in which Tortoise is too clever by half and suffers defeat.

A tale called 'Tortoise Shows Why' (pp. 78–80) is a specimen of the former variety. Yen, the hyena, is prowling round a village when he sees two men fighting; puzzled over why this should happen, he consults Tortoise, addressng him with the opening compliment, 'There's no doubt you're the wisest of us all' – to which Tortoise bows in dignified assent. Yen explains his problem. 'It seems to me so strange and so foolish', he says, 'to carry on like that. They ought to know better.' Ingenious Tortoise at once arranges an experiment to demonstrate man's innate foolishness. From a hunter's trap he takes a dead squirrel and carries it to the river, where he empties a fisherman's basket and puts in the squirrel. The fish he now places in the hunter's trap and invites Yen to sit with him and await developments. The hunter arrives and is furious at the sight of the fish. 'By the grey hairs of my ancestors', he swears, 'I'll teach the fisherman who did this a lesson. And I know who it is.' However, at the fisherman's house, he is greeted by a torrent of abuse: 'Thief . . . Rogue . . . good-for-nothing hunter. What kind of a man are you? Stealing all my fish, and then you had the cheek to put a dead squirrel in my fishing-basket. You'll pay for it.' A fight starts in which the villagers quickly, and rashly, take sides. Tortoise and Yen watch for a while, then move quietly away, Yen sadly pointing the moral, 'If only man could be a little bit patient.' Tortoise laughs knowingly, before replying in a nice paradox, 'Man is much too clever to see the wisdom of your words.' And there the story ends!

In 'The Laughing Tree', however, which is a too-clever-by-half tale, Tortoise's brain lands him in trouble. This is a longer and more complex story than most in the volume, beautifully poetic in parts, and offering a 'how and why' explanation of a certain aspect of Tortoise's behaviour. A thief is at large in the village, stealing palm kernels. Attempts to catch him are in vain: this is no ordinary thief but one possessed of a high degree of cunning. The villagers are perplexed. Perhaps the gods are angry, they think, and so, by way of appeasement, sacrifice rams, goats, and chickens. But all to no avail. The thief of course is Tortoise, who, with equal facility (and here is a moral point), can use his intelligence for good or evil. Carrying a rope, sack, and knife, he creeps forth at the darkest hour each night and slowly climbs the palms to do his mischief. But eventually his greed conquers his wisdom; he insists on setting out one night even after

140

his wife has had a premonition of disaster. Stumbling along in the dark, he bumps into a fat tree which terrifies him by swaying suddenly from side to side and laughing hideously. He hurries back home. But such, now, is his greed, that he sets out yet again the following night. This time, however, Alumo the laughing tree spreads news of his coming throughout the forest, and a delightful colloquy is heard in the silence of the night (p. 73):

> 'Thief!' said the Coconut Tree.
> 'He's wicked!' said the Mango Tree.
> 'He'll come to a bad end!' said the Cashew Tree.
> 'We must do something about it!' said the Guava Tree.
> 'What shall we do?' asked the Kola Tree.
> 'Teach him a lesson!' replied the Orange Tree.
> 'What sort of a lesson?' asked the Pawpaw Tree.
> 'Let's help the villagers!' shouted the other trees.

And so, in an example of the natural world helping humans in the fight against evil (it occurs in folktales across Africa, those of the Luo in Kenya, for example, providing many instances), the trees decide to broadcast their secret to the world. The following night, therefore, at a signal from Alumo, thieving Tortoise is greeted by all the trees singing in chorus (pp. 73–4):

> Tortoise is on his way
> Alumo, the king of laughter, Alumo,
> To steal the palm kernels,
> Alumo, the king of laughter, Alumo,
> In his right hand, a knife,
> Alumo, the king of laughter, Alumo,
> In his left hand, a rope,
> Alumo, the king of laughter, Alumo,
> On his back, a sack,
> Alumo, the king of laughter, Alumo.

Their singing, followed by hissing and booing, angers Tortoise who hurries back home. But a farmer returning late from his fields has heard and seen everything. The village elders are informed, and a plan is laid to catch Tortoise red-handed. The cunning thief lies low for a while; but when he sets forth once more, the villagers are ready for him. The trees warn of his approach and as Tortoise reaches the top of the tree, the villagers rush out and startle him; he falls with a thud into his own sack; and now, ashamed and outwitted, he is carried back to the village and flung into jail. On his release, 'he was so ashamed of what he had done that he always hid his face if he saw anyone looking at him. And so has every Tortoise from that day to this.'

The texts we have discussed so far are samples of the material that African writers are now offering to their own schoolchildren. A healthy situation has developed in which African children are reading literature woven from the stuff of their own lives and culture. The emphasis has been largely on prose texts, though, of course, many of the tales drawn from oral tradition contain both song and verse. One volume devoted entirely to poetry, however, is *The Moon Cannot Fight,* an anthology of Yoruba children's poems collected and translated by Beier and Gbadamosi.[5] This pioneering anthology covers a broad range of subject and mood. It includes lullabies, riddles, finger games, and songs of abuse – songs that mark the early skirmishes in the battle of the sexes. The collection also contains the following *oriki* or praise song composed in honour of all children. There are lines here often heard in the Yoruba Folk Operas – lines that emphasise the immense value which the Yoruba attach to their children:

A child is like a rare bird.
A child is precious like coral.
A child is precious like brass.
You cannot buy a child on the market.
Not for all the money in the world.
The child you can buy for money is a slave.
We may have twenty slaves,
We may have thirty labourers,
Only a child brings us joy,
Ones child is ones child.

Among the Yoruba, the children have their own special Egbe society, a junior branch of the adult Egungun society, which is responsible for contact with the dead. Beier tells us that once a year the children have a mask of their own at which the following song is sung:

We assemble under a great shade tree.
It is a hot shade.
They killed the cock in their mouth,
And said: 'Rain will beat you!'
No rain can beat us as long as Egbe exists.
We belong to Egbe. Listen to us, Egbe.
Companions must know each other.
Akanbi show me my Egbe.
Nobody shall dare to mock us.

Yoruba candour, so vigorously displayed in Beier and Gbadamosi's *Not Even God is Ripe Enough,* extends even among the children. Here are two poems on the subject of housetraining:

> Lagbada shits in the house
> We do not blame him
> Lagbada pisses in the house
> We do not blame him.
> But the flies will give him away.
> The flies will give him away.

The second is called 'You Broke the Rule':

> You broke the rule
> you are not worthy to play with
> you are like stale yam
> you are like watery soup
> yesterday's piss – you are the one who pissed it
> yesterday's shit – you are the one who shitted it
> don't shit don't shit
> bow down and clean it
> bow down and clean it.

In a 'Song to Drive a Boy from a Girls' Game' we find:

> Penis penis plays by itself
> Vagina vagina plays by itself
> We shall not play with somebody
> Who has 16 testicles.

Finally, there are the riddles, popular with children, as devices for showing off their intelligence, or as payment for a bedtime story. Here are three riddles from *The Moon Cannot Fight,* whose answers appear in parentheses in the final line of each example. With their distinct sense of metaphor, of calling familiar objects by other names, these riddles take on one of the essential marks of poetry:

> We call the dead – they answer.
> We call the living – they do not answer.
> (Dry leaves sound when trodden on. Fresh ones don't)

> Two tiny birds jump over two hundred trees.
> (Eyes)

> The bereaved one has stopped weeping.
> The compassionate friend is still crying.
> (Rain dripping from the leaves)

A use for literacy: Nigerian popular literature

A curious by-product of the gradual spread of literacy in Nigeria has been the genesis of not one but two literatures. For alongside the verse of Okara or the prose of Achebe – work aimed at a world audience – there has blossomed a rare species of sub-literature, remarkably vigorous in its way, yet modestly intended for an audience of only semi-literate Africans. Ulli Beier first called attention to this strange phenomenon in his article 'Public Opinion on Lovers', published in *Black Orpheus,* No. 14.

This new growth is confined mainly to the big market town of Onitsha in Eastern Nigeria. With a population of 88,000, Onitsha is an old town that sprawls along the east bank of the Niger, offering farmers and river folk from a wide area the biggest open market in West Africa. Here will congregate fishermen from the Niger creeks, Fulani cattlemen from the North, and Yoruba cocoa merchants from the West. Furthermore, the town has enjoyed trading links with the outside world that date back over several centuries. Among the vendors of fish and bananas at Onitsha Market, there are booksellers, too, whose stock-in-trade once rarely went beyond exercise books, writing materials, and simplified versions of whatever literary text the West African Examination Council was currently prescribing. The past few years, however, have brought to the stalls a motley array of cheap, indigenous, ephemeral literature.

Pamphlet size, and poorly printed on hand presses, the books are usually about forty-five pages long, and range widely in subject matter. Books of advice and warning rub shoulders with novelettes; romantic tragedies jostle with guides to prosperity and political pamphlets. *Beware of Harlots and Many Friends* and *How to Get a Lady in Love* appear on the same shelf as *Many Things You Must Know About Ogbuefi Azikiwe* and *How John Kennedy Suffered in Life and Death Suddenly.*

While the University of Ibadan has produced its Clarks and Soyinkas, Onitsha has been spawning its own writers – a generation of schoolboys, taxi-drivers, and minor journalists who gaily wield the pen to produce a saleable manuscript on any topic the local people will enjoy. They are responsible for a new literature that combines the luxuriant abundance of the forest with the dionysian energy of the people. They are, moreover, men who in literary matters refuse to consult oracles or adore idols.

It would take a reckless commentator to offer blanket generalisations about the Onitsha writing. However, after a careful scrutiny of the texts, one can, at least, affirm that it is largely free of the melancholia and nostalgia which figure so prominently in Nigeria's more respectable literature. There is, to be sure, a reflection of social change in the writing; but the nuances of Africa's great cultural debates, the agony of

144

the disciples of negritude – these appear to hold no attraction for a class of authors who cast their vote simply for life itself, which they live with verve and good humour.

Their work, however, is essentially ephemeral, and its interest lies in the implications it holds for the growth of indigenous popular reading rather than for any special artistry it might reveal. Behind discussion of African literature there usually lurks the problem of audience. Thanks to Achebe, the belief that African writers *must* address an overseas audience has now gone to its proper place; but there was a time when the local audience for African writing was severely limited, and it is still true that African writers are conscious of a world audience and market for their wares. What must be insisted upon, however, because it helps to define a basic point of difference between Nigeria's two species of literature, is that the Onitsha writers have never faced a problem of this sort. A semi-literate, entirely local, audience created a demand which a school of semi-literate authors swiftly satisfied. Though western attitudes permeate the texts (there is little love for Old Africa here), the Onitsha pamphlets are emphatically *not* addressed to a white audience; they are offered purely for local consumption, and Nigerians devour them avidly, and in large quantities.

Drawing literary parallels between Europe and Africa can be a perilous exercise; but there *are* times when European history does seem to repeat itself in Africa. British experience, for example, holds an interesting precedent for the Onitsha phenomenon; for, surely, the chapbooks of seventeenth- and eighteenth-century England, with their crude composition and their easy diet of spice and old morality, are of a kind with the Nigerian writings. Though Onitsha literature pursues a more realistic and consciously modern line than the chapbooks, which dealt largely in the traditional and the fantastic, they are alike in that each of them is truly a people's literature – cheap reading matter for the poor and half-educated; alike, too, in their scarcely noticed existence beside a more lofty and laurelled species of art.

It would be absurd to imagine that great literature is pouring from the presses at Onitsha; but it would be equally absurd coldly to dismiss writing that appears at this level, for critical arrogance is apt to cause critical myopia. Grub Street journalists, those busy men whose abiding interest lay quite simply in *quicquid agunt homines,* were cruelly spurned by the Augustan literary establishment; but the English novel was fathered by the despised Defoe and Richardson, not by Swift or Pope. It was low-born, springing from the common soil of life, and taking on the people's energy and resilience. Events at Onitsha have not been materially different. Indeed, the town has already produced

Cyprian Ekwensi, whose writing shares with Defoe's a common rootedness in the street-level realities, in the day-to-day problems of ordinary city life. Ekwensi and the Onitsha writers do not look out on the world from the Senior Common Room windows at Ibadan, Nsukka, or Lagos. It is not the imponderables of national or racial destiny that excite them, but the difficulties of ordinary people in real-life situations. How to live successfully in the city: how to handle money; how to avoid shame and scandal; how to write letters; how, in short, to chart your way through the rough waters of urban life – these are the questions to which Onitsha writers address themselves, for these are the questions to which the new town-dwelling classes require an answer.

And, of course, the Onitsha phenomenon is essentially an urban one. City living is usually the focus of attention, though it is often contrasted with the traditional patterns of rural life. Printed on the jacket of *Beware of Harlots and Many Friends* by M. Okenwa Olisah, a prolific author who writes under the pseudonyms of Master of Life and Strong Man of the Pen, we find the following lay sermon; a sermon which, in one form or another, is heard throughout the whole continent as urbanisation spreads:

> I want to say more about the life in the township. The type of life in it spoils many people, not only girls. Some womanisers have forgotten their home towns and people. Harlots and some women spoil their brains. These womanisers do not write letters to their people at home and no longer care to visit homes. Bad life and 'women' have spoilt their brains. They plan every time how to get women in love. They give women all the money they get for the day but their parents at home go hungry and wear raggy clothes. Nothing is sent to them from year to year. Shame to these people.

The Master of Life is a connoisseur of the new order which so powerfully attracts his people. Like Ekwensi, he can glance coolly over his shoulder at the old dispensation and offer patronising advice to those dizzy with the freedom of escape from it. And yet, in these comparative descriptions of rural and city life, a note of moral ambivalence is often heard, as if the object of attack is secretly an object of affection, and vice versa. One feels, for instance, that while the authors preach the values of rural life, they are, at the same time, wallowing in the joys of a different life entirely; a life which ruthlessly tramples the breath from the old morality of the countryside. If we see this ambivalence as an unwitting reflection of the cultural conflict affecting Africa as a whole, it helps to explain the twin, and apparently con-

146

tradictory, elements of conservatism and iconoclasm that lie at the heart of so much Onitsha writing. The society reflected in the pamphlets is, for the most part, *newly* urban, and has yet to escape the emotional pull of rural life, which haunts it like a bad conscience.

Those who pour into town from the countryside move into alluring but difficult waters for which they possess neither chart nor compass. Hence the Onitsha manuals of advice and guidance which are pulled off the presses in their scores. And yet the newcomers are constantly reminded of the life they have deserted. As soon as they espouse city ways, the innocence and unpretence of country life is recalled for them. In *Beware of Harlots and Many Friends,* for instance, they are told by the Master of Life that youths in rural areas are to be admired for their lack of interest in dress, fashion, and money; and the same is true of country girls (pp.15–16):

> The girl born and trained in the township lives different life from the girl born and trained in the rural area. The girl born and trained in the township loves to play 'highlife' and knows in and out about love making. She attends the cinema and sees how kissing is made and how love is played. She attends dances and other things. All this things can spoil her.
>
> The girl born and trained in the rural area have no chance to go to all those things. She goes farm after School. She returns from the farm and faces domestic duty. She is not much after dresses and have no idea about dancing. Before a boy gets her in love, it will be very hard for the boy.
>
> I will like to recommend to my Readers to marry girls trained in the rural areas. Those trained in the townships play 'Highlife' and too 'wise' in love business.

Yet such is the Master's ambivalent attitude, that alongside songs of praise for rustic innocence, with their hints of nostalgia for old values and the simple life, we find an insistence on ideas that belong firmly in the western economic ethic. Where the old order accepted the security of mutual help in the extended family system, the new dispensation (so memorably explored in Achebe's *No Longer at Ease*) calls for rugged independence. The Master strikes a distinctly modern note when, elsewhere in his book, he warns, 'Do not depend upon any person. Struggle to have your own money. Man does not dash his fellow man money.' A brand of African Puritanism seems to be advocated here, and the author's remarks are reinforced by some terse comments on the importance of work (p.14):

> The lazy man loves to chop but hates to work. To work is hard but to eat is not. He who hates work do not want progress in his life.

We work to get money, and eat to have the strength to do job.
Eating and working are brothers. If you chop you work and if you
work you chop.

So much for the communal sharing of the old order! A purely cash
economy dictates that from now on it is every man for himself.

Though the old order is praised from time to time, the Onitsha
writers often heap ashes on its head. Sermons like those from the
Master of Life are needed as correctives to a general attitude of scorn
and disrespect. In innumerable romantic pieces, where an educated girl
is coerced by illiterate parents who want her to marry a man she does
not love, the parents become a laughing stock, speak an absurd form of
pidgin English, and are abused for their hostility to the sacred code of
romantic love, that powerful infection from the West. Love always
triumphs and the modern miss gets her man, educated and westernised
like herself.

A typical specimen of this sort is *Veronica My Daughter,* a playlet
by Ogali A. Ogali (Snr). Veronica is a modern young lady (who,
therefore, does not use her African name) being forced into an arranged
marriage by her father, Chief Jombo. The fiancé is Chief Bassey, a man
of substance and highly respected under the old order, but an
impossible match for Veronica, who has eyes only for Mike, a smart
journalist who can quote Goethe and Bishop Latimer, and who already
has taken a sparkling Intermediate B.A. Ogali rushes to attack traditional society soon after the play begins, in a speech where Veronica
outlines her problem (p.5):

That is where I have disagreed with my old illiterate father who
wants me to marry a person of his choice. If my father Chief
Jombo had attended even infant school as to be able to write and
read simple English, I am sure he would have known that girls of
nowadays choose their own husbands themselves. I am in love
with a young boy by name Michael popularly known as Mike. He
is the only person I can marry. But father wants me to marry one
old money-monger of the first order whose name is Chief Bassey a
grade one illiterate.

Partly for comic effect, but mainly to underline the justice of the lady's
cause, Ogali pokes fun at Chief Jombo, portraying him as an ignorant
fool whose English never rises above pidgin. On his first entry, for
example, he is heard shouting: 'What kind trouble be dis. My daughter
get strong ear too much' – a style whose illiteracy we are meant to
contrast with the 'educated' (though of course faulty) style of Veronica
herself. The denouement is predictable. True love must inevitably
triumph over such bucolic harshness and ignorance. Veronica wins

148

Mike, and Chief Bassey is left disappointed with his gold. Exulting in the righteousness of his cause, Ogali whips up the euphoria and brings the play to a grandiose climax, with the conversion of the traditionalists, a lavish Cathedral wedding for the young couple, and a clinching, though mutilated, quotation from Confucius (spelt 'Confusion'): 'Our great test glory is not in never be falling but in rising every time we fall.' As the final curtain goes down, there is a strong feeling that one more nail has been driven into the coffin of Old Africa.

For those who read the history of the English novel as the history of the emancipation of women, the basic message of Ogali's play ('in this modern age and indeed at all times, it is unfair and improper to impose a husband on a girl') must sound like yet another echo from the past; from the eighteenth century, in fact, where the social position of women, dramatised so often as the lonely heart pitting itself against tyrannical convention, was a constant theme in the writings of Richardson and Fielding. It is destined to become an increasingly important theme in African writing too.

How often the Onitsha authors treat the subject of romantic love and its accompanying problems can be seen from the following list of pamphlets published by one firm alone, Njoku and Sons:

How to make love with girls
Why boys of nowadays never marry early again
Beware of women
How to get a lady in love
How to write love letters
Life story of boys and girls
The work of love
A guide to marriage
How to marry a good girl and live in peace with her
How to write and speak to girls for friendship
How to play love (in printing)
The prize of love
The joy of love
A guide to lovers (in printing)
The game of love and how to play it

The neophyte, on entering a strange urban world, must learn new rules and skills for the most ancient of pursuits! Hence, of course, the enormous demand for manuals on the art of composing love-letters. The love-letter is a vital item in the high-lifer's equipment and authors are apt to include a few specimens even in pamphlets devoted ostensibly to quite different topics. Typically, in *Never Trust All that Love You* (Third Edition, Enlarged), a book carrying the banner-headline warning 'The world is so corrupted that it has become difficult to trust all people', R. Okonkwo offers a chapter on *billets doux*. The letters he offers are characteristic in their use of impressive business and academic addresses, their comic parading of proverbs and cliches, and their inclusion of socio-economic data as though this is essential fuel for stoking the fires of love. Here is an epistle from a certain Miss Lucy Mojoke, whose address is given as Government College, Calabar (pp. 6–7):

My dear lover,

I am acknowledging your letter addressed to me and dated 29th March 1960, the contents which were easily digested. Thanks very much. I received the letter with mixed feelings. I felt happy to read that your employers have promoted you to executive post. I congratulate you. I was also unhappy to read that you are ill, that you have been attacked by Malaria. I am sorry and my happiness have been threatened by the illness ... Please contact a good Doctor for an expert treatment. Never look money 'on face' life is certainly precious. If you have no money for treatment, wire me I will send you at least £10 through the Post Office. It is true that I am a student, doing no job, but as you know my parents are capitalists. Any amount I demand, they will urgently send it.

As you know, dear, I believe in 'natural love'. I love you not because of money, as for money my parents have it plenty. You know the cause of my love for you is cleanliness, sincerity and socialism ...

I am
Your sweet heart,
Lucy Mojoke

What an astonishing confusion of the material and the spiritual results as Lucy strives to insist that the one in no way depends on the other! Her lover, Christian Ibete of the Veterinary Department at Fakados (presumably Forcados), replies in the same vein. He warmly thanks Lucy for her offer of assistance but assures her that he has £400 in the bank and has withdrawn a mere fifty for his medical bills. Having scored his points in this bout of financial gamesmanship, he now assumes a fittingly superior attitude by exhorting Lucy to greater efforts in her studies. 'You are expected of Grade I', he says, 'try to have it. I strongly promise you the following if you pass it; Two shoes, one wrist watch, one fine parker pen and Five guineas.' Should the heroine conquer, she will be decorated with the appropriate emblems of status and success!

The mistakes of grammar and idiom in the letters are legion. But what emerges here, and indeed throughout the Onitsha writing as a whole, is that the authors believe they are making successful attempts to write good English prose. Alas, with few exceptions, the finished product is a rubble-heap of broken rules and half-digested idioms; a style with the inelegance and unwitting comedy of a proud miss sporting high heels and silk stockings for the first time. Head held high, it can neither strut nor strike a pose without a trip and a fall. But for the authors such disasters go unseen. Indeed, it is this very unawareness, this sense of the crooked nose innocently parading itself as beauty, that the outside reader finds so comic. But the pamphlets, it must be repeated, are *not aimed* at the outside reader; and, leafing through their pages, one gets, besides this accidental mirth, a guilty feeling of trespassing on private land.

And yet, for all his clumsiness, the Onitsha writer usually makes his meaning clear. A feeling for the rhetorical flourish can sometimes pull a sentence clear of the rocks, as when Miss Eunice in Amala Dede's play *How to Get a Lady in Love* asks, 'Will this type of thing continue as it is just beginning or is it a mere catelogue of deceit in skeleton form?' Combined with a sudden flash of the imagination, a good ear for rhetoric can also save gems such as the following from the same play (p. 24): 'Likeness can well seen be in the eyes and if there is any love x-ray machine that can expose the mind of men to those whom they desire to woo, then I shall be ready to surrender myself for rescrutiny.'

At times, the Onitsha writing reveals how English words can be wrongly spelt because they have been *heard* often enough (pronounced inaccurately), but rarely *seen*. Anozie here speaks of 'the introduction of the unexpected into what ought to be bass upon sincerity and uprightness'; there is a reference to two men who are 'leaving together in one room', and to the 'simpless terms of culture.' Often new work is found for old phrases. A man in Dede's play will be 'accessed to the lady of his own choice', and another declares that further endurance 'would only tantamount to nothing short of foolishness'. The lovers in the play look for a priest to get them 'into a holy wedlock', and when the ceremony is finally arranged the priest gravely counsels, 'don't forget to love yourselves'. In the Strong Man of the Pen's book *Life Turns Man up and down*, one finds the following curious versions of familiar expressions: 'It is shameful to drive car this year and ride on a bicycle next year because of brokage'; 'Cleanliness is holiness so it is very foolish to think that those who keep themselves clean do so in order to attract women'; 'Whether a man is poorer than church rat he is liable to tax'; 'Do you know that an independent woman has no way to refute the charge that she is a prostitute? That is very hard to resist the trials of men? That people will look you very down?'

Some of the main features of the Onitsha style and ethos can be found in an amusing scene from Dede's ostensibly serious play where the love-affair between Eunice and Anozie burns to its climax. Here it is complete with stage directions, mis-spellings, and curious punctuation (p. 26):

Anozie: I am not rested. It is time for me to be pratical enough. But I must ask, will you be ready if I come to you for a legal marriage?

Eunice: I shall be fully prepared my dear, Even now. (*Both of them sit in one chair, face to face and chest to chest. Anozie holding his arm around her upper part and nothing but true romance becomes the entire show.*) O, Dear, you are a wonderful chaser. *Y-o-u r-o-m-a-n-c-e slowly.* Your romance, sweet and lovely, has made me lose my senses.

Anozie: (*Scratching out blood from his right arm and also from Eunice's right arm. Both of them suck each other's blood.*) This is in keeping with the tradition of our people. It simply indicates, our everlasting devotion one person to the other. Today, you have become my own wife and apart and parcel of me. It is by my blood that I, did swear.

Eunice: (*Solemnly*) You have also became my own husband in life.

At a time when English prose style has been refined to ever greater degrees of sophistication, it is not unrefreshing to encounter the gawky efforts of Onitsha. If semantic violence is often done to the language, it seems, nevertheless, to sustain little harm. But while the Onitsha style certainly represents progress beyond the crude pidgin of the 'Brudder George' letter cited by Wauthier, it is not always far beyond that. On the whole, one finds a sort of linguistic half-way house that coincides with the stage these semi-literate people have reached in their gadarene rush to assume western ways. They are young Africans who are not particularly proud of their cultural heritage. To understate the matter, they are negritude's least enthusiastic apostles; whose assimilationist zeal, indeed, suggests they might even prefer to be white! They are people at whom an advertisement inside the cover of Eze's *Little John in Love* screams, 'HELLO! GAY BOYS! REMEMBER OSAJI TAILORS, MAKERS OF YOUR FAVOURITE SUITS, JEANS, AMERICAN JACKETS AND MODERN MENS TROUSERS', while another advertisement addresses them with the words, 'MODERN FASHIONABLE GENTLEMEN, GO GAY WITH WOOLLEN TROUSERS, SMART SHIRTS, JACKET, TERYLENE, BOTH STRIPE AND PLAIN OF ALL KINDS.'

Beier in his *Black Orpheus* article on Onitsha drew attention to some brief but remarkable examples of imaginative writing. But it would be wrong to pretend that we have here in Onitsha a pool of untapped literary genuis. The Onitsha phenomenon is important mainly because of the direct bond which it displays between writer and audience, which, with its complete lack of reference to the outside world, makes this the first wholly 'private' and wholly popular writing in English that West Africa has ever seen. Africans here are writing purely for one another, authors addressing a reading public that is just emerging from a traditional rural background dominated by the spoken word. The Onitsha writer cannot be accused of keeping an eye on the overseas reader whose patronage he requires; he cannot be accused of garnering grist for the examination mills. What we have in effect is the world of the glossy magazine and Peg's Papers reborn in an African setting, and guarded over by the twin spirits of genuine moral concern and naked commercialism. These, of course, are familiar spirits and both were in attendance at the birth of the English novel itself. Now, side by side, they hover over the labouring presses of Onitsha. One can feel, for instance, the breath of their inspiration behind the following advertisc-ment for the books of the indomitable Master of Life. It appears in *Beware of Harlots and Many Friends* (p. 18):

Read and Have Sense

Always read pamphlets published by Mr. Okenwa Publications and acquire sense and wisdom. The Author, Mr. Okenwa Olisah, is your famous Author. He has been publishing wonderful books, novels and pamphlets which no family can afford to miss. His publications bring love and peace in the families.

Do not borrow copies of our publications. Buy your own copies and have them in your house in order to help your-self and entertain your visitors.

Whenever you have any family problem or any other problem conernig life, write to us for solution. We will give you best ADVICE free of charge. We have been helping so many Readers with ADVICE.

Buy this pamphlet and send to some-one you love. He will receive it with happiness.

Few critics would look to Onitsha for signs of new frontiers or new directions in West African writing. Onitsha has not yet produced innovators like Okara or Soyinka. Yet there is a riotously free atmosphere here in which anything might happen. There is an audience ready for novelty and authors bold enough for experiment. From socially low ranks came Defoe and the English novel. From Onitsha we have already witnessed the rise of Cyprian Ekwensi, Nigeria's most prolific author and the acknowledged leader in urban fiction. Who can say that others will not follow him? There is no divine law decreeing that a nation must rely for its literature exclusively on Senior Common Rooms and University Departments of English. This, surely, is a fact which Africa has known longer than anyone.

Political writing

The corpus of spoken and written literature that has emerged from Nigeria in recent years has not all come from aspiring poets, novelists, and dramatists. Political men have made their contribution, too, sometimes in the conventional literary forms (there is, for example, Balewa's long story, Osadebay's book of verse, and Awolowo's unpublished short stories), but mainly in the form of political writing and oratory. It would be hard to find a Nigerian schoolboy who cannot recall the day when he was asked to write on, or debate, the familiar dictum, 'the pen is mightier than the sword'. It is a saying that caught the imagination of colonised Africans in a remarkably strong way; and the reasons are not hard to unearth. They can be found in the basic facts of the colonial situation where a poor and disorganised population was dominated by a foreign power overwhelmingly superior in terms of military might. It was a saying that gave a shred of comfort to sensitive spirits who laboured under the shame of conquest and dreamt of the day when their country might break her chains. But how to bring dreams to actuality? If the sword was both useless and unavailable, then why not explore the proverbial power of the pen?

An early nationalist who seized the pen and turned the language of England against its owners was the redoubtable Nnamdi Azikiwe, whose tireless efforts in the cause of freedom justly earned him the title Zik of Africa. Zik became a master of the art of political writing, bringing to his task much of the skill and sensitivity expected from more conventional literary craftsmen. Essays and speeches show him using the word in a brilliantly creative way: the imagination soars high and lifts the language with it. A rare clarity of vision and a rare candour of expression, useful aids to style, are qualities he possesses in a high degree. Zik's work gives us not only a detailed account of life in colonial West Africa – from the viewpoint of the colonised – but a faithful record of the dreams of one nationalist committed to the unshackling of his fellow men. We have heard of late bitter words spoken against Nigerian politicians by artists such as Soyinka; and the lamentable history of Nigeria since 1963 provides a measure of justification. But in the career and writing of Nnamdi Azikiwe, there is, one feels, more to admire than to scorn.

A man who has excelled in the roles of statesman, journalist, athlete, businessman, and reformer, Zik has long been a figure of controversy with more than his share of detractors, even for a politician. In the early sixties, among expatriates drinking in their clubs, he was a target of undisguised contempt. They whispered of bank deposits in Geneva. He had grown fat, they hinted, in the fight for freedom. His compatriots, however, held him in awe, marvelling at his scholarship, and lauding his challenge of the white man.

Much learned commentary has been published on Zik's career; but to understand the popular view of him, the view held by the Nigerian masses, one cannot do better than dip into the pages of a 1964 Onitsha pamphlet by Okenwa Olisah graced with the burdensome title *Many Things You Must Know About Ogbuefi Azikiwe and Republican Nigeria*. From the trumpet fanfare of the Preface, which declares that the great man's full name is Dr Ogbuefi Nnanyelu-uge Nnamdi Azikiwe, and affirms that 'the story of a great man like Zik has no end', Olisah's account glows with the reflected admiration of the people. For them he was an African hero cast in the epic mould, a modern-day Chaka or Sundiata, ennobling himself during long battles with the oppressor. 'It is a general fact, and an accepted one, as well,' writes Olisah, his style rising in exquisite Gibbonian flights, 'that Nnamdi Azikiwe – "Zik" – was Nigeria's No. 1 hero in the political emancipation of the Federal Republic of Nigeria.' Such lofty flights, however, are hard to sustain; for, after informing us that Zik was born on Wednesday, 16 November 1904, at Zungeru in Northern Nigeria, of Ibo parents, the author announces, in very low key, 'His original Christian name was "Benjamin" but he dropped it in July 1934, after the British Empire Games Council refused to allow him to compete in the Half Mile and one Mile race at the British Empire Games of 1934, on technical grounds.'[6] Yet the biography soon recovers its stride, sweeping forward with the mounting excitement of an adventure story. There is the prophetic award of a prize at Methodist Boys' High School, Lagos, consisting, as Olisah tells us, of 'a book entitled "FROM LOG CABIN TO WHITE HOUSE LIFE OF JAMES A. GARFIELD",' followed by the incident enshrined for ever in Nigerian folklore when Zik in his first, abortive, attempt to reach America, stowed away on a ship; only to be detected off the Gold Coast and discharged with ignominy at Sekondi, after 'paying the cost to Elder Dempster Lines Limited'. On his eventual return from America, his pockets stuffed with degrees, Zik became a marked man. He was refused a post at King's College, Lagos, because, as Olisah claims, 'the then colonial Government was afraid of his influence and what could be the result of his mixing with its Obedient Servants . . .'[7]

Though Zik began his political writing in Accra, where he was journalist in charge of the *African Morning Post* (motto: *Independent in all things and neutral in nothing affecting the destiny of Africa*), his career as Nigeria's Lord Thomson of Fleet did not begin until 1937 when he started the *West African Pilot* (motto: *Show the light and the people will find the way*). Chief Awolowo, in his autobiography, gives us the most vivid account of Zik's sudden appearance on a torpid home scene (p. 84):

> As there was no effective vehicle for the vigorous ventilation of supressed grievances, a journalistic vacuum was thus created which Dr. Azikiwe very cleverly exploited and usefully filled when he returned to the country in 1937 to establish the *West African Pilot* which, whatever its literary defects, was a fire-eating and aggressive nationalist paper of the highest order, ranking in this regard with the *Nigerian Daily Telegraph* under Ikoli, and the *Lagos Daily News*, but much better produced. It was naturally very popular, the very thing the youth of the country had been waiting for. Newspapermen in the employ of the *West African Pilot* were better paid and they assumed a new status in society. Civil servants, teachers and mercantile employees resigned good and pensionable posts to lend a hand in the new journalistic awakening.

A string of newspapers was soon established, including, under the parent company of Zik's Press Limited, the *Eastern Nigeria Guardian* at Port Harcourt, the *Nigerian Spokesman* at Onitsha, the *Southern Nigeria Defender* at Ibadan, the *Daily Comet* at Kano, and the *Eastern Sentinel* at Enugu. Zik thus owned news media throughout the entire country, and guaranteed for himself the airing of his own nationalistic propaganda.

But he had already been active in other areas, too, most notably as a public speaker. We must return to Awolowo for another memorable, if rather mischievous, account of Zik at this point in his career. There was his first lecture, given in 1934, at Methodist Boys' High School on the subject 'There is Joy in Scholarship', a virtuoso performance whose fame spread rapidly. At a second oration, at Faji School, the crowd was so vast

156

that Awo, a reporter covering the event, had to stand outside beneath an open window and take notes from there. So huge were the crowds at Zik's third lecture, in Alakoro, that the performance had to be given in the open air. Awo writes eloquently of Zik's rhetorical style (p. 87):

In a manner which was both charming and disarming, he subtly and implicitly laid claims to fields of learning which were truly catholic and almost limitless. 'Now let us run through the pages of history,' he proclaimed at Faji School; and there was thunderous applause which lasted some two minutes. It was the first time in Nigeria, so we his hearers believed, that any Nigerian was academically competent and self-confident enough not only to enter just a few of the pages of British History, British Empire history, or European history, but to run through the pages of *all* history, as we were made to understand. Dr. Azikiwe's reputation had preceded him to Nigeria through his book *Liberia in World Politics*, and there was a general belief that he was the most outstanding Nigerian scholar in the academic history of the country. Now this declaration by him proved it. Whether he actually succeeded in running through the pages of history, whether he was accurate in the route he chose in the race, or whether the milestones and landmarks to which he pointed were genuine and true to fact, no one cared to inquire. The genius of New Africa had spoken, and there was an end of the matter.

The passage is not only revealing in the light it sheds on Zik's early popular acclaim; it also displays something of the animus he provoked in certain quarters. He soon aroused opposition, and not only from the ruling power. As Olisah sadly remarks, Zik deplored the fact that although he had undertaken the task of racial regeneration with zeal and sincerity, he had, alas, failed to reckon with the vagaries of human nature. In the *Eastern Nigeria Guardian* for 31 October 1949, he felt compelled to write:

... I expected those who had been comrades-in-arms with me, those who had toed the line of action with me, those who had faced the front line fire of racial prejudice abroad, to co-operate wholeheartedly, forgetting self in this great adventure. Day by day, my eyes are being opened and I am beginning to appreciate that when Mary Kingsley said that Africa killed her benefactors, she was not very wrong.[8]

Meanwhile, he was a constant thorn in the flesh of the administration, to whom his name, if we can believe Olisah, was 'the sound of terror'. To the people, however, buoyed up by his vision of liberty and unity, his name sounded 'magical and fairy-like ... they associated it with the

157

name of a redeemer'. This fairy note rings loud in the closing section of Olisah's biography, when, briefly, he lifts us into the company of the gods with the question, 'IS ZIK A SPIRIT OR HUMAN BEING?' Many of his fellow countrymen, Olisah remarks, believe that 'he *is* a spirit and can change into a fly or any other thing when he meets a fatal danger'. We are returned to earth, however, with the reassurance that although Zik is 'beyond human destruction', he is, in fact, 'a pure human being with extensive stock of knowledge, talent, democracy etc'.[9] It is easy to see how this folk belief took root, for in 1937, after conviction for seditious libel in Accra, Zik made assertions which were readily construed by the people to mean precisely this. In periods vibrant with allusions to Calvary, Golgotha, and Gethsemane, there issued forth the following declaration:

> Gethsemane was there to be conquered. Golgotha was there to be trodden under the feet of man. Calvary was to be overcome. And when a son of the New Africa is faced with the travails and tribulations of Gethsemane, and Golgotha and Calvary, there is no need for the spirit to weaken. At this stage of my life, I cannot be mere flesh. I cannot be part of the corruptible phase of man's organism. I am a living spirit of an idea – the idea of a New Africa. I am a living spirit of an ideal – the ideal of man's humanity to man. I am a living spirit of an ideology – the ideology of the effacement of man's inhumanity to man.[10]

Stirring stuff that sends the blood singing along the veins, but unhappily (and deliberately?) rather ambiguous.

This Cambridge selection of speeches delivered between 1927 and 1960 offers testimony to the skill with which Zik can put the language to work. Whatever the topic, whether national unity or the founding of a new university, he argues with force and eloquence, his mind ranging magisterially over his subject, and stooping at times to shape an image that would flatter an Okara and quote a saying that would flatter an oracle priest. In addition to citations of Lincoln and Jefferson, two of his favourite heroes, there are quotations from Spenser ('A fool I do him firmly hold that loves his fetters, though they were of gold!'); from Burke ('Tell me what are the prevailing sentiments that occupy the mind of your young men, and I will tell you what is to be the character of the next generation.'); from Tacitus ('A desire to resist oppression is implanted in the nature of man.'), and allusions to Jesus, St Paul, Socrates, and Thomas More. There is much of the natural advocate about Zik, and when a natural gift combines with West African flamboyancy, the result is a style of oratory of a truly formidable kind. One should recall here his 'reinforcing' experience among the Blacks of

North America. Zik shares, for example, the typical black preacher's love of the sublime, his constant reaching out for spiritual and transcendental glory. He, too, can paint rapturous and visionary scenes of peace and harmony; he, too, dreams of justice and rehabilitation for the black race. Zik has much to say and little time to say it. The urgency of the cause makes it imperative that his style be terse, pungent, and memorable; and, for the most part, these are qualities which he achieves.

In 1946, at Ikare in Nigeria, Zik delivered himself of his political Creed, a skilfully worked manifesto whose liturgical format is obviously meant to suggest spiritual conviction, political commitment, and personal integrity (pp. 59–60):

I believe in the God of Africa.

I believe in the black people of Africa.

I believe that it is not the will of the God of Africa to sentence the black people of Africa to servitude for ever.

I believe that there is a destiny for the black people of Africa, and that such destiny can only be realized successfully under the aegis of free and independent African nations.

I believe that by a firm resolve on the part of the black people of Africa, undaunted by fear of imprisonment or exile or death, unaffected by ostracization or victimization or persecution, the black people of Africa will live in free and independent African States in the community of a world society of free and independent nations.

I believe that if I am obliged to pay the price of leadership, in the cause of African freedom, no matter how extreme and severe are the penalties, the prosperity of the black people of Africa shall enshrine my memory for ever in the national pantheon of Africa.

I believe that Nigeria will pass through the acid test of oppression, to which we are now subjected, and shall emerge triumphant.

I believe that the freedom of Nigeria shall come to pass and Nigeria shall become a sovereign State in our life-time, in spite of the might of the conqueror.

I believe that the God of Africa has so willed it.

His inaugural speech made during his own installation as Premier of Eastern Nigeria in 1954 contains some inferior couplets:

So let it be, Creator mine,

Whose skilful hands and thought divine

Did mould my frame without a blame.

And gave to me this fleeting flame

159

but also his more impressive 'sixteen canons of rectitude in public life.'
He pledges (pp. 90–1):

> that we shall not seek to reap where we have not sown; that we
> shall not covet our neighbour's yam patch or his pay-packet or his
> material wealth; that we shall not deliberately exploit the ignor-
> ance of our underprivileged folk; that we shall not design or
> manipulate the downfall of the upright; that we shall not conceal
> or adulterate the truth; that we shall not pervert the court of
> justice; that we shall not allow ourselves to be corrupted; that we
> shall not worship filthy lucre; that we shall not be a conscious
> vehicle for the immolation of the guiltless; that we shall not
> mislead the innocent; that we shall expose and excoriate evil in
> any shape or form; that we shall be constructive in all we say or
> do; that we shall resist injustice with all our might; that we shall
> commend and not discredit merited achievement; that we shall
> serve without the hope of gain; that we shall willingly surrender
> the reins of office in the usual democratic manner.

There is an impressive sense of occasion about this speech and an
enormous weight of conviction in the repeated hammer-stroke enuncia-
tion of the canons. Here is a noble manifesto for any man assuming
high office. Nor were these canons merely the brilliant bubbles of a
hollow rhetoric. Their liberal spirit became manifest during Zik's
performance in office. His role in the final destruction of the Osu system
is a case in point. In 1956, a bill was introduced into the Eastern House
of Assembly designed finally to remove from the face of Ibo society one
of its more disgusting blemishes. Zik's speech supporting the bill's
second reading equates the measure with Magna Carta, the Petition of
Right, the Abolition of Slavery, and the Indian Untouchability Act.
After sketching for his audience the history and evils of the system, he
reaches for the heart of the matter with a series of searching questions
(p. 93):

> What right have we to destroy their [Osus'] personality on the
> altar of tradition? What kind of tradition shall we revere? A
> tradition which enslaves the human soul and destroys human
> virtues? A tradition which sacrifices man's humanity to the
> passions of man's inhumanity? Why must we question the need
> for a law of this kind, when it is obvious that it is the right thing to
> do so as to justify our faith in our ability to rule ourselves justly
> and righteously?

The attack thus pressed forward, he establishes his position with
powerful affirmations of his own view of the matter:

> I will not be a party to any social proscription of my fellow man. I

will not support any stigmatization of human beings simply because they are said to be descended from a certain family ... I submit that it is devilish and most uncharitable to brand any human being with a label of inferiority, due to the accidents of history.

To borrow a rhetorical device from Zik himself, who cannot hear in this speech the voice of a genuine liberal reformer and the rhythmic skill of a great orator?

In countries striving for unity and a sense of nationhood, it is usually left for the poet, the novelist, or the composer to evoke a sense of place, to fix the hills-and-rivers fact of the new entity on the imagination of the people. In Nigeria, where enormity of size and cultural diversity have long militated against national cohesion, Zik's dream of unity drove him to this task long before it was faced by literary men. Listen, for example, to part of an address he made at Enugu in 1952, to a group of political supporters (p. 53):

> Here you are, leaders in your own right – from the cold and temperate plains of Awgu and Nsukka, to the mountainous terrain of Buea and Bamenda; from the jagged and rugged littoral of Brass and Calabar to the undulating plains of Okigwi and Wum; from the shining serpentine course of the lordly Niger, to the muffled and winding trails of the Cross River.

The fact that Awolowo in his autobiography (p. 139) cites a similar effusion offered on the occasion of a school's soccer match (in which an Ibo team beat a western team), does not destroy the argument that Zik, in his writing and in his speeches, made a creative effort to establish the map of Nigeria in the minds of her widely differing peoples.

Like Nnamdi Azikiwe, Chief Obafemi Awolowo has enjoyed the same nomadic career that has marked a generation of African politicians. Turning his hand to the assorted tasks of teacher, trader, journalist, clerk, and advocate, he chose, at last, the realm of political life, wherein he has been Prime Minister of the Western Region, Opposition Leader in the Federal Parliament, and, latterly, an adviser in the military government of Major General Gowon.

A Yoruba from Nigeria's Western Region, Awo has less of the visionary about him than Zik; he is much more the cool pragmatist, with a flare for efficiency and organisation. We are not surprised when he confesses in his autobiography that his talents did not run in the direction of the short story. His consolation was to find that they ran, in a quite formidable way, towards the art of political writing. If Awo lacks the soaring imagination of Zik, and the grandiose swell of his

161

style, he possesses, in a high degree, qualities of equal importance; for there is a precision, a clarity, and a continuous strength in his prose, given just enough salt by a nice command of irony – a gift which it was not Zik's fortune to possess. For political writing, what further qualities are required?

The weapon of irony he appears to have forged rather late in his career. Its delicate use against 'the genius of New Africa' we have already witnessed in passages from his autobiography, written in the easy reflective years of middle life. It was not in evidence thirteen years earlier when he published his coldly skilful *Path to Nigerian Freedom*.[11] The mood, then, was different; the objective called for a different style of polemic. Here was a masterful indictment of British attitudes towards Nigeria during the colonial era; but an indictment tempered always by a cool insistence on Britannia's achievements, on the import-ance of Empire for collective security in a perilous world, and on Nigeria's own sins – including, at that time, ignorance, apathy, and complete unfitness for self-rule. Constructive ideas on progress emerge. There are suggestions for law reform, for a federal structure of govern-ment, and for genuine partnership with the mother country. There is also a prophecy of conflict in Nigeria's Northern Region – the fruit, he argues, of a British policy which keeps native and stranger apart. Seldom has disaster been prophesied with quite such precision and exactitude.

In her Foreword to Awo's book, Dame Margery Perham declares that it is written in 'the forthright, almost sledgehammer tradition of political pamphleteering'. This is too crude a judgement. From its careful choice of audience to its skilful manner of attack, there is a delicacy present in its pages; and, as Strachey once remarked about the prose of Macaulay, 'one cannot hammer with delicacy'. The document is addressed – in its entirety – not to Awo's countrymen (whom too often he tends to despise) but to his British overlords. Fresh from the chambers of the Inns of Court, Awo stands at the bar and argues his case before an imperial nation. A trained legal mind goes to work, carefully and shrewdly organising its material.

In the opening stages, the audience must not be antagonised. Arias sung on its virtues will engage its sympathy. Since it is rumoured to revere objectivity, chastisement, when the precise moment comes, must be inflicted in a manifestly objective way. Since this same audience boasts of worship at the shrine of reason, then reason, in her purest dress, must be seen to guide and inspire the cause at every turn. It would be useless here to look for such soaring flights as Zik's 'I have the vision and the imagination to appreciate the need to dedicate myself to this romance of nation-building in Africa.' Awo's mind is cast in a quite different mould. In any case, he was shrewd enough to know that, faced by such emotion, the great British public would have remained contemptuously unimpressed. Awo's text is a skilful piece of persuasion precisely because its author understands so well the correct approach to his audience – how an apt quotation here, and a scholarly reference there, can soften a blow, or sweeten the palate. Distinguished British figures are invoked; men who, for a moment, seem to step forward and stand with him in his cause. They range impressively from Mill and Laski to Churchill and Milton. Where Zik quotes Spenser's 'A fool I do him firmly hold . . .', Awo quotes Milton: 'Better to reign in hell than serve in Heaven.' And the book's opening leaves are garnished with assorted pieties from Shakespeare: ideal fare for British consumption:

This above all, to thine own self be true;
And it must follow, as the night the day,
Thou canst not then be false to any man.

*

Those who cover faults, at last shame them derides.
The candour thus promised is faithfully delivered; the frank vein of the following is not untypical of the text as a whole (p. 32):

Given a choice from among white officials, Chiefs, and educated Nigerians, as the principal rulers of the country, the illiterate man, today, would exercise his preference for the three in the order which they are named. He is convinced, and has good reason to be, that he can always get better treatment from the white man than he could hope to get from the Chiefs, and the educated elements.

Passages of this sort carry the twin advantages of flattering the audience and displaying the author's integrity. Equally candid, and equally clever (though in a less admirable way), is the following reflection on international ethics. Eleven years after Nigerian Independence, it makes strange reading; but it displays all the plain-speaking, the pragmatism, and the efficiency which mark both the man and his style (p. 33):

The second world war has shown of what strategic and economic importance Nigeria is to Britain. Necessity does not admit of much ethics. We live in an immoral world. The watchword of national security, as exemplified in the diplomatic and military moves of great nations, is: 'If the independence of a weaker or smaller nation endangers or threatens to endanger your security, do not hesitate for a second to bring it under subjection, if you can.' And there is no earthly reason on our planet now why

163

Britain should allow Nigeria's independence to endanger her national security.

So far we have examined figures from two of Nigeria's main regions: Nnamdi Azikiwe is an Ibo from the East, and Obafemi Awolowo a Yoruba from the West. With the autobiography of the late Alhaji Sir Ahmadu Bello, Sardauna of Sokoto, we hear a representative voice from the North.

My Life marks itself off from the main work of Zik and Awo in one fundamental way: it is a post-independence document and does not, therefore, concern itself with arguing a case for political freedom. It is more an outline of Northern attitudes during the colonial period, the Sardauna reflecting on the years before 1960, and calmly explaining his own, and his region's, position during the long struggle for independence. His purpose in writing is implicit in the fourth paragraph of his Preface (pp. viii-ix):

> I am not unaware that I have often been a controversial figure. I have been accused of lack of nationalism and political awareness because I considered that independence must wait until a country has the resources to support and make a success of independence. I have been accused of conservatism because I believe in retaining all that is good in our old traditions and customs and refusing to copy all aspects of other alien civilisations. I have been accused of many other things, but the views of others have never made me deviate from the path which I am certain is the one which will benefit my people and country. I have always based my actions on my inward convictions, on my conscience and on the dictates of my religion.

The text, then, is an *apologia*, written in a style and mood which reflect massive self-confidence, a feeling for history, and an unshakeable religious faith. This is a blend of qualities which some might describe as aloofness, and which Bello's enemies insist on calling feudal arrogance. The Sardauna's background is quite different from Awo's and Zik's. While the southern leaders rose to eminence from rather humble origins, Bello was a Muslim aristocrat whose ancestors had built an empire. He was a man born to rule.

'I could not avoid the obligation of my birth and destiny', he writes (p. viii):

> My great-great-grandfather built an Empire in the Western Sudan. It has fallen to my lot to play a not inconsiderable part in building a new nation. My ancestor was chosen to lead the Holy War which set up his Empire. I have been chosen by a free electorate to help build a modern nation.

With such a pedigree, Bello was the natural spokesman for the Hausa States of the North, an area covering more than seventy per cent of the Federation's land mass, and containing perhaps sixty per cent of its population. *My Life* is not only the autobiography of the region's leader; it is also an evocative picturing of the region itself. What emerges, above all, is that this region comprised a world and tradition which Bello's southern colleagues neither shared nor understood. It was a region complete in itself, and content with its own pattern of existence; an historic entity which, with only two major tribes, a dominant language, and almost total allegiance to Islam, enjoyed greater cohesion, greater unity, than either the Ibo East or the Yoruba West. Its mood in politics was conservative; in religion, fideistic. Bello portrays a land in which an ancient way of life went on under a pattern of government that exerted its authority over huge territories – a pattern on which new structures might be built, but built slowly. As he remarked in a speech made to the Northern House of Chiefs in 1951 (p. 75):

> When the British came to this country they found that we had our Chiefs, Schools, Judges, and all that was necessary for civilisation. They made some slight changes which were accepted by all the people. It can only be said today that changes would be welcomed but not drastic ones that might bring the country to a state of chaos.

The note of restraint, of support for a traditional pattern that has worked effectively, echoes on from the beginning of this book to its close. The restless southerners might get giddy over the idea of political independence; but temporal matters like this could hardly fire the minds of a people forever contemplating eternity, and whose contemplation the British had chosen not to disturb.

This, in part, explains Bello's calm approach to the Lagos independence debates, and southern fury at what was called his colonial and backward mentality. As a devout Muslim, the Sardauna saw himself in the hands of God, who would arrange all things in His own good time. He affected no hatred of the colonial power. Indeed, with typical coolness, he writes: 'I do not think that there was any particular antipathy against the British. It was the will of Allah that they should be there; they were not evil men and their administration was not harsh.' In a similar relaxed strain, when reflecting on the struggle for freedom, he quietly admits (p. 86):

> ... we were never militant 'nationalists' as some were. We were sure that in God's good time we would get the power. The British had promised this frequently and we were content to rest on these

promises; there was plenty of work ready at our hands for us to do.

And then, in an egregious example of the fatalism that must have exasperated activists like Zik and Awo, he writes (p. 131):

The hand of God was moving as always, using us men as its pieces on the wide field of world events. Nothing which we could have said or done would have moved the date of Independence forward, or put it back a single hour from the moment in which it was ordained from the dawn of time itself.

There is little to disturb the cool waters of *My Life's* opening chapters. The author is in a reflective mood, offering idyllic scenes from his childhood and useful glimpses into the history and customs of the Hausa States. Signs of an approaching storm appear only when we reach the chapter called 'Crisis in Lagos'. The crisis was the famous one of 1953 which erupted during a budget session in the Lagos House. It arose after Chief Enahoro suddenly put down a private member's motion reading: 'that this house accepts as a primary political objective the attainment of self-government for Nigeria in 1956'. Unable to consult his people on the issue, Bello opposed its being debated, drawing down on himself the combined fury of Enahoro, Akintola, Thomas, Awolowo, and Azikiwe. The episode provokes a rare burst of spleen from the author and a flash of sardonic humour. Unflattering portraits of several Nigerian leaders are sketched. Chief Enahoro (who has now written his own life, *Fugitive Offender*) has his chieftancy title ridiculed before being tartly dismissed as 'a back-bencher from the Action Group, a very talkative man'. Enahoro's speech on the motion receives equally brusque treatment: 'It was long; it enlarged upon the obvious; it magnified the conspicuous; it slipped conveniently over the dangers that lay ahead.' Jaja Wachuku, later to become Nigeria's Foreign Minister, he calls 'an ingenious man, quick to take advantage of any situation that might arise to further the ends he was interested in at the moment'. But his most withering attack is reserved for the late Bode Thomas, a figure to whom the Sardauna reacted with particular animus. The life of Awo paints Thomas in glowing terms as a man whom 'we all adored for his unique endowments'. Bello's portrait is different. It opens with the terse comment, 'Bode Thomas was not a likeable man'; and continues (p. 129):

He was a clever lawyer but was ungracious and arrogant and never went out of his way to help: it is not surprising that the Action Group thought a lot of him, for he was the kind of political bulldozer they admired and wanted. They have named a dredger after him in Lagos harbour – it is not inappropriate when you think of its functions. He thought that we were a lot of uneducated savages and never attempted to conceal this opinion. He is dead now, but no one was really surprised that a veil of mystery and suspicion cloaked the circumstances of his death.

According to Bello, the cry of 'Self-government NOW' would always raise a mob in the Coast towns and the large centres of the Yoruba and Ibo. Thus it was no shock that the end of the Independence debate brought the Northern delegates howling disapproval from the Lagos populace. All the way north, even as far as Kaduna, they were hooted and booed by what Bello calls, with disdain, 'Railwaymen and other Southern elements'. And now he describes events which are crucial for an understanding of the recent civil war; for just six weeks after the Lagos crisis, there erupted in Kano the first real inter-tribal fighting since the arrival of the British – events, as we have seen, prophesied by Awolowo six years earlier. Here is Bello's detailed account (pp. 136–7):

... trouble broke out between Kano City and Sabon Gari, the area outside the walls occupied by 'native foreigners' (mostly southerners). This was the culmination of a series of incidents in the past few weeks which had had their origin in the troubles in Lagos. While the Action Group in Lagos had been the prime mover, they had been supported by the NCNC. Here in Kano, as things fell out, the fighting took place between the Hausas (specially from the 'tough' suburb of Fagge) and the Ibos; the Yorubas (of the Action Group persuasion) were, oddly enough, out of it. Very large numbers were involved on both sides and the casualties were severe in numbers, though not in proportion to the crowds involved. The rioting went on all through Sunday and into Monday morning: peace was reluctantly accepted by the combatants, though they were in fact very tired by then. In the end there were 31 deaths and 241 wounded.

The Sardauna readily concedes that the North, politically immature in any modern sense, was progressing more slowly than the rest of Nigeria; and he expresses admiration for the expertise of Southerners like Zik. But behind the admission and the admiration there lies – plainly and potently – a basic divergence of culture and philosophy. From Bello's *own* account, one senses a bustling dynamic southern Nigeria reluctantly heaving along a huge, tranquil, and contented North. Repeatedly, Bello drives home the fact of separateness. While the Southerners, he complains, are a hedonistic lot, given to drink and merriment, his people are a more sober breed, quietly cultivating the life of the spirit. Indirectly, the point is reiterated in what sounds like a thrust at southern politicians – especially perhaps at Azikiwe – when

167

he remarks that 'Nigeria is so large and the people . . . so varied that no person of any real intellectual integrity would be so foolish as to pretend that he speaks for the country as a whole.'

The note of separateness and conservation, sounded so firmly in the Preface, remains vibrating to the end. It can be heard, for example, in the following paragraph from the closing chapter. The new, independent, North has changed but slightly; it is still, by and large, the same united Muslim state that it was before the coming of the British (p. 227):

I think that it is fitting to bring my narrative to an end with the grant to us of our long-sought self-government. It might be called the restoration of the pre-1900 era, modernised, polished, democratised, refined, but not out of recognition; reconstructed, but still within the same framework and on the same foundations; comprehensible by all and appreciated by all. The train, the car, the lorry, the aeroplane, the telephone, the hospital, the dispensary, the school, the college, the fertiliser, the hypodermic syringe have transformed Othman dan Fodio's world, but the basis is still there. The old loyalties, the old decencies, the old beliefs still hold the people of this varied Region together.

The fact that this quietly aloof Muslim aristocrat was so feared and hated by his Southern colleagues (who, three years after Independence, still saw him as the grey eminence behind the throne of Prime Minister Tafawa Balewa), testifies to his skill and stature as the leader of Northern Nigeria. *My Life* is a restrained exposition of Bello's inner qualities and those of the varied, but cohesive, region of Nigeria that produced him. One of the ironies of his career was that he should meet with a fate similar to that which he darkly hinted at for Bode Thomas.

For a man whose background and lineage made him more the autocrat than either Zik or Awo, the autobiography rather than the political essay would seem to be the natural medium of expression. Stylistically, where the former push the language about in the service of rhetoric, Bello writes a steadier-paced prose that is more a reflection of inner qualities than an instrument of political persuasion.

In one important respect, their apparent indifference to local art and culture, all three are alike. Despite Zik's encouragement of the poet-politician Osadebay (he is warmly acknowledged in the Introduction to Osadebay's *Africa Sings*), despite his own handful of poems, and Awo's abortive attempts at the short story, there is no one here who combined political eminence with a genuine zeal for indigenous art and literature. There was no Léopold Senghor in Nigeria. Zik, at times, speaks of freeing his countrymen from 'superstition and ignorance'. Awo stresses the need for law and order to facilitate commercial growth, and, in a passing reference to India, actually sneers at local culture as having bedevilled the struggle for independence. Bello ruefully admits to being 'more practical than artistic', confessing that Islam 'does not encourage appreciation of art, except in its own stylised forms'. Small wonder that a yawning rift was to open up between Nigeria's politicians on the one hand, and her writers and artists on the other.

It is useless to look to history for justice. The men whom she assures of immortality are chosen on no such lofty principle. Unchronicled saints lie in scattered oblivion throughout the dusty graveyards of the world, while the corruption of a Borgia and the sickness of a de Sade are kept festering by the votaries of history. When, in a remote future, the curious examine Nigeria's history as an independent state, certain figures will arise for scrutiny. Zik will be there; Awo will be there; Bello will be there; even Akintola will be there. The historians, by their writings, have already signed the decree. Others, alas, will sink swiftly into the quicksands of oblivion. Through no fault of their own, they will be entirely forgotten.

Among them, one suspects, will be Mr Tai Solarin. In a land where the teacher's calling is held in low repute, where, at best, it is seen as a stepping-stone to loftier spheres, Solarin chose to be a teacher. Indeed, he was doubly unfortunate; for having chosen one despised profession, he turned, in a part-time way, to another, journalism. Like teachers, journalists are not much remembered by history either.

Yet, to a generation of Nigerians, Tai Solarin has been as inspiring a figure as a host of his political contemporaries. He, as much as they, deserves to go down in history as an apostle of the new order. But his chances are slender. They rest, for the moment, on a slim volume of his writings, and on yellowing heaps of the Lagos *Daily Times* – which will see corruption in the archives of Ibadan and Nsukka.[12] Neither provides a very firm guarantee of immortality. Perhaps this is too gloomy. Perhaps in some freak outbreak of headmaster-worship, Solarin will be the subject of golden biographies. Perhaps, like an Arnold or a Thring, he will see his ideals carried abroad by a band of zealous former pupils. It does not seem likely. Unlike the lawyer, the doctor, and the politician, the schoolmaster has never been revered by the world at large. To 'rear the tender thought' or 'teach the young idea how to shoot' has never been granted equality with the lancing of a boil, the defence of a criminal, or the casting up of gold. Read the mighty Boswell (who wisely chose law) and find the extraordinary claim that for teaching, great minds, such as Dr Johnson's, are not only unnecessary, but a positive hindrance. In his patronising way, Boswell did, in fact, concede that the 'art of communicating instruction, of whatever kind, is much to be valued', and observed that 'those who devote themselves to this employment, and do their duty with diligence and success, are entitled to very high respect from the community' – as one might respect a faithful doorman, or the peasant who dutifully tugs his forelock whenever quality is present. 'The greatest abilities', however, 'are not only not required for this office, but render a man less fit for it.'[13] Do they indeed? One must applaud such frankness. Nigerian politicians, Solarin complains, who used the profession like a whore and then thrust her aside, were never so elegantly candid.

Returning from England in 1957, with degrees from London and Manchester, Solarin founded an experimental school at Ikenne in Western Nigeria. It was to be his object lesson on the basic educational needs of his country, as he saw them. As a pioneer opening up a new frontier, he christened his brainchild The Mayflower School. It began with an initial enrolment of seventy boys, who, acting on one of the basic principles of Solarin's philosophy, had cleared the bush and dug the first foundations. By 1962, about 400 pupils had built thirty-five buildings, and the project was arousing comment on all sides. There was no antique Latin motto, no absurd cap and blazer to ward off the tropical blizzards. 'Our mission is clear', Solarin tersely remarked. 'It is to foster absolute freedom of thought . . . and we don't intend to turn out any gentlemen.'

Ikenne was one channel through which Solarin contributed to the new order; a column in the *Daily Times* provided another. His weekly essays here ranged widely over the contemporary scene. Whilst education was clearly his *forte*, many other aspects of national life also came within his purview. The essay titles in the Longmans collection are evidence enough: 'The True Purpose of Life'; 'Take Mr Devil's Scholarship' (an appeal to Nigerian youth to get an education anywhere, at any price); 'Open Letter to the Adjutant General'; 'Our Society Stinks' (in which he urges jail for every bribe-giver, the firing squad for a nurse who sleeps on night duty, and execution for the teacher who spends class time checking his football coupon) and 'May Your Road Be Rough'. Further titles are, 'Braggart Africans'; 'Lecture delivered 50 Years Hence'; 'An Open Letter to Chief Akintola' (who is given a verbal lashing for sending his son to Eton); 'Nehru – My Perennial Beacon'; 'What the Nigerian Worker Wants', and 'Public Morality'. Whatever the topic, Solarin, in his unvarnished way, will speak his mind. Nor does he shrink from speaking hard words to the great.

It is astonishing how many aptitudes can be squeezed into one human frame. Examine the writings of Solarin and discover that in one essay, he is the scourge of corruption or the visionary reformer, in another, a schoolmaster ombudsman, a virulent iconoclast, an idealist, a socialist, a pragmatist, or a humanist. His likes and dislikes are bellowed from the rooftops. He does not like the missions; he does not like British education – for Nigeria; he does not like opulence; he does not like waste; he abominates sloth; he hates corruption; he detests private education; he has a horror of selective schools; white collars make his blood run cold. Jingoism turns his stomach; complacency makes him sick at heart; judicial leniency sticks in his throat.

We should hear him first on education, especially on the British system he is striving to replace. 'Our education in the three R's', he writes, 'divorced of the real substance of education – the use of our hands and our skills – is a paltry sham. He continues:

The education we had from the British was the education that was specially geared to prop the imperial administrators of the British Empire. It was not meant for a people that was going to take over self-government. It was, according to Sir Alan Burns in his *History of Nigeria*, an education that enabled men 'to become Ministers of the Christian religion or learned in the laws of England'.

One can enter into government offices or commercial houses in Lagos ... and find stenographers not, as in other lands, women whose deft fingers seem to be specially made for typewriters but men with shoulders three feet across sitting on tiny stools, stiff and choking in starched high collars ... They become quickly and painfully bored being saddled to professions which have nothing to do with their interests but which fate has bestowed on them as a legacy of their education. They talk of nothing but the leave just taken or of the one imminent or of the reminiscences of the one they had several years before.

They spend most of their hours 'in the latrine' and when illness, apparent or imagined, shows up on their faces, they are off to the hospital and their discharge is followed by a week or two of convalescence. I cannot blame them.[14]

On balance, it is the ex-colonial power which is blamed here. Elsewhere Nigerian society itself is put in the dock. Indeed, Solarin's frequent satiric forays against his countrymen are a solid rejoinder to Awolowo's complaint in *Path to Nigerian Freedom* about his country's lack of 'that searching and impartial self-examination which characterizes the history of great nations'. Awo himself could hardly wish for

171

anything more forthright than the following broadside against what Solarin sees as national irresponsibility:

> We, in Nigeria, were satisfied with our 'Voluntary Agency' schools because as Nigerians, we were, and are, the most irresponsible people this bulge of Africa has produced. We are so used to getting other people to carry our loads for us ... A few years back, the *Daily Times* published the story of an English-woman who cared for, and brought up, a Nigerian girl of five. She is now 21, and still living with her English 'parents' in England. This poor Englishwoman received over 100 letters from other Nigerians who were ready to 'give' – till maturity – their children to be so brought up – at the expense of that same Englishwoman! Nigeria is very clever at pulling its chestnut out of the fire with somebody else's paw.[15]

Solarin agrees with a Peace Corps official who was worried because 'from the discussions he had had with many Nigerians, it would seem that the Peace Corps had come to do what we ourselves would only do when we had to'. The pedagogue is not valued by the nation and a radical shift of attitude is needed. Solarin makes one of his many refreshingly 'extreme' suggestions when he urges that all teachers should be paid the same salaries as Permanent Secretaries! The politicians, he says (only five per cent of whom have *not*, at some time in their careers, been teachers), have done much to downgrade the profession, despite their familiar cajolery:

> I try not to laugh when our politicians deliver their rhetoric on the significance of the noble teaching profession. I know, and so do you, that they have no positive belief in what they are saying. If they do, one of the first acts for a radical change in this country is to break the old colonial prop that the teacher was, and is pitched on. If I had the power I would break it within the first five minutes of my being in office.[16]

But of course the point is that Solarin has *not* got the power. He deplores the fact that it is the politicians who have, and grows indignant about a system which considers politicians and civil servants superior to the teacher and pays them salaries which bear no relation whatever to their 'intrinsic value' to the country.

Behind much of Solarin's thinking lies an Arnoldian viewpoint which sees the state as the sum total of all that is fine and useful in a nation and urges that this should be available for every citizen: it is an impressive view quite free of the totalitarian shades the word raises in, say, modern America. Arnold saw the idea dramatically exemplified in the state school system of Prussia. Solarin does not illustrate this notion with quite the same elegance as his Victorian predecessor (he is a coarse stylist who never learnt the distinction between the present perfect and pluperfect tenses), but in a futuristic essay called 'Lecture Delivered 50 Years Hence' – which begins with the suggestion that we 'hop over' the first ten years of Independence as years of 'erratic wanderings' – he sketches clearly enough what he hopes will be the shape of things to come. It is interesting to note that even his own school is detailed for absorption into a vast new state system:

> I think the first great sign of the rejuvenated country showed most glaringly in its educational set up. All the King's Colleges and the Queen's Colleges and all the Saint Dominics, Mayflowers and Coronas were assimilated into the huge body of Nigeria. All private schools and all highbrow institutions for the sons of the great were proscribed by law. All the nation's schools outside the primary and teacher training were pooled and transformed into comprehensive high schools . . .
>
> Today, as we celebrate our 50th anniversary, there is not a single Nigerian of school age who is not in school. At least in literacy, we have caught up with the United States of America and the U.S.S.R. We have surpassed Spain, Portugal and Mexico . . .
>
> Today, our politicians are a different calibre compared with their pygmean predecessors. If you read your papers regularly, you probably read only yesterday, of the State Minister in Yola who got ten years for withdrawing his two sons from the carpentry section of the state school, and sneaking them into the stream with children going to do geology. All who aided and abetted the deceit got five years each. Such corrective measures were unknown whilst the republic was young and badly needed such measures.[17]

Solid thinking too easily melts into absurdity as Solarin's ideas pour forth, his pen wandering across the page wherever the spirit might lead. In one short article, he is likely to attack on many fronts. Take his column in the *Daily Times* for 27 June 1963, a piece perhaps excluded from the Longmans collection because of its very formlessness. It begins with a call for universal compulsory education in Nigeria by 1970. And then, developing an argument about the possible funding of such a scheme, Solarin seizes a chance to lay down a powerful barrage against national corruption. Stylistic blemishes aside, the argument is forcefully presented:

> Let us first and foremost consider our present assets. Do you know that in the year 1959/60 in the Western Region of Nigeria, out of the total grants paid to schools, a sum of over £970,000,

that is almost £1,000,000, disappeared in the hands of those who took it from the public coffers and those who paid it to the teachers in the Western Region?

Some of the money was paid to teachers who had been dead for years; some were paid to teachers who were non-existing; some were simply paid – into the pockets of the payers!

Our second asset. Do you know how much money goes as straightforward bribes into the hands of school headmasters and principals of schools in Nigeria each year? I suggest a figure of £2,000,000.

The reckoning continues, and a sum of £12,000,000 is finally reached, the loot thieved by what he calls Nigeria's 'educational cutpurses'. With the rock pulled up and the worms exposed to daylight, Solarin calls for remedies, including national sacrifice that should begin from the *top* of society and work downwards. At a time when the famous Coker Commission reported the building by the Nigersol Company of twenty-eight houses for prominent politicians (many at a cost exceeding £14,000 and none below £8,000), Solarin urges a drastic reversal of this trend towards ministerial opulence. Dr Onabamiro is praised for arriving at his ministry in a Volkswagen, and the author hopes he will set a fashion!

A rebel is a necessity among our state Ministers if we mean to engender an entirely new way of life to create a new Nigeria. For a Minister, any Minister, the outrageously gorgeous and opulent gown must go. It is an anachronism in these very lean days in the Federation.

The cocktail party, that handy symbol of diplomatic high living, should go too. And as for the Independence Layout at Enugu ('a more luscious ministerial haven than Los Angeles' Hollywood'), the 'damned lot', as Solarin delicately puts it, 'should be sold to the highest bidders and the money turned in for public education'. This last word brings him back to his original theme, and he launches into a description of the ideal school syllabus, a programme which includes, amongst other items, cooking, midwifery, painting, carpentry, brick-laying, and radio-engineering. He then suggests that each town in Nigeria should build, by communal labour, a school big enough for every child up to the age of twelve. Asking 'What type of classrooms do we need in Nigeria?' he supplies his own answer:

The simplest – roof on top and concrete floor if you can afford it, at the bottom. If you cannot, the army of the children's shod and unshod feet would turn the floor into a glassy surface.

All windows, anywhere in Nigeria, are foolish luxuries.

174

He takes the case of a small town like Shagamu. It needs, he says, only two schools to house all its children in the relevant age group. But the townsfolk must build these themselves. Solarin, in his forthright way, suggests how it should be done:

> Every adult member to carry his own sand or fell trees on school site. Those who are too big or too fat to condescend to contribute their own physical exertion to pay heavily for it in money – or special purchases, say 20 bags of cement in lieu of a day at foundation digging. The schools are to be built entirely by communal labour. 'Big men' to be made to pay by the nose.

And so the prose pushes its way forward with Solarin prodding the nation's conscience, exposing folly here, suggesting a cure there. It is not, to put it succinctly, good prose – it displays neither Zik's soaring flights nor Awo's cool irony – but it has the rough strength of unvarnished oak. The mind and vision behind it are, one might almost say, those of a prophet; and certainly, like Strachey's stern child of Ecclefechan, this opinionated Nigerian possesses some of the essential qualifications for the prophet's calling – a loud voice, a bold face, and a bad temper! History will complete the requirements. For, despite his labours, and despite the Longmans tribute to him, Tai Solarin will *not* be honoured in his own country.

The new writing from Africa gives literary criticism an opportunity to break free from traditional practice and turn its attention to forms not customarily within its purview. Hence this chapter's examination of children's literature, of writing by politicians, journalists, and even the semi-literate. Such work is important, not because it might be shown to feed or prepare the ground for more laurelled forms (this, in any case, would often be hard to demonstrate), but rather because it has an importance in its own right. For *all* literary activity in modern Africa, no matter what its type and rank, stands, in one way or another, as a manifestation of the cultural changes and the great debates that are presently occurring throughout the continent.

5. Drama

Africa and drama

Tragedy, claimed Aristotle, began with the leaders of the dithryamb, and comedy with the leaders of the phallic performances, and it is hard to find scholars who would seriously challenge this view, that drama's roots lie deep in religious and quasi-religious practices. The religious background to the development of English drama is familiar enough, if non-Greek examples are needed. These observations are made by way of introducing a suggestion that modern Africa should be rich in signs of dramatic phenomena; for, unlike Europe, Africa has only recently begun to suffer (and then but marginally) an invasion by philosophical materialism and its respected fellow-travellers, humanism and agnosticism. Africa has passed through no great age of doubt, and the twin engines of slavery and colonialism inflicted wounds upon the continent's psyche rather than upon its soul. If, then, religion in its various manifestations is linked with the nature and growth of drama, Africa should prove to be dramatically fertile ground, for its religious systems, or (for those who believe that Christianity has made a telling impact on African life) its sense of the religious, has remained largely intact. When Doob says that 'the traditional society meaningfully survives', this, in part, is what he means. The ancestral cosmology and the ritualistic life lived in harmony with the seasons still largely hold sway. Christianity, so often pilloried as the blind destroyer of African culture, has made an important contribution, too, keeping alive a sense of the spiritual and introducing to its converts a ceremonial which itself helped to generate a dramatic tradition in other lands.

The signs

The presence of dramatic forms in Africa and the possession by its people of strong mimetic instincts are first documented by Equiano. Though torn from his homeland at the age of nine, he remembered enough about West Africa to claim of his people, 'We are almost a nation of dancers, musicians, and poets.' This, in itself, is a bold

176

testimony to the artistic health of West Africa in the eighteenth century; but of more interest to us is the remainder of the paragraph from which the assertion comes:

Thus every great event such as a triumphant return from battle or other cause of public rejoicing is celebrated in public dances, which are accompanied with songs and music suited to the occasion. The assembly is separated into four divisions, which dance either apart or in succession, and each with a character peculiar to itself. The first division contains the married men, who in their dances frequently exhibit feats of arms and the representation of a battle. To these succeed the married women, who dance in the second division. The young men occupy the third and the maidens the fourth. Each represents some interesting scene of real life, such as a great achievement, domestic employment, a pathetic story, or some rural sport, and as the subject is generally founded on some recent event, it is therefore ever new.[1]

On the face of it, this is a simple description of a village dance. But notice that Equiano mentions 'the representation of a battle', and also says that each section of the dancers 'represents some interesting scene of real life, such as a great achievement . . . a pathetic story' and so on. With the representational element so strongly present, this, surely, is almost as much drama as it is dance. It is a peculiarly African phenomenon, part ballet, part drama, part opera (certainly a precursor of the vernacular folk opera currently thriving in West Africa), in which the entire community is the cast and the village square the stage. The whole performance is clearly a synthesis of the major indigenous art forms in a truly 'popular' and theatrical activity; and the claim that 'the subject is generally founded on some recent event' suggests a marvellous capacity for rapid dramatic improvisation.

Equiano was writing in 1789. But the modern scene, too, is teeming with similar examples of nascent drama, and since a basic aim of this chapter is to argue a promising future for West African theatre in English, let us examine some further specimens of interest to our study. The pages of the magazine *Nigeria* offer abundant examples. A typical case is described by Ulli Beier in an article called 'The Agbegijo Masqueraders'.[2] The *agbegijo* (literal transation 'we take wood to dance') represent the entertainments branch of the Egun, 'a secret society of men who are specially trained to communicate with the dead'. Beier offers the following account of Egun activities (pp.188–9):

An Egungun festival . . . is a very serious occasion and the big masqueraders impersonate the spirits of the dead, who are believed to reside in them while the dance is on. No wonder these

177

masqueraders are considered sacrosanct, and it is absolutely forbidden to touch them. The young boys wielding whips who surround them are there to protect the onlookers from the charged and dangerous touch of the masqueraders.

The Yoruba do not draw sharp dividing lines between the sacred and the profane however, or between awe and humour. It is not surprising therefore, that the Egun are at the same time the principal entertainers in Yoruba life. Not all the masqueraders are impersonations of ancestors. Some are simply caricatures which are intended to draw a laugh from the audience.

Notice here the signs of drama: the wearing of masks, the disguising, the impersonation of ancestors. Notice, too, the existence side by side of the sacred and the temporal; the performing for profoundly religious purposes and also for worldly entertainment. The same cult, the same society, is responsible for both. The *agbegijo,* then, are the special group of the Egun society whose duty it is to entertain, and they appear to dance 'on the occasions of funerals, marriage ceremonies, wedding feasts', and at the annual sacrifices of *orisha* worshippers.[3] Trained especially in comic entertainment, they do not wear the serious masks of the ancestors, but the grossly carved masks of caricatured human types and eccentrics. Beier observed at the town of Oshogbo that these subjects fell into four easily distinguished categories: 'those imitating other ethnic groups (Hausa, Europeans, Nupe, etc.); those imitating people with odd physical features (big ears, big nose, small mouth, etc.); those making fun of social types (the prostitute, the policeman, the drunkard); and those imitating animals (baboons, leopards, snakes, etc.)'.

The entertainment, however, is no carelessly improvised farce. There is a set pattern, an order of events which begins when the masqueraders first appear singing *iwi,* 'a kind of poetry which is sung exclusively by Egungun'. Beier cites a typical, humorously satiric *iwi* about Ibadan (p.192):

> Mighty Ibadan – We must ask for permission
> Before we enter this town.
> Ibadan is the town where the thief is found
> innocent
> And the owner of property is guilty.
> Ibadan, the town where the owner of the land
> Does not prosper like the stranger.
> Nobody comes into this world
> Without some disease in his body.
> Riots in all the compounds
> Is the disease of Ibadan.

178

You may think you have friends in Ibadan
But they will not care if they sell your
   own child.

This is usually followed by popular mat-tricks, and then by the appearance of *ekun* the leopard, who dashes suddenly into the crowd and
disappears, until he is seen on the top of a nearby roof making
threatening gestures. He will not come down unless somebody in the
audience produces a chicken for him. Beier aptly conveys the excitement of what follows (pp.197-9):

> After this exciting scene numerous masqueraders appear in fairly
> quick succession: there is *Gambari,* the Hausaman; *Tapa,* the
> Nupeman; and *Idahomey,* a warrior from Dahomey. Sango
> dances with Oya, his wife, and more animals follow: the python
> wriggles on the ground; *obo,* the baboon, is portrayed with the
> help of an old gas mask from the 1914 war. *Omuti farasofo* – the
> drunkard who throws his body about, performs a staggering,
> comical dance. A highlight are the *Oimbo* – the Europeans
> with enormous hooked noses and smooth black hair made from
> Colobus Monkey skin. They shake hands, say 'how do you do'
> and perform a ridiculous ballroom dance. *Asewo* – the prostitute,
> is often accompanied by a policemen; and the creditor usually
> appears squatting, as *osomolo*: I will squat and will not go. All
> kinds of masks appear that make fun of people with weird
> features: *eleti kolobo* – the one with big ears; *elekedidi* – the one
> with large cheeks; *enimuoru,* the one with a pot nose; and *elenu
> robo* – the one whose mouth is as small as *robo,* a cake made of
> melon curd.
>
>   Generally, the final piece is a mask known as *iyawo palo* – the
> parlour wife, or the beautiful wife of whom the husband boasts to
> his friends and guests. Iyawo Palo appears wrapped in a great deal
> of cloth. She gradually takes off several layers of wrappers until
> she reveals a baby on her back. These beautifully carved dolls are
> then taken forward and fed from long, flat cloth breasts.

This closing gesture is a rather moving way of signifying the restored
harmony that universally marks the final scene of comedy. The
agbegijo, then, offer a humorous and noisy spectacle, and also a
representation. The performance is supported by poetry, song, and
dance, and by a drumming accompaniment; the properties consist of
bizarre costumes and grotesque masks; the cast is like a regular
company of players, all male, and all members of the Egun society.
The 'theatre' is again the village square, and, as with all genuinely
popular art, the audience is strongly linked with the performance. The

village people meet here acknowledging the fears and views which they hold in common, so that the entertainment is, in a way, an instrument of social peace and conformity.

If the comic antics of the *agbegijo* are only indirectly religious (Beier stresses that this is only one side of Egun work, the other being serious, and both probably aimed against the power of witches), there is plenty of evidence to show that the traditional kinds of religious observance still flourishing in Africa also contain marked dramatic features. 'Drama is manifest', claims J. A. Adedeji, 'during the observance of most of the principal divinities of Yoruba especially during the annual festivals when everybody in the community is involved either as a participant or as a spectator. It is an occasion when the whole community shares a kind of spiritual experience with their gods by making offerings or sacrifices for atonement or appeasement.'[4]

One of the most important of these festivals is held annually in honour of Obatala, the great Yoruba god of creation, the father of peace and father of laughter. According to Yoruba belief, Obatala was sent by Olodumare, the Supreme God, to come down and create the earth; but, feeling thirsty on his journey, he drank too much palm-wine and thus bungled his work, creating blind men, albinos, and hunchbacks. For this, he was imprisoned in the sacred city of Ife, a sojourn that has become the subject of several literary works. Because the rest of creation begins to droop and drowse, he is released from prison and his sufferings enable him to emerge morally triumphant and purged of guilt.

According to Adedeji, Obatala and his sins are the subject of the annual festival of the god Moremi at Ife, the city where, according to Yoruba belief, creation began. Here the ritual is clearly divided into a plot of three acts: first there is the conflict in which Obatala is captured; second, the ransoming of the imprisoned Obatala; and thirdly the release of Obatala and the restoring of peace to Ife. Such elaborate festivals, it must be emphasised, are still commonplace in West Africa. On their dramatic elements Adedeji, a scholar who teaches drama at Ibadan, can speak with authority (p. 92):

> Essentially, the ritual performance is an 'act of worship'. The re-enactment is only a design to give material existence to a state of belief in the worship of Obatala ... The dramatization of the epic is to give the religious observance a significance and a reality that the worshippers need to confirm their faith in the *orisa*. The ritual performancè creates a religious experience but it is not without an artistic form. Although the ritual play is not 'staged', the whole festival has a form or an outward appearance which

180

gives it an artistic pattern: there is a procession – a mass movement of people who gather in the market place (arena) for their
participation in the festival either as participants or spectators.
There are music and song which furnish the poetic element. It is in
the chant and drumming that the scene is laid and background
information furnished. Together, these form the 'choric element'
and they combine rather effectively to communicate thoughts and
interpret moods which add to a better understanding of the
performance.

The ritual play calls up the spirit of Obatala, the priest acts as his
deputy and momentarily becomes 'ridden' or possessed by his spirit so
that this spell 'may serve as an indication of the presence of the divinity
in the "theatrical arena" '. While the essentially religious nature of the
festival precludes any *deliberate* attempts at histrionic effects, an
outsider would see the performance as aesthetic, artistic, and dramatic.

Doob also notes some interesting dramatic phenomena. Like the
Yoruba of Nigeria, he claims, the Mende of Sierre Leone also have their
secret society, whose members are paid to impersonate spirits and visit
the client's home dressed in wooden masks and a cape of raffia and
there 'resort to miming and mimicry' to convey their message from the
dead. But he cites a more unusual form of embryonic drama which
exists among the story-tellers of the Akan of Ghana. A simple yet subtle
form of satire is practised here by raconteurs who begin their performance, rather like the allegorists of English letters, with the words, 'We
don't really mean to say so; we don't really mean to say so' – a
protective device allowing them to give full vent to their complaints and
social criticisms. Responsibility neatly disclaimed, they can now
narrate a tale 'dealing with ordinarily sacred subjects such as gods,
fetishes, ancestors, chiefs, the sick, and sexual matters in a profane
manner and sometimes too with ridicule'.[5] This is interesting enough;
but what really concerns us here is that we have a narrator, 'on stage' as
it were, and an audience who have willingly suspended their disbelief.
What is more, to vivify and drive home the message of the tale, two or
three actors are brought in who can skilfully impersonate the characters
to whom allusion is being made. Hence, with plot, narrator, audience,
and actors, we have a simple form of drama whose function is to
provide for the utterance, in a dignified, harmless way, of social
satire. A similar purpose is served by another custom in which one
African suffering at the hands of another will stand with a friend
outside the offender's house and then proceed violently to abuse his
friend in the loudest possible voice and fight a mock brawl with him.
The listening offender understands well enough the significance of this

performance, and thus real social turmoil is avoided in a manner that can only be described as 'histrionic' in the most literal sense of the word.

Doob's discoveries can be reinforced by the researches of Professor Molly Mahood. Looking for signs of what she calls African 'pre-drama', she menions a Kikuyu dance witnessed in 1903 by W. K. Routledge:

It had excellent staging 'in the round' on a saddle between two hills, so that long effective entrances could be made from the valleys on either side. There was scenery (an artificially planted tree), lively impersonation and highly dramatic entrances in the modern style by actors breaking their noisy way through the ranks of spectators. In fact it was a drama in its own right and, in consequence, it was impossible to tell if its origins were the commemoration of a successful battle against the Masai or a ritual attempt to ensure success in the next encounter with the enemy.[6]

Another form of pre-drama mentioned by Professor Mahood is seen in the funeral dances of the Nyakyusa of Tanzania, for which she quotes the dancers' own remarkable explanation: 'We dance because there is war in our hearts; a passion of grief and fear exasperates us.' This is remarkable, not only because explanations of this sort are rare, but because it recalls the ancient Aristotelian view of tragedy and its catharsis of the emotions of fear and pity.

It is safe to say that because so many 'dramatic' phenomena crowd the contemporary African scene, there has never before been so much living material at hand for those who would enquire into the nature, origins, and development of drama. Miss Mahood herself takes the explanation of the Nyakyusa as the starting point for an interesting line of argument. It suggests, she feels, a probable reason why drama has developed from narration and ritual:

It would seem that, in the former, there was need to become *less* involved than the rite demanded, to be detached from these supernatural happenings; in the latter, there was a compulsion on the part of the hearers to throw themselves into the event narrated and to become more involved. And when we find a modern critic redefining the Aristotelian catharsis as a state of equipoise between the impulse to approach and the impulse to retreat, we may feel that there already existed in African society, long before the *Poetics* became required reading in African Universities, a spontaneous understanding of the nature of drama.[7]

Clearly, Africa as a whole is only too familiar with the idea of the dramatic illusion. In West Africa, where ritual in its various forms is still cultivated, along with representational dancing and dramatised story-telling – where, indeed, the mask is a common sight in the streets – there is, surely, a fertile soil for the growth of a written, developed, and recognisably modern form of drama – a drama that will reflect those changing circumstances and social strains which have become the themes of neo-African prose and verse. We should now, therefore, examine the extent to which West Africa's modern dramatists have taken advantage of their opportunities.

Modern African drama

With the arrival in the twentieth century of more fully developed dramatic forms, recognisably distinct from, though developing along-side, religious and quasi-religious growths, Africa presents a fascinating scene in which drama can be seen, uniquely, flourishing in all those stages which scholars have usually supposed European drama to have passed through. Religious ritual, by which indigenous cults honour and bind themselves to the sources of human and vegetable creation; the oral tale acted out to a willing audience – such embryonic forms have now been joined by drama that approaches western norms – drama, sometimes extempore, sometimes based on a text, whose primary aim is to entertain and which is performed by travelling bands of players. The finest illustration of what is happening lies in what has come to be called the Yoruba Folk Opera of Western Nigeria.

The history of this species of drama (for drama it is, despite its name) is not well documented. Critics who note the predominantly Christian and moral nature of its themes conclude that its origins were mission-inspired. But the evident maturity of the form and the astonishing cohesion of the performances lead one to suspect that its ancestry (not, of course, its present form) predates the arrival of Christianity. Indeed, one must stress that the fusion of song, dance, mime and drumming, which is the very essence of this form, differs only in theme and organisation from the 'public dances' which Equiano described in the eighteenth century. It is a case of new wine in old bottles, an example of Christianity once again taking ancestral 'pagan' forms and moulding them to its own purpose.

Yoruba Folk Opera, as its name suggests, is performed, and frequently nowadays written, in the vernacular. We must examine it because it provides a link between the embryonic drama which we have discussed and the English-language drama of Clark and Soyinka towards which this chapter is moving. Not only is this Yoruba form the natural outgrowth of historical dramatic practice, it is also a seed-bed, a source of creative strength for the new school of literate anglophone dramatists.

The power of Yoruba Opera, especially in its impact on a European audience, is astonishing. In his interesting study *Le Théâtre Négro-Africaine et ses Fonctions Sociales*, Bakary Traoré describes the development of a similar form of drama at the William Ponty School in Gorée, Senegal. When a group from the school went to perform in Paris in 1937, this is how they were received by one enthusiastic critic:

> La race que représente Keïta Fodeba et ses camarades vit au maximum, tant son spectacle est d'une extraordinaire beauté. Ne parlons pas seulement de cette musique qui est rhythme et vie . . . Joie, tristesse, complainte ou cérémonie, tout est prétexte à ballet, mais un ballet qui s'organise spontanément et reçoit, comme par enchantement, un ordre supérieure et naturel. C'est l'Afrique tout entière, l'âme exquise et fraîche d'un peuple merveilleusement élégant dans ses gestes et ses pas . . . ou toute musique est rhythme et toute parole devient mélodie . . .

A reasonably similar style of entertainment given in Toronto in 1967 was described by *The Globe and Mail* critic (16 August 1967, p. 12) as follows:

> Les Ballets Africains offered an evening which was quite simply sensational: thrilling, extravagantly colorful and almost compulsively theatrical. It was a performance of virtually limitless range and variety, encompassing tribal myth, superstition, social commentary, humor, and simple exhibitionism . . .

Description here cannot hope to substitute for experience. Pure European drama is often intensely absorbing; pure European singing can be uplifting, and the European dance a fine spectacle. When two or more of these join together, as in ballet or opera, their combined effect can indeed be thrilling. But Yoruba Folk Opera (in which, one critic wrote, 'tout est mouvement') combines freely and fully, at their highest possible pitch, all of these arts, to produce a synthesis whose brilliance is at once electrifying and overwhelming. The whole text, now normally constructed around traditional poetry and hence resplendent with natural imagery, is sung by solo actors and chorus. A drumming orchestra and frequently a variety of other instruments (flutes, bells, for instance) accompanies the action; and the talking drums of the Yoruba (the drum is not the dead instrument it is in the west) can 'speak poetry, and . . . often add to the text, or play poetic refrains'.[8] The actors use song, dance and gesture to play out their roles and a chorus drives home the major themes of the play.

184

In the hands of two distinguished men, Hubert Ogunde and Duro Ladipo, Yoruba Opera has grown rapidly in strength and ambition. There are now at least a dozen companies regularly touring the Western Region of Nigeria. 'Ogunde', says Beier, 'was the first and is still the most famous of these company directors, who are dramatist, composer, director and lead actor in one.'[9] Ogunde, however, uses no written texts and it was left to Ladipo to write a text and thus fix the form and content of this genre more precisely. Ladipo, too, a poet and musician, first made a serious attempt to draw on traditional Yoruba verse, using the three main types which we have already mentioned: the *oriki* (praise verses), the *ijala* (hunter's songs), and the *iwi* (masqueraders' poetry). And whereas the Folk Opera had previously concerned itself with Biblical stories, and beast allegories, Ladipo extended its range by including what Beier calls 'historical tragedies'. In 1964, Mbari published three plays by Ladipo, *Oba Koso, Oba Moro,* and *Oba Waja,* all of which were translated by Ulli Beier.[10]

The texts are recognisably those of a play; but since they are texts for singing, in their printed state they cannot possibly convey the music and energy that their live performances possess; and although Ladipo does survive translation (his *Oba Koso* was performed with great success in German at the Berlin Festival of 1964), the English language cannot adequately convey the musicality of an essentially tonal language such as Yoruba. Nevertheless, something of the richness of the original comes through; and certainly the strength of Yoruba vernacular traditions leaps out from every page.

Oba Koso (The King Does Not Hang) is an eight-scene dramatisation of the death of Sango, the Yoruba god of thunder, who, like all Yoruba gods, led an earthly life among men before his death and deification. He is still the god of a flourishing cult among the Yoruba, and his festivals are noisy and alarming affairs. This play, therefore, while it is 'theatre' as opposed to 'ritual', will often be acted for, and perhaps by, Sango worshippers themselves, for whom it must partake of a religious experience.

Yoruba plots are simple; texts are brief but can be enormously extended by improvisation, which is in the spirit of the traditional dramatic forms. Here, Sango, the King and founder of modern Oyo, finds himself at the end of a war being pressed for a lasting peace by his people. His two generals, Timi and Gbonka, despise peace, and Sango therefore tries to get rid of them. Timi is sent to Ede, ostensibly to defend the frontiers of the kingdom, but the people there welcome him as their king. Sango then dispatches Gbonka to go and destroy Timi (in the hope that they will destroy each other), but after magically knocking Timi unconscious, Gbonka brings him back to Oyo. The people, horrified by the return of both men alive, persuade Sango to have the men repeat the fight in the market place. This is done, with the same result; but now with Gbonka cutting off Timi's head. Gbonka suspects Sango's treachery, and, turning on him, drives him out of the city, whereupon the King goes and hangs himself in a forest. Thunder is heard and the voice of the deified Sango demanding homage from his people; henceforth Sango is accepted as their god, while at Ede a long line of Timis begins, stretching down to the present day.

The opening of the play is a show of praise and honour towards Sango, by his wives (Oloris), by the court poet, Iwarefa, and a group of drummers; it combines poetry, song, dance, and ceremonious prostration (p. 7):

IWAREFA:	We greet you
	Father of mankind
	Of divine power
	Second only to God.
OLORIS:	Kabiyesi, we prostrate before you.
IWAREFA:	Mighty one!
	You control the most stubborn!
	You bring trouble to your disobedient
	Children!
OLORIS:	Born to be a king!
IWAREFA:	You are a huge sacrifice, too heavy for
	the vulture,
	He staggers under your weight.
OLORIS:	Of divine power, second to God.
IWAREFA:	You are a bigger morsel than any of us
	can chew!
	If anyone tries to swallow you –
	You come out of his anus at once.
	The leopard is merely taking his rest –
	Yet the hunter is afraid!
OLORIS:	Kabiyesi! Born to be king!
	Of divine power, second only to God.

'Kabiyesi', 'Born to be king', 'Of divine power', 'Second only to God' – these are the key praises that are repeated in an antiphonal way by the poet and the choric group of wives: this is a standard feature of Ladipo's plays and, since it represents the use of *oriki* or praise verse, it is directly linked with ancestral tradition.

Typical, too, is the nature imagery of the verse: Sango is 'too heavy for the vulture', he is a 'leopard' who is 'merely taking his rest'.

186

Ladipo tries hard to create credible characters for his drama, and though they remain essentially uncomplicated figures, they do, at times, show a good deal of liveliness. Timi, for example, reveals himself with the frankness of a Jacobean villain: 'I am small but I am evil/No fight has ever seen me hesitate./I am small but I defy the elders,/I defy the elders who are forging weapons.' In the same confident manner, he approaches the city of Ede and courts the affection of the people in lines of fine verse which are built, typically, around parallel assertions and repeated injunctions that have an urgent, cumulative effect on the listener. The imagery derives as ever from familiar details of the physical world and from the elements (p. 15):

> I come gently like rain in the evening
> I come swiftly like rain in the morning,
> I come suddenly like rain in bright sunlight.
> Spirits of the place:
> Asarewa, Arintona, Atuyanya,
> Let the people move quickly to meet me,
> Let them walk swiftly towards me on the road,
> Let the wind blow them all towards me,
> Let them all come rushing to me.
> If we throw our net into the sea
> It catches all the fish in the shallow waters.
> I am coming to Ede today,
> I know nobody,
> Nobody knows me,
> Asarewa, Arintona, Atuyanya,
> Let them all rush towards me.
>
> *
>
> My net draws them in,
> All the fish who will not stay in the deep waters,
> My net gathers them towards me.

The play has several other good moments. Scene Eight, an open field, reveals Sango, like Lear or Oedipus, in the wilderness, deserted by his people and now, finally, deserted by his wife, Oya. Her song of farewell, undoubtedly pure lyricism in the original, retains some of its simple quality even in translation: the imagery, especially in the closing lines, reflects Sango's reduced circumstances with some poignancy (pp. 27–8):

> My Lord, my husband, the one I trust,
> The one I adore, the one whose tongue commands,
> Small bird, whose song carries far in the forest,
> Though small, he is still the husband of all the queens.

Ajala Iji,
I have tried much for you – but I will follow you no further.
Let me go back to my town at Ira, where I was born.
Small bird whose song carries far in the forest,
Farewell.

This desertion is what finally breaks Sango's heart and he runs and hangs himself. 'Sango hangs' then becomes a wild and repeated cry in the mouth of Oya who tries to convince herself that he will return: 'Sango hangs, Sango hangs/O let it not be heard/That Sango hangs at Koso'. At this point, the people of Oyo enter, declaring that their town is in utter confusion, and, prostrating themselves before the hanging Sango, ask him when he will return. The Magbas, Sango's friends, upbraid the townfolk for driving out their king and announce the king's immortality (p. 30):

Has a stone ever died?
If you cut open the chest of a bat,
You will meet a new bat inside it.
The bat, that has children upon children,
Ever renewing itself!
The King does not hang!
When the kite flies high into the sky,
People think he is lost,
Yet he returns to his nest.
Those who will say, Sango is dead,
Will know his wrath today.

A great clap of thunder is heard, and Sango speaks from on high offering his people peace, wealth and happiness, if they will pay homage to him. The people shout out all the key praises and chants that have underpinned the text of the play and end with a joyful 'Kabiyesi O!/The King does not hang!' At the conclusion of the play, we feel that we have seen the dramatization of a series of events that began a cult – Sango's life and death on earth. There is also a strong feeling that social harmony and cohesion will be assured if the people remain faithful to their deity and his sacred rites.

Clearly, *Oba Koso* is not a political play. Its *raison d'être* has nothing to do with Nigerian Independence, Africa's continuing struggle against the remnants of colonialism, or with negritude's battle against the white world. It shares with the work of Fagunwa and Tutuola a lack of concern with such issues: it is inward- rather than outward-looking; it is 'conservative' in the way that folk art is by custom conservative; it thrives on ancestral themes because it is the outgrowth of a stable and ancestrally oriented society. And it stands as a fair example of the species to which it belongs.

The demands of tradition weigh heavily on the Yoruba dramatists; they are close to the ancestral society and their commitment to the vernacular must carry with it a number of unconsciously felt cultural obligations. This is not to say, however, that the Yoruba plays deliberately and consistently shun the contemporary world, or that they are an insufficiently flexible medium for dealing with it. *Oba Waja,* the third play in Ladipo's collection, is an example of how the form can deal with a modern theme; for the events on which the play is based actually took place at Oyo in the Western Region of Nigeria, in 1946, and, dramatised by Ladipo, become a most telling indictment of European interference in African affairs.

The Alafin, or King, of Oyo dies, and custom demands that Olori Elesin, commander of the King's Horse, should also die to act as a servant and companion on his master's journey to heaven. This office has been in Olori's family for generations, and he knew his fate when he inherited the position. The logic of tradition is moving smoothly ahead when the intrusion of the British District Officer (on the prompting of a wife who will 'take the next boat home', if this 'human sacrifice' is not stopped) causes it to grind to a halt; the suicide is forbidden and Olori is left, half-relieved, half-alarmed, in an intolerable situation. He is caught between two worlds in an agony of self-doubt and mortification, despising himself and despised by his people. While he is caught in this situation, his son, Dawodu, disgusted with a father who has broken faith with tradition, decides to take upon himself the burden of office, and so commits suicide, reviling his father as he dies and crying shame on the unnaturalness of his behaviour (pp. 68–9):

> Today a child must carry a father's burden.
> The falling leaf does not stop to rest
> Before it touches the ground.
> The river will never return to its source.
> Today will I face the gatekeeper of heaven
> Preparing the glorious entry of my king!

Dawodu's death brings Olori's agony and disgrace to new heights. Cheated by the white man of a glorious death under the traditional code, he has suffered the further disaster of losing his own son. Only an infamous death is left for him and after cursing the District Officer's intervention – 'This is the white man's doing,/The white man with his new law!' – he too kills himself. The British official, trying to save one life, has caused two deaths, and is a wiser man for his mistake (p. 72):

I was trying to save a life –
And I have caused a double death.
Man only understands the good he does unto himself,
When he acts for others,
Good is turned into evil; evil is turned into good!

The Oyo people console him, however, arguing that he has been deliberately confused by Eshu, the troublesome god of fate who leads men astray. But they offer a polite word of advice: 'With Eshu/Wisdom counts for more than good intentions,/And understanding is greater than justice' – sentiments that are fraught with Yoruba pragmatic morality. On balance, the fault is laid at Olori's door; but even towards him the people are disposed to be merciful, despite the cataclysmic implications of his behaviour; this is the note struck by the women of Oyo whose final chorus provides a neat recovery of the play's material (p. 72):

Olori Elesin, Commander of the Horse:
You believed the stranger
And the world broke over your head.
You believed in the new time –
As yet we cannot tell
How much of our world you have destroyed
Cross now the river in peace.
Today you shall see the king of the river.
Today you shall face the king of the sun.

A fine principle of construction is at work in the play, for it is built around three or four central ideas that are realised in key images and expressions. There is the central theme of disintegration, for example, which is carried by a constantly reiterated allusion to the world being spoilt or the world breaking over the heads of the people. 'Let not the world spoil in our own time!' the citizens of Oyo cry near the beginning of the play. Then, immediately after the District Officer's interference, they lament, 'The world is spoilt in the white man's time/. . . The white man's rule has spoiled our world.' Similarly, their most crushing insult to Olori is to tell him 'Our town has spoiled in your time!/. . .. The world has spoiled in your time.' The voice of the Dead Alafin echoes the same motif, 'The world is spoilt in my time,' and Olori's recognition of his own guilty misfortune is rendered in his cry, 'Oyo people – the world is spoilt in my time/The world has broken over my head.' The effect of the metaphor is to make us feel that these people are standing before the whole of their assembled tribe, dead and alive, and confessing that the sacred gifts of life and the earth, handed on to them for safe-keeping, have now been irreparably desecrated.

190

To be caught thus between two worlds is, as we have seen, a commonplace of modern African writing; but it *is* a contemporary fact of life and it involves precisely that conflict of forces and the necessity to choose which lie at the heart of good drama. What happened at Oyo was an isolated incident; but in Ladipo's hands, it is dramatically magnified to become symbolic of the collapse of a whole way of life.

The basic material of the play, therefore, is rich in dramatic potential, and Ladipo exploits it with some skill. At the same time, and as part of this process, he decorates and reinforces his theme with memorable verse drawn from vernacular sources. Take, for instance, the lament that rises at the death of Dawodu (p. 69):

> O pain, O pain! O cruel death!
> Death breaks the honeycomb
> And spills its sweetness.
> Commander of the horse!
> Weep!

or Dawodu's own account of the inscrutability of Death, which is typically Yoruba in conception and a vivid example of how the Yoruba imagination likes to leap up to metaphysics from buttresses that are solidly embedded in the earth (p. 66):

> O merciless death.
> The house of joy collapses when you arrive.
> You break the honeycomb and spill its sweetness.
> You do not allow a man to pack his loads
> before he follows you.
> You kill the King of Ara, you do not respect
> the King of Esa either!
>
> *
>
> O merciless death,
> You are the short man in the afternoon
> You are the tall man at night.
> When you enter the house
> The whole compound breaks out into noise.
> When you enter the back-yard,
> The entire house begins to shake in its foundations.
> Death, you turn the house into a forest,
> You turn the verandah into a pile of rubble
> Death, you cross the river,
> And wailing is your companion.

In its attempt to probe the unknown through the familiar, in its combination of the tangible with the abstract, Dawodu's verse (and indeed so much of the verse in these Yoruba plays) calls to mind a

191

remark made by Coleridge in *Biographia Literaria*: 'Most interesting is
it to consider the effect when the feelings are wrought above the natural
pitch by the belief of something mysterious while all the images are
purely natural. Then is it that religion and poetry strike deepest.'
Dawodu comments poetically, too, on the death of one's parents. 'The
day our mother dies', he says, 'Our gold turns to trash./The day our
father dies,/Our mirror sinks into the deep sea.' To show the unnatural
behaviour of Olori, to drive home, as Dawodu did, the broken logic of
his conduct, the Oyo people describe the scene of the living father
standing over his dead son in an image which we have previously
encountered in a funeral poem from Abeokuta: 'The palm tree should
die, being weighed down by his fruit/See now the old stem erect, and his
fruit rotting on the ground.' Skilful in construction, and rich in verse
that survives translation, *Oba Waja* demontrates the strength and
adaptability of Yoruba drama, and suggests once again the solid
foundations on which the English-speaking dramatists can build. It
marks, too, a trend in vernacular drama towards a concern with the
contemporary scene. Indeed, by 1964, we find Ogunde's troupe being
banned from performing anywhere in Nigeria's Western Region after
its production of *Yoruba Ronu,* a frankly satirical piece aimed at the
corruption of S. A. Akintola's government. Ogunde then moved into
the Federal territory of Lagos and immediately staged a reply called *O
Tito Koro – The Truth is Bitter.'*[11]

No account of Yoruba theatre would be complete without a glance at
Obatunde Ijimere, one of Ladipo's actors who now writes plays for the
company. Inspired to write by *Oba Koso,* in his hands Yoruba theatre
has gained noticeably in sophistication and flexibility. His plays are
still largely made up of chanting and singing; but they mark a
departure from Ladipo in their inclusion of conventional stage dialogue; and the verse, while retaining many of the familiar devices of
Yoruba dramatic poetry, is not quite so repetitive of basic motifs and
formulae. The imagery remains rooted in nature and the physical
world; but there is a concern to fill in more detail, so that the scenes and
characterisation do not share Ladipo's stark and spare quality. They
are theatrically more alive; and his gods, while retaining the idiosyncrasies which Yoruba tradition has celebrated in them, appear more
like human beings; they are equally god-like, yet more warmly human.

A volume of Ijimere's plays was published in 1966, comprising
Woyengi, a play based on an Ijaw myth recorded by the poet Gabriel
Okara; *Everyman,* a Yoruba version of the Middle English and German
play; and *The Imprisonment of Obatala.*[12] All are interesting pieces –
Everyman, it seems, has already been performed with great acclaim by

Ladipo's company in Switzerland, Belgium, Germany, and Austria, as well as in Nigeria – but of the three the Obatala play represents the most complex achievement. We have encountered Obatala already in our discussion of pre-drama: he is a god of creation, father of peace, father of laughter, and the myths about him provide a rich source of literary inspiration. He, or at least, his imprisonment, lies at the core of the play; but Ijimere has usefully brought together several major deities in this work, so that we find, along with Obatala, Shango, King of Oyo, god of Thunder, and Obatala's friend; Eshu, the god of fate who leads men into mischief; and Ogun, the god of war and iron. They are included for a special purpose; for one of the central aims behind the play is to present a full picture of the Yoruba cosmology; to present a complete picture, where others, Ladipo for example, have provided only glimpses and fragments.

The play makes use of the familiar myth about Obatala's imprisonment for bungling the work of creation. A Babalawo sings his praises, but here reminds him of his errors (p. 10):

You made the blind man who cannot see
The whiteness of the cattle egret,
Nor the blackness of the hornbill,
Nor the redness of the cuckal.
You made the red-eyed albino
Who is frightened of the sun,
Whose skin is sore like the leper's.
You made the hunchback,
Laughing stock of children,
Shunned by women,
A living calabash of medicine.

His punishment will be meted out by Eshu, whose tricks and torments he must undergo as he begs his way to Oyo 'Disguised as a mendicant priest'.

The lesson in humility and suffering which Obatala teaches is an important theme; but what is more crucial is the cosmic effect of his ten years' imprisonment. We must remember that these are creation myths that Ijimere is using, myths that explain not only the origin of life but the way it is maintained and propagated. Thus, when a god of creation is jailed, the creative and procreative processes dry up. Children die in the womb; crops fail to ripen; the yam will not grow; women bleed to death in childbirth; large stomachs are a death sentence and no more a sign of joy and fruitfulness. Women dread intercourse in 'cold sweat and fear'. All creation shudders to a halt. Such a development illustrates a basic cornerstone of Yoruba thinking since it stems directly from the concept

193

of their pantheon (in itself a divine, though 'human', representation of the cosmic order) as a grouping and balancing of forces in which, as it were, all subsists by elemental strife. Obatala balances Ogun, who balances Shango, and so on; and thus is harmony maintained. When a 'good' god lies fettered, therefore, the whole cosmos falls into chaos as the forces of destruction seize their chance and rampage unhindered around the universe. Hence, during Obatala's incarceration, those gods preponderate who embody the opposites of his powers and qualities; instead of his laughter and peace, procreation and fulfilment, savage war breaks out, stirred up by Ogun, and there begins a long period of life under the shadow of slaughter. Even at the moment of Obatala's imprisonment (at the hands of his best friend Shango, though Eshu is ultimately to blame) misfortune erupts, as Shango's wife, Oya, reports (p. 27):

> My Lord,
> Even now the imprisonment of Obatala spells
>   disaster.
> The bringer of peace, the father of laughter
>   is in jail,
> You have unleashed Ogun, who bathes in blood.
> Even now his reign begins:
> He kills suddenly in the house and suddenly
>   in the field.
> He kills the child with iron with which
>   it plays.
> Ogun kills the owner of the slaves and the
>   slaves as well.
> He kills the owner of the house and paints
>   the hearth with his blood!

Meanwhile shouts and screams, heavy drum rolls and gunfire are heard outside, and after replying to his wife's announcement, Shango leads his soldiers off to war, with the cry, 'Ogun shall have his due today./ . . . The curdling blood shall form black swamps/Reeking by the wayside/And the vulture at last shall be rewarded'. With war and death now in the ascendant, Ogun receives the praise chants of the women (pp. 29–31):

> The leopard claws the earth,
> Blood oozes from his nostrils,
> His eyes stare white towards the sky
> When he is hit by Ogun.
> The elephant roars like the *kakaki* trumpet
> His trunk threatens to tear the sky
> Like an old rag.

> But when he is struck by Ogun,
> His tree-trunk legs snap like broomsticks,
> And his weight comes thundering down
> As camwood and iroko are crushed
> Under his load.
> And the forest dove shrieks and flutters in
>   the sky
> When its nest hits the ground with the iroko
> And the yolk of its eggs are scattered.

But for all this, 'A curse has fallen on Oyo'.

> The corn on its stalk is worm-eaten
> And hollow like an old honeycomb;
> The yam in the earth is dry and stringy like
> Palm wood . . . Creation comes to a standstill
> When he who turns blood into children
> Is lingering in jail.

At this point the elemental strife which keeps the cosmos in harmony is reduced to human terms and dramatised in a refreshingly concrete and democratic way. If Shango's wife is to make complaints of this sort in defence of Obatala and his powers of creation, then she had better realise that Ogun, as the god of iron and slaughter, has grounds for complaint, too. 'Let us not hear of him', he cries, leaping up in anger (p. 31):

> We had his peace too long!
> The iron rusted in the smithy
> And the smith grew rings round his waist.
> I had grown tired of the blood of dogs
> Offered as substitute by men
> Who had grown soft and fat like eunuchs.
> The king of laughter had his time
> Now let me quench my thirst!

However, when Obatala has expiated his crime and is released from prison in an immaculate white gown to symbolise the beginning of a new era of peace and prosperity, and when the chorus of women enter triumphantly, as they did at the start of the play, bringing in the new yam that symbolises new growth and well-being, Ogun gracefully bows out and salutes the god of creation with dignity and good humour (pp. 37–8):

> Father of laughter
> Your reign has begun.
> Once more you have come to us
> To turn blood into children.

I shall retire from your dazzling presence,
Your immaculate whiteness
Drives me back into the darkness of my forest.
Now the blood will dry on swords and arrows
The elders forging weapons in the smithy
Will grow fat.
The river of blood that fed me has dried up.
I will have to be satisfied with a trickle
That flows from circumcisions and tribal
Markings.

He reminds Obatala, nevertheless, of the closeness of the link between them, the delicacy of the balance they represent, and the likelihood that it will be disturbed again in the not-too-distant future (pp. 38–9):

I will return to the silent darkness of my forest.
Death and creation
Cannot live too close together.
Yet remember: They cannot live too far apart either.
The iron you despise
The iron you wish to imprison
It is the same iron
Used to carve your sacred images.
The iron makes the mahogany weep
When it chisels out the bulging eyes
That stare in a trance.
The iron makes the mahogany groan
When it moulds the mango breasts
Heavy and pendulous, as if with milk.

. . .

Father of laughter:
I yield to you now;
But the iron that serves you
Will one day shout for blood!

The calm waters of the Epilogue, which takes the form of a soliloquy by the god Eshu, are ruffled only by a repetition of the same warning. Everyone is happy; Obatala rests in the sky 'like a swarm of bees'; Ogun has returned to the forest of Ekiti and idly watches the woodcock and tree creeper, listens to the weaver birds and the prophecies of the owl; admires the wisdom of the bombill and enjoys the humour of the cuckal. The people of Oyo are asleep, their stomachs filled with new yam, the wine still fermenting in their heads. They will wake to halcyon days, in which the earth will never fail them; the palm-tree will provide oil and wine, and women will bear a multitude of children.

Weavers, gold-smiths, and drummers will grow fat on the vanity of women and the appalling reign of Ogun will be completely forgotten. And yet they will still need the attributes of Ogun. It is iron that is used in circumcision and in the slaughter of the goat sacrificed to Obatala. 'The child that Obatala moulds in the womb/Is begot and born with blood.' A time will come, however, when Oludumare, the Supreme god, will send down Eshu, the god of fate, to cause confusion once again – it is he who has been responsible for the events of the play. Eshu explains all this in a passage that again reminds us of the Yoruba view of the cosmos (pp. 43–4):

> The time will come when the owner of Heaven
> Will send me back to confuse the heads of men.
> Then Ogun will burst out of his forest
> To cool his parched throat with blood.
> Then the father of laughter will be driven
>   from the city.
> And the rule of iron returns.
> For if Obatala is the right arm of the owner
>   of Heaven
> Ogun is his left arm.
> If Obatala's love is the right eye of the
>   owner of the sun,
> Ogun's iron is his left eye.
> For the owner of the world has interlocked
>   creation and death
> Inseparably like mating dogs.

Ijimere is writing in the same tradition as Ladipo, although he is prepared to use subjects, such as we find in *Everyman* and *Woyengi,* which are taken from outside Yoruba oral tradition but seem adaptable to Yoruba tastes and values. The verse is still largely the verse of Ladipo, or rather of the oral tradition, and the device of rhyming images and motifs is used with only slightly less frequency. The plays, after all, are written expressly for Ladipo's company, and we should not be surprised to find that much of Ijimere's art is in the same vein as Ladipo's. We can see, for instance, that there is the same feeling for the great tableau as a fitting opening for a play. *The Imprisonment* opens with Obatala seated on his throne in his palace at Ife, listening to his wife singing the ceremonial praises of the new yam. At the beginning of *Everyman,* Olodumare is seated on his heavenly throne magnificently garbed in the white robes of a Yoruba Oba, his face hidden by a veil of white beads hanging from his crown, while beside him are bearers carrying the ceremonial sword, symbolic of his power over life and death. A chorus of sword-bearers is chanting the praises of Olodumare, Supreme god of Heaven and owner of the world. *Woyengi* also begins in Heaven. 'The stage is bare, except for a platform and a huge sun, suspended high.' Woyengi is the great mother of creation in Ijaw mythology; and thus an appropriate, though visually startling, element of the tableau over which she magisterially presides is a crouching figure completely wrapped in brown cloth – symbolising a lump of common clay about to be moulded into human form by the creative power of the goddess.

There are, then, basic similarities between Ijimere and Ladipo. But there are important differences, too, and one of these is the marked increase in stage activity found in Ijimere's work. In the Obatala play, for instance, Eshu, the god of confusion, is a lively comic figure, making the action go with a swing, always dressed to deceive in a coat half red and half black. He causes endless trouble to Obatala on his penitential walk to Oyo, tipping a jar of oil over him, causing him to be beaten by a farmer in a dispute over the true colour of the god's coat, and constantly singing a refrain most appropriate to his character and present vocation: 'The hunter thinks the monkey is not wise./The monkey *is* wise/But he has his own logic.'

Nor does Ladipo offer us any character so fully drawn as Ijimere's Obatala. Depth of characterisation and the play's moral aims are united in the god's acceptance of his guilt, his willingness to do penance, and his steadfastness in its performance. Once he has decided to accept his punishment, he is inspired by the Babalawo, who recites to him the prophecy of the king of Awe, 'who conquered his foes through patience', and this strikes the keynote for Obatala's conduct from this point onwards. The prophecy is couched in a familiar concrete and repetitive African style (p. 11):

> The river abuses the rock –
> The rock keeps quiet.
> The river attacks the rock –
> The rock does not fight back.
> The river swallows the rock –
> The rock holds still.
> But when the dry season comes
> The river is lost in the sand
> His fishes turn white bellies to heaven,
> But the rock remains immobile
> Where God has planted it.
> Shango may thrive in war,
> Orunmila may thrive through wisdom
> But you will thrive in suffering.

Hence Obatala's stoic acceptance of Eshu's tricks, his refusal to strike him, his willingness to undergo captivity and his patient endurance of years in jail. He nobly refuses to defend himself when Shango, his best friend, wrongfully accuses him of horse theft – the charge which leads to his incarceration. On his release he can show magnanimity to the friend who has wronged him (p. 36):

> True friendship never takes offence
> I asked you to be patient,
> You were wildly impatient
> And I loved you for it.
> I asked you to be peaceful,
> You steeped your arms in blood
> But I still loved you for it.

All this, of course, is a powerful lesson to the laity in their daily struggles to bear up beneath the burdens of adversity.

The convincing portrayal of Obatala, and his lively exchanges with Eshu, contribute largely to the success of a play that is at once more theatrically alive and thematically complex than its predecessors. There is a quality of resonance here, a sense of the play working in many different directions. Where Ladipo baldly states, Ijimere hints or vaguely suggests, what the work is trying to put across. An easy summary is not so readily achieved as it was with *Oba Koso* or *Oba Waja*. As we have seen, there is an overall impression of a complete Yoruba reading of the universe: the great cosmic mysteries are not mysteries at all, but are accounted for and reduced to memorable simplicity by the action itself. And while the audience is instructed in the details of the Yoruba cosmology, it gains at the same time a certain reassurance: the world is not a meaningless bundle of chaotic forces, but respects an order that can be detected and explained. On the religious level, this reassurance serves to confirm the people's faith in a divine system whose legends and myths have provided the materials of the drama. Similarly, knowledge of the pantheon and faith in its members provide the key to a philosophical understanding of the strangely dual nature of human existence. There is no unrealistic assumption of religious blinkers here, for the Yoruba know that both Obatala and Ogun, both creation and death, must be accounted for. They know that both gods have their rights and that, since they work alongside each other, joy and sorrow in life will always be close together. By bringing a god like Obatala down amongst men, there is a suggestion as to how these central facts of the human situation can best be faced; how, indeed, man's social behaviour should be conducted. By dramatising the dignity and ultimate triumph of Obatala's acceptance of suffering, the play offers a compelling example to the people, who no doubt feel, 'If even the great god of creation can humble himself to accept the hardships of this cruel earthly life, then surely mere creatures such as we are can do so too.'

We should remind ourselves at this point that Ladipo and Ijimere are vernacular writers: we have been discussing texts translated out of Yoruba into English. Granted the abiding problems of translation, one must still marvel at the splendour and strength of the vernacular poetic and dramatic traditions – qualities which are solid enough to survive pretty well the killing act of translation. Clearly, then, with a cornucopia of dramatic and pre-dramatic wealth at their disposal, African writers who choose the drama as their medium of expression begin with a significant advantage. It remains for us now to examine precisely how, and to what extent, the new dramatists in English have made use of this inheritance.

J. P. Clark

When, in 1961, just one year after completing his university education, John Pepper Clark published his first play, *Song of a Goat,* he seemed doubtful about the advantages which the indigenous tradition had to offer; hence the play bears the marks of indecision and is clearly a work of low voltage.[13] And yet it is evident that Clark is attempting to marry some features of his African heritage with those of the western tradition which he had encountered as an undergraduate at Ibadan. Indeed, the very title of his play is suggestive enough, being a literal translation of the Greek elements that are usually assumed to make up the word 'tragedy'. It is as if Clark, recalling the ritualistic origins of Greek drama, felt that here was a rare opportunity to write a Graeco-African tragedy; for, after all, are not ritual and the sacrifice of animals still commonplace practices among his people? He decided, then, that he would write a modern tragedy which respected the classical unities of time, place, and action, and use a strictly limited number of *personae.* The theme of fertility would be explored – a theme appropriate in an African context and yet fittingly universal as well. African villagers would conveniently form a chorus and a local medicine man could play the oracle.

The plan was perfect, and the plot memorably simple. Zifa, a fisherman and part-time ship's pilot, has become impotent. His wife, Ebiere, upon the advice of the village Masseur, who is the local doctor, confessor, and oracle, warmly encourages Tonye, his younger brother, to take his place; and this he eventually does. During the sacrifice of a goat, and after the ceaseless, and senseless, ululations of a half-possessed aunt, Zifa discovers his misfortune. As a result, Tonye hangs himself, Ebiere dies, and Zifa drowns himself, an event which takes place off-stage in the best classical manner.

The play does not succeed, or rather it partially succeeds as poetry but not as drama. There might be various reasons for this; but one suspects that the basic truth of the matter is simply that Clark, in 1961, was a young writer with a fair command of verse but no sense of theatre: his skill in verse he had cultivated over a number of years, but in the dramatic crafts he had served no apprenticeship. Thus he was able to bring to the play's theme, setting, and structure, all the critical taste of the Honours School of English, but none of the life-giving sense of real theatre.

Perhaps, too, Greek tragedy is deceptively simple. Its thin contours require a heavy clothing of pity and terror for it to succeed artistically; there is, after all, little else to hold the imagination in a form where richness of colour and variety of scene and *personae* are all severely pruned. *Song of a Goat* possesses this same thinness of texture, without the complementary charge of pity and terror – except that Clark finally stumbles across a certain amount of both qualities when Zifa and Tonye commit suicide. But pity for those who suffer unnecessary death is a universal emotion which arises spontaneously. Here it is not felt to rise from an artistically prepared situation within the play, for we have not really felt much sympathy with any of the three protagonists before they are destroyed at the denouement. The chorus, too, is unsatisfactory; it is simply a crowd of busybodies, who help neither to carry the play's values – whatever these might be – nor to focus attention on the hero's decline; and the whole movement of the action fails to demonstrate that inexorability of fate, that relentless turning of the slowly grinding mills of god that so fascinates in Greek tragedy.

The play's merits lie rather in its poetic qualities, though even these are an indication of why the play as a whole fails; for they are those qualities that evoke a sense of place and atmosphere rather than the movements of a soul; qualities which describe an outer, rather than an inner, landscape. This is hardly surprising when we recall Clark's professed concern for 'nature and actuality' and his 'attempts to realize natural concrete subjects ... in a personal memorable way'. It is significant, then, that *Song of a Goat* is strong in descriptive pieces. Its landscape is at once recognisably different from the Yorubaland scenes of Ladipo, Ijimere, or Tutuola. The sense of darkness that goes with high equatorial forest gives way to the more open ground found among the creeks of the Niger Delta, where the Ijaw live. It is a land of

rivers, backwaters, tides, and beaches, subject to enormous rainfall and
providing the people with fishing, farming, and, for a few families,
bush-navigation on the great freighters that come in from the sea.[14] A
sense of this locale is called up in the lines of Orukorere when she asks
her neighbour about the fate of Zifa (pp. 42–3):

> Speak up, man, what effect
> Can the words you bring have now? Don't you
> See it is raining over the sea tonight?
> On the sands sprawling out to dazzle
> Point till eyes are scales
> This outpouring should be impression
> Indeed. Here only waves pour out
> On waves, only dunes upon dunes.

and again in the neighbour's reply, which is an example of reported
action in the classical style (pp. 43–4):

> Well, you saw how he
> Went out of here as one in sleep. He said
> Nothing more and so, silent, we followed
> On his heels. It was a heavy walk, the fishing
> Baskets scattered all about, the new canoes
> Carving on the shore. And the grass was wet
> On our feet. Presently, fording the sands,
> We saw him reach the water's edge. Just then
> That noise you said you heard as distant
> Thunder rolled out to where we stood. It was
> A steamer calling out for a pilot
> To pass beyond the bar. At the sound of it,
> Zifa seemed to start out of his sleep: Blow,
> Blow, sirens, blow he bellowed as in reply,
> And blow till your hooting drown
> The moaning of the sea. No blow
> Will be stronger. The owls, he said, that should
> Hoot at night have this afternoon blown down
> His house as they have the ancestral hall
> Open in the market place. And the stalls there
> That should crowd with voices are filled now
> Not even with the buzz of houseflies. All
> Are fled, fled, and left behind
> Bats to show their beards by day.

The view of the sands, with its boats and baskets scattered about, the
view of the ancestral hall blown down in the market place – these have
the making of fine insets, though they stand amidst verse whose halting

movement suggests a need for more discipline and control; verse which suffers from obvious infelicities while displaying, at times, signs of developing power. There are some fine passages, too, near the beginning of the play, where a conversation about the impotency problem is carried on in a continuously oblique vein between Zifa and the Masseur. Significantly, the verse here gains its vitality from basing itself on typical African modes of expression. The oblique style is itself a common feature of Ijaw conversation about delicate subjects; also the Masseur describes Ebiere's impatience with Zifa's impotence in imagery culled directly from the African environment – the storehouse which Ladipo and Ijimere drew on so successfully (pp. 6–7):

> Don't you see the entire grass is gone
> Overlush, and with the harmattan may
> Catch fire though you spread over it
> Your cloak of dew?
>
> . . .
>
> She has waited too long already,
> Too long in harmattan. The rains
> Are here once more and the forest getting
> Moist. Soon the earth will put on her green
> Skirt, the wind fanning her cheeks flushed
> From the new dawn. Will you let the woman
> Wait still when all the world is astir
> With seed and heady from flow of sap?

Zifa's reply to Masseur's offer of help is in the same vein (p. 6):

> You talk of help, What help can one expect
> That is placed where I stand? People
> Will only be too pleased to pick at me
> As birds at worm squirming in the mud. What,
> Shall I show myself a pond drained dry
> Of water so their laughter will crack up the
> floor of my being?

And yet, unfortunately, Clark's poetic talent works erratically. Alongside lines as mature as the following (p. 48):

> Do not, my people, venture overmuch
> Else in unravelling the knot, you
> Entangle yourselves. It is enough
> You know now that each day we live
> Hints at why we cried out at birth.

we find lines of astonishing ineptness, which introduce either absurd notions or grave disruptions of tone: 'Say', cries Orukorere, 'has/ Lightning struck him down that walked/Into the storm, his head covered with basin?' Masseur offers us the unpoetic lines: 'But now you/Have lived to this day, perhaps you are ripe/To hazard a crack at life's nut', while Orukorere, wondering why she cannot find her leopard, asks herself, 'sports him no spoors?'

The Masquerade is evidently meant to share an organic link with *Song of a Goat,* for we find Diribi, the heroine's father, talking about his daughter's mysterious suitor, Tufa, in the following terms (p. 68):

> Did he tell you also his father
> Usurped the bed of his elder brother, yes,
> Brazenly in his lifetime, and for shame
> Of it after hanged himself in broad daylight
> While this unfortunate abused husband
> Walked of his own will into the sea?

This is a clear reference to the events of the first play. Tufa is the son of Tonye, who 'stole' the wife of Zifa, his brother. The connection, however, is of little importance, since it is not woven artistically into the fabric of the play. Despite this deliberate suggestion of continuity (perhaps Clark in these first three plays has the idea of a trilogy in mind), the events of *The Masquerade* do not grow naturally out of those in *Song of a Goat*. The reference to Tufa's origins is important in so far as it gives him a bad family background. This in turn sets up one of the themes of the play (albeit a theme not pursued very far), which is the conflict between traditional and modern attitudes, especially over a subject like marriage. Diribi is a traditionalist; Titi his daughter a modernist. Hence her reply to the attack on Tufa's parentage:

> Well, is the seed to be crushed and cast
> Away because of aberration
> And blunder by those who laid out
> The field?

But, curiously enough, this information about Tufa – that he had 'real' parents and a 'real' blot on his pedigree – while conveniently getting some dramatic conflict started, virtually destroys what seems to be offered as a basic idea in the play, namely *that Tufa has magical origins,* that he is not, in fact, a real human at all. The dramatist cannot have it both ways; he tries, but fails.

The faults of *Song of a Goat* are repeated in this second play. Essentially, *The Masquerade* is not very dramatic, though, again, it contains some good descriptive verse. The embryo of good drama is here, but it is doomed to a still-birth. The mystery surrounding Tufa might have been exploited much more skilfully. It is hinted at, even in the opening scene when the villagers see an upturned moon and prophesy disaster 'down the whole delta'. With the ground thus prepared, and despite the spoiling effects of Diribi's revelation about Tufa, we are built up, in a rather flat kind of way, for a revelation of earth-shaking proportions. But we are disappointed. The denouement leaves us coldly unimpressed, a little angry at the villagers' cruel treatment of a stranger, but not really sympathetic to the stranger himself. If the mystery surrounding Tufa is inadequately exploited, so, too, is the fundamental conflict between Titi and the traditionalists.

With such chances missed, the play lacks life. That vigorous interplay of opposing forces which generates good drama is missing. Neither is there a sufficient charge of mystery to excite the audience into an active, reaching-out curiosity about the nature of the main *persona*. The play fails to engage us closely; it seldom shocks and rarely stirs our sympathy. The hero is dull; the heroine, for all her modernism, is little better; the minor figures are scarcely worthy of mention. Perhaps in plays as short as this, in-depth portraits are hard to do; but Clark succeeds much better in *The Raft,* where he is faced with precisely the same restrictions.

The dialogue, on the whole, is modelled in shallow relief. There is little variety in tone and vocabulary firmly to distinguish one speaker from another. Doubtless Clark would argue that all his Delta people share the same stock of phrases and images; that they are, in a sense, linguistically homogeneous. But to succeed at this shallow modelling, where a slight shift of tone, a slight change in the turn of a familiar phrase, and a slight disordering of a standard sentence pattern, can give the lie to character, change the meaning of a whole situation, or subtly force the reader to modify an established view – to succeed in this exercise demands the prodigious skill of a Pope, a Racine, or a Jane Austen.

The Masquerade is designed around a tragic diagram, and one notes again Clark's concern for something close to classical unities: there is a concentration of scene; the *personae* are few; it is a *Drama of one night.* What is more important, however, is that the play advances the local-rootedness of Clark's work. The plot, for example, is based on a legend widely known along the West Coast of Africa. It centres on the magical suitor who suddenly appears in the market-place and lures away a local maiden – usually a girl who has defied convention in some way and delayed marriage. Perhaps she has refused the man who is her father's choice; perhaps, like Titi, she is a modernist who has her own strong views about love and marriage. The suitor in the legend turns out to be made up of false parts; his beauty is all spurious. He is a sort of *ignis fatuus,* a will-o'-the-wisp who leads girls astray as a punishment for their independence, for their rebellion against accepted social

convention. The same legend is alluded to in Achebe's short story
'Akueke', and, of course, appears in the Complete Gentleman section of
Tutuola's *Palm-Wine Drinkard,* where the suitor, in grisly fashion,
hands back all his hired parts. Clark's version is far less horrific than
Tutuola's. In the final scene of *The Masquerade,* we merely find Tufa,
once 'so tall and strong', now a cripple. He is 'Splintered to the
ground', and the villagers say, 'Let us help to pick up his scattered-
/Scotched pieces . . .'

The Ijaw setting is, once more, beautifully evoked. The play is
decorated with vivid images of the Delta creeks, of boats, tides, fishing,
and the sea – all that fills the lives of the Ijaw people. When Clark's
figures speak, they express themselves naturally in images and allusions
that arise from their background. Listen to Diribi lamenting his
daughter's waywardness before Orise, the Sky-God (p. 74):

> . . . I have
> Fathered maidens as well as male – all
> By the labour of my loin – so that
> The river that took root at the earth's
> Deep centre, come drought, come disease, may never
> Run out. In all that course have I not shed
> My own self to several distributaries
> And seen to it each, wayward or weakling,
> Has a firm foot, a full mouth past heart's
> Common content? But Titi, Titi I loved
> To think sat innocent between my laps and
> Who I have hugged to myself as
> A river laps an island, now seeks
> To dam my path, even as I answer
> The unavoidable call to sea. Look at
> It, fathers and mothers already arrived
> Home, look at it close, what single harm
> Have I done that this poison more catching
> Than fruit from the piassava palm should
> At this late tide be bailed into the stream
> Of my blood?

The chorus of women answer Diribi in the same idiom:

> One mother-salt does not season the stream,
> One crook of the valley does not trip up
> The river, and the turn up of one
> Water lettuce need not mean the flood
> Is close on the swimmer's heels, and the terrible
> Pilgrimage year after year begun.

With its images of tide, stream, and blood, the verse is attractive in its home-rootedness; it successfully calls up the environment whence it springs. And yet, isn't there a vague sense of contrivance about it? Doesn't it all seem too self-conscious? It is the dramatic poet's task, having decided on his idiom, to make the verse pour from these people in a wholly natural, free-flowing way. Yet it does not. The metaphors seem to have been forced into the verse pattern with spanner and wrench. One can almost hear Clark saying: 'now Diribi has to speak, let's be sure he's given all the right images and allusions'.

More successful are the insets we get from time to time, where a straightforward description of a reported scene is offered – a description that does not involve the unburdening of the speaker's heart and mind; one that could be taken out of the tapestry of the play and offered as a separate poem, complete in itself. The first meeting between Titi and Tufa is a case in point. It comes as a picture provided by a witness (pp. 57–8):

> You should have seen their first meeting. It was
> In the market place. Nine maids all aglow
> With cam fresh from stem formed her vanguard train.
> Another four of a bigger blossom,
> All of them wearing skirts trimmed with cowrie
> And coins, mounted props for a canopy
> Of pure scarlet and lace, and cool under it
> Walked Titi, in fact some said afloat, doing the last
> Of her pageants. How can I describe
> The bride? Oh, you should have been there!
> Her head high in that silver tiara so
> Brilliant it was blindness trying to tell
> Its characters of leaves and birds, and
> The ivory stick between her lips, the rings,
> The necklaces especially fashioned by a goldsmith
> All the way from Yoruba country, and
> Then those bangles, those beads of coral! But
> What is this I'm saying? The bride herself
> Beat this treasury flung so lavishly
> Upon the world.

the echo of Shakespeare and Egypt is faint enough not to detract from Clark's achievement. The description is richly vivid and the scene was obviously created when the poet's imagination was on the boil. It is an example of the external painting that Clark does so well.

But the inherent faults of *The Masquerade* as drama are not fully compensated by an achievement of this sort. Surface glitter in dramatic verse can never make up for the absence of life below or within. It is not until Clark's third play, *The Raft,* that this kind of inner life is arrived at.

Take a log raft, place four men aboard, free it from its moorings, and float it off at night down the labyrinthine creeks of the Niger, and you have the formula for what is by far Clark's most successful piece of dramatic writing. There is a natural simplicity about the situation. It is set, like Clark's two previous plays, in Ijawland, where the creeks of the Delta are an essential element in the people's lives, and where hard-woods from the interior are floated down to the coast to be shipped to all corners of the globe. What more natural setting could an Ijaw writer choose?

And yet the choice is a masterly one, for this basic situation contains both naked simplicity and endless complexity. This commonplace situation vibrates with a meaning that reaches far and wide, into problems that are individual, national, continental, and humanly universal. Even the separate items in the formula can clearly have a dual significance. The rivers and creeks *are* the rivers and creeks of this part of Nigeria. The tides encountered on them *are* the real tides that flow in from the Atlantic, bringing ships and sometimes fog. Yet the reader feels there is more here; and this is precisely what Clark wants him to feel so that the underlying ideas of the play can be appreciated. Hence one senses that the waters of life and the river of life are being alluded to; and, having reached this far, the imagination soon begins to conjure other meanings – the idea of water as a spiritual cleansing agent, for instance, its use in ritual, and so on; meanings which arise naturally in an African context. Indeed, the practice of expelling evil by water-borne means is still known in this area of Nigeria. Then there is the powerful suggestiveness of the tides, with their ebbing hints of death and their flowing associations with birth, new growth, and optimism. The raft is a real workaday raft; but also, on a political level, the ship of state, and, for the individual, the vessel of life of which each of us is skipper. The situation, then, is fraught with suggestiveness, and Clark exploits it to the utmost. Loading his play with as much meaning as it can bear, without its sinking into sheer confusion, he can make subtle allusion to the human condition in all its aspects, be they private, national, racial, or universal. Although the focus is essentially on Nigeria's own situation, the debates set going in the play effortlessly assume a wider significance.

The play, then, invites, and withstands, close scrutiny. It is a play that puzzles, that leaves questions unanswered. It has a moral

208

ambiguity which is at once honest and consciously modern. The fearful questions of the four characters – 'Who are we?' 'Where are we from?' 'Where are we going?' – have echoes all round the modern world. The play does not pretend to provide answers.

The predicament of the four men on the raft – Olotu, Kengide, Ogro, and Ibobo – drifting helplessly in the night, is meant to be taken as the predicament of the Nigerian nation as a whole as it looks for directions, searches for a teleology while floating about in the dangerous waters of the modern world. The raft is adrift, its moorings gone. Who or what cut it loose? Will anyone tell the four men where they are? Can anyone tell them where they are going? Without stars or moon to guide them (where Clark presumably means the certainties of the old order), they are lost. These cardinal facts are established early in the play (p. 93):

Ibobo:	Olotu, Kengide, are you asleep
	Still? Wake up quick! We are adrift.
Kengide:	No-o!
Olotu:	Adrift, you say?
Ibobo:	Yes, no doubt about that.
	Ogro found it out.
Olotu:	Have you tried the moorings?
Ibobo:	We have already.
Ogro:	Yes, we have.
Kengide:	All of them?
Olotu:	How come all the knottings are
	Unfastened at once?

Ibobo is inclined to believe that sea-cows have eaten them out of their roots. Soon the following dialogue occurs (p. 95):

Ogro:	Will anyone tell where we are?
Olotu:	Yes, where exactly are we going now?
Ibobo:	I can't see through the grey baft spread
	Of the night. The moon has long turned in, and not
	A single star in the skies. Why doesn't
	Someone turn up the lamp?

When Ogro says he can see trees on the bank drifting past, Kengide insists, rather obviously, but with a special charge of meaning, 'Don't be an idiot; it's we/Who are doing the drifting.' The symbolic nature of their predicament is now increasingly pressed home. It can be felt in an angry exchange between Olotu and Kengide, when the latter shouts, with obvious ambiguity (p. 96):

> Slime and entrails! You and I
> And every fool that ever set foot on this raft
> Are on the same payroll . . .

And then, a few lines later, the same symbolic weight is again felt to be present. Ogro is speaking about the difference of opinion that emerges as the four men react to their dangerous situation:

> Whenever we are at the crossroads, Kengide
> Takes one road, and Olotu rushes up
> Another, but here we're at the fork still,
> And not one of you can tell the forces
> To get us out.

When a bowl is placed in the water to determine the direction of the tide, it is found to be spinning. The raft, it seems, is in the arms of Osikoboro, a great whirlpool said to lie at the confluence of all the creeks. Again, this situation is, on one level, real enough, and yet symbolic too; for the whirlpool is often appealed to as an image for West Africa's predicament in the modern world. One recalls Okara's heroes in *The Voice* being sucked down to their doom in an obvious defeat for the traditional order. Then, too, we have Awoonor-Williams' memorable lines:

> Sew the old days for us, our fathers
> That we can wear them under our new garment,
> After we have washed ourselves in
> The whirlpool of the many river's estuary –

To add a touch of repugnance to a perilous situation, Clark describes Osikoboro as the 'drain pit of all the earth'. However, the whirlpool hazard is safely negotiated, and now the stagnation of a becalmed situation becomes the subject of complaint. This is the moment for a sly thrust at national corrupion. Kengide, who seems to carry a good deal of the play's message, says:

> The pilot fish now smell rot among
> The logs: they don't jump on board any more.

To which Olotu caustically replies, 'The ghost smell is more on some people/Than on the logs.' Soon, in an obvious and rather prophetic reference to the divisive forces at work in the ship of state, the raft breaks in half after a sail has been hoisted to help move the vessel out of its becalmed state. Olotu is now on one section of the craft and his three companions on the other. Ogro wants to swim to Olotu and save him; but Kengide discourages him and Olotu is swept out of sight to his doom. The scene ends with a restatement of their basic plight: 'We are all adrift/And lost, Ogrope, we are all adrift and lost.'

The raft floats helplessly on, until a big steamer passes. Ogro confidently swims to it for help; but he is beaten back into the water and drowns. Clearly this is a foreign vessel, a representation of the outside world, and the West in particular. The point of the incident is clear. Ogro, his friends, and their broken raft are not wanted by the crew of the passing ship; they receive no help in their calamitous situation. They are alone. They are powerless. Their situation, to use a happy phrase of Clark's that occurs here and as the title of his book of verse, is that of 'a reed in the tide', moving at the mercy of forces beyond its control. There seems to be no hope. Even when, near the end of the play, the raft approaches Burutu, its destination, a brief eruption of hope is smothered by a blanket of fog. The two survivors can see nothing; they are drifting helplessly past Burutu towards the open sea. The tension here mounts rapidly (pp.132–3):

Ibobo: Burutu is there floating past – I hear
           Voices of people as in a market,
           And the beating of drums, the smell of food
           In the air, and we are drifting past – I
           Shall jump and swim!

Kengide: No, Ibobo, no, not when you yourself
           Say you cannot see your own hand! Why, here
           We are, holding hands, but can you see me?
           Fog has stuffed its soot and
           Smoke in our eyes, has shut up the world
           Like a bat its wings. Don't you see?
           All is blindness and scales!

There is something approaching great art about the close of this play: two men, holding hands, shouting hopelessly in the night. They have no control over their situation; they drift on to an unknown fate. Even on land, at Burutu, the destination they had been happily anticipating, all is confusion and alarm, with the noise *of men crying and calling out to one another in fear*. A fact stressed at the close is the aloneness of Ibobo and Kengide now, an aloneness which stands out starkly as a modern feature against a traditional African background of family and tribal togetherness. The modern predicament is heavily underscored by this final emphasis. When Ibobo wants to swim ashore, Kengide, now a very frightened and rather cowardly man, tries to stop him. There is a struggle (p. 133):

Ibobo: Let me go! Let me go – will you?
           Or are
           You afraid to be alone?

Kengide: Aren't you, too, Ibobo,
           Aren't you afraid to be left alone
           In this world, aren't you?

               . . .

> Shout, shout, Ibobo, let's shout
> To the world – we woodsmen lost in the bush.
> Ibobo: We're adrift, adrift and lost! Ee-ee-eee!

There seems to be a final harsh judgement on these castaways when Clark in his closing stage direction mischievously remarks that the shout which the two men send echoing over the water is *that long squeal as used when women go woods-gathering and by nightfall have still not found their way home.*

The play, then, concentrates on a central predicament that is richly allusive. In addition, however, Clark achieves a more convincing characterisation here than he did in his first two plays. His figures now have a life of their own; they are more strongly individualised and their differing attitudes make for dramatic colour and conflict. Kengide is a man who knows the modern world and its ways – or thinks he does. He wears his moral outlook (a mixture of materialism, selfishness, and tough realism) like armour to protect him from the blows of a cruel world. Life has soured him; he has seen corruption at work; he has witnessed the amassing of fortunes by illicit means. His country, he feels, is dominated by a dog-eat-dog morality (p. 120):

> In this game
> Of getting rich, it is eat me or I eat
> You, and no man wants to stew in the pot,
> Not if he can help it.

He speaks of policemen who are feeding fat on bribery and failing to put down crime. And then, in a complaint which, for western readers, has echoes right down the course of English Literature from *Seconda Pastorum* through the Jacobeans down to *Animal Farm,* he bewails the plight of the underdog in an unjust class society:

> Man, it is
> We ordinary grass and shrubs who get crushed
> As the mahoganies fall.

Ibobo is more a traditional man, rather ignorant of the modern world. He holds a traditional view of marriage, is naïve in his attitude to officialdom, too ready to believe he will be treated with justice and honesty. He knows nothing of such strange practices as homosexuality, respects the dead, and chides Kengide for not doing so. Unlike Kengide, he is not soured by life, but retains a delightful innocence of mind and soul. Kengide calls him 'the boy from the bush full of taboos'; but he wins our respect more readily than his companion, who, for all his worldly wisdom, has a good deal of cowardice and selfishness in him. When the two men are left alone at the close, however, it looks as though we are meant to feel that neither of them – neither Kengide the modernist nor Ibobo the traditionalist – has the answer to the nation's problem as it drifts helplessly on the reef-strewn waters of the modern world. In the final clinging together, it is Kengide who is the more afraid of being left alone, of being deserted by tradition. But there is no neat resolution to the play because there can be no neat resolution to the situation the author is exploring.

Song of a Goat was published in 1961. When we turn to *Ozidi,* published in 1966, we can detect a critical change that has taken place since Clark's career began. This is no Graeco-African play, but a work that is solidly African. A prefatory note informs us that 'the play is based on the Ijaw saga of Ozidi, told in seven days to dance, music and mime', and this at once suggests that if, in *Song of a Goat,* Clark was uncertain of the direction in which his art should move, he has now, five years later, made up his mind. He has decided that to write successful neo-African drama, his work must sink a taproot into his own indigenous culture; *Ozidi* represents a deliberate and wholesale 'return to roots'. We should notice also that his material is drawn directly from one of Africa's ancient, and yet still flourishing, species of pre-drama; for *Ozidi,* in its oral form, as Clark's note announces, is an elaborate specimen of the 'drama-supported narrative' discussed earlier in this chapter; indeed, in a gesture that indicates how concerned he is to adhere to the ancestral form (and also to inject more sense of theatre into his work, a stronger impression of the dramatic illusion), Clark retains the Story-teller, who introduces the play and tells the audience that he will play several roles in it.

The differences between *Song of a Goat* and *Ozidi* are numerous and basic. The first was spare in outline, displaying all the economy necessary for a successful imitation of classical practice. The unities were respected. The action was uncomplicated and played out in one central setting. The characters were few and we saw them at one crucial moment in their lives. 'There was a chorus but little or no music, dancing, and spectacle. *Ozidi* is *not* in the classical tradition. The prefatory note about its origin leads us into a list of dramatic *personae* that would have adequately covered the communal 'dance' described by Equiano. This is crowded drama, teeming alike with characters, scenes, and events. It calls for an orchestra consisting of master drummer, side drums and a horn blower; and, in the manner of Yoruba theatre, almost every scene is alive with singing and dancing. There is, too, a great deal of processing, solemn ritual, magic rites, mime, and horrific stage spectacle in an enormous amalgam of those dramatic phenomena that Africa has kept alive for centuries. If the characters in *Song of a Goat* are seen at one crucial moment in their lives, the central figures of *Ozidi* grow from youth to old age before our eyes: the hero indeed is not born until after the play has begun and, thereafter, we watch him develop from childhood to adolescence and manhood, and then fall to his doom. A static, marble-cold Greek quality is replaced by a frantic sweep of hot gory action, epic in its proportions and African in its abundance.

Scene One provides an impressive opening in which the Story-teller involves the audience in the play, poses for them problems associated with tradition, displays in disarming manner the nature of the dramatic illusion, and introduces a strongly religious element into the proceedings. The Story-teller's address, and the author's stage directions accompanying it, are worth quoting at length, for they provide, in themselves, a graphic illustration of Clark's radical shift into an indigenous mode (pp. 1–3):

Attention please, all you who have come to see our show, will you please give me your ears? I am afraid there's a hitch. Look, don't let that turn your bowels sore; we are first to admit this a most shaky thing to happen with old hands. However, it is a hitch, one out of which we hope you can help us. You see, our cast is incomplete. We need seven young women right now. Seven young women, and whatever for? I can see some of you raising eyebrows. I hasten to assure you we intend nothing dishonourable! Trouble is that, before we can perform for your pleasure and benefit tonight, we must first have a sacrifice to placate our hosts from the sea. Oh, yes, there are special spectators streaming all around you right now, even though you may not see or touch them. And the seven girls we ask of you, all virgins mind you, alone can bear offerings to our guests from the sea, and so establish between us a bridge. Perhaps, you think this a quaint custom, that we are propping up cobwebs that with broom and brush we ought to sweep clean out of the house. Well, that is your own opinion and you are quite entitled to hold it; for aren't we living in a free, democratic country? But you may as well know that opinion expressed by our principal player; he will not put up appearance in any show that looks down on tradition. You see, the oracle has warned him of a swift finish to the act if the programme is not followed properly, and he's nothing if not pious. I know him well; why, I am the fellow himself when I am not the plain narrator of our story; in the actual drama I play brother to the king as well as father to, and in fact your hero himself. Quite some intricate and interesting relationship that, isn't it? But wait until you see the whole epic; that is, on the condition that you grant us our seven virgins. There, I see a number of fair hands shooting up already; yes, all three of you there please come up this way. That's not all; oh, yes, you are coming along, too, are you? Good show, and you beautiful girl over there, let not the forest cover up your head of fountain. No more willing maids for us? Now, come, come, only two more now, and we shall be satisfied. And here they come – I knew they would – two springs tripping in the sun. Well, this really is most generous of you! Here we are, our glass already flowing over the brim before we have even opened mouth to drink. Now, who was it said our country lacks the fertile soil to produce sweet innocent flowers? Let him come and view these sprigs to the garland we have gathered in one spot, all of them undefiled still by bird or wind.

[*While he is speaking, the orchestra and chorus of actors and dancers gradually emerge behind and swirl around him, singing the solemn, processional song* Beni yo yo, beni yo yo. *As a group, they are all dressed up as our first man, although running in the general wash of white is a dash of black, indigo and scarlet. At their sudden appearance, the story-teller starts in great excitement, and turns to the seven virgins now also clustered about him, all in mixed emotions of expectation.*]

Here, to your right you see seven rich dishes all set in readiness. They are not for you to eat, you understand? For that, you will have to wait till you get to the fattening house. Now, each of you take one and step out this way one after the other to the stream. All others will follow.

[*To the spectators at large, his finger to his lips.*]
Hush, please, hush, or don't you people kneel to any god?

[*Meanwhile the procession to the stream has begun. The virgins, each holding out her dish of offerings, are led in front by a man; then close behind him the whole group of actors and dancers. The orchestra, of a master drummer and three side drummers, remains stationary to the left at the back. The procession moves slowly round the open place of play, and then towards its far end where nobody sits all through the performance. At this stage the chorus of actors and dancers open out to either side of the story-teller, who stands a little out of line at the head of the seven virgins. Close by, an assistant steps forward and directs the girls when to give and take back their dishes of offerings from the story-teller, who now assumes the powers and posture of a priest. When he begins his prayer and invocation, all the singing and music come to a stop.*]

215

After assuming 'the powers and posture of a priest', the narrator invokes the help of the people of the sea, giving us a clear sign of the socio-religious nature of the gathering when he tells them that members of the community 'in all their numbers/And from all quarters' have come tonight 'sinking here their quarrels/And washing themselves of all colours and taint . . .' He offers up food and drink on their behalf and asks for good wives, good children, and, since the sea people control the flow of the world's wealth, good money, too. Finally, with the prefatory rites complete, the entire group becomes the Council of State of the town of Orua, and the narrator becomes Ozidi himself.

It is easy to see, then, the direction in which Clark has moved since *A Song of a Goat*. And this opening scene, with its invoking of the sea spirits, its offering of libation, and its procession to the stream; with its use of a narrator-cum-leading actor, and its involvement of the audience in the ceremonies, not only partakes of indigenous practice, but, by this very fact, gains that exciting tingle and anticipation of live theatre which Clark's first two plays so patently lacked. It is as though this play had been written with the aim of a live village performance in mind, and *Song of a Goat* for perusal as a text in the library. The dancing, ritual, and singing set a pattern which is continued throughout the play. Indeed, the work ends with a dance led by the narrator, who, though still dressed as Ozidi, recalls his initial function by now casting away the dramatic illusion. This final dance 'draws all the players into its wake, so that a long processional dance finally forms in which all spectators may join'.

The play describes the murder of the first Ozidi, the birth and rise of his son as an avenger, and the son's decline into a condition of loneliness and humiliation. It exhibits, therefore, the simple rise and fall of the tragic diagram. Richer dramatically than *Song of a Goat, Ozidi* also represents a successful poetic endeavour, even if one still has a sense of perusing fine material that is often insufficiently controlled and organised. The play's proximity to indigenous modes is stylistic as well as thematic; hence it is not surprising to find that the imagery once more rises consistently out of the natural environment of Clark's people. 'The rains/May soak my skin', blubbers the demented Temugedege, pushed rapidly from the throne of Orua, 'but I am not salt, and/In the sun I like to bask as a crocodile/On the river bank.' When Ozidi arrogantly insults three women in the forest who have stopped to help him, one of them very properly condemns his ingratitude: 'It is like the cobra,' she observes, 'he puffs his cheeks/After spitting into your eyes rank venom.' Oreame, a witch who helps Ozidi to avenge his father's death, upbraids Temugedege, the boy's uncle, who refuses to espouse the cause of vengeance: 'Temugedege,' she cries, 'make way for the boy! Not all/Are wall-geckoes forever hugging/The kitchen wall.'

Such usage is well enough for it gives the play an African flavour. But Clark has more artistic considerations in mind. Not only must his imagery be drawn from the Ijaw locale; it must also be so woven into the texture of the play as to poetically carry its themes and reflect its movement. Hence we find rain, river, tide, and flood – those basic elements of the Ijaw scene – providing an artistically appropriate background to a play dealing with the rise and fall of a young hero and his enemies. For instance, the villains of Orua, those who savagely slew the first Ozidi and set their hearts on slaying the second, forever use hunting imagery, which both reflects their daily lives and vivifies their role in the play. Listen to Sigirisi talking (p. 80):

> Let me hunt the fellow down with my net, and
>> call me the fool
> Who went to the stream with a sieve if I do
>> not
> Return with that butterfly in my bag.

or to Ofe, Ozidi's arch-enemy (pp. 79–80):

> Now we are how many left in the chase,
> Badoba? The whole circle of us
> Set out after a quarry we thought was
> A grass cutter: we threw about him our ring;
> With loud taunts and shooing followed
> On his heels till at one stage it was like
> A hurricane raging full above his head.

and again, the same villain (p. 81):

> Oh, who knew that woman Orea
> Could bear? Kill her, kill her too, Azezabife
>> said, but
> I was such a fool, believing the catfish cannot
>> come
> Out of a bamboo trap. Now I am pricked on
> All sides by its thorns.

The rise of the second Ozidi, and his return to Orua, the scene of his father's slaughter, are frequently rendered in harvest imagery that suggests growth and ripeness. Indeed, by means of this type of imagery Clark, in Act III, skilfully crystallises the main events of the play (p. 81):

> Third Citizen: Now it is harvest time, and the yam
>> Has thrown such a tuber it taps
>> The bowels of the earth.

Fourth Citizen: Above the ground, its leaves and
                Tendrils spread so wide, if you do not shore up
                The plant, it certainly will choke all the land.
First Citizen: So please trim down this blossom.
Second Citizen: Dig up the treasure to its last root.
Third Citizen: A whole season now there has been
                No masquerade.
Fourth Citizen: Nor any offering to the gods and dead; and
                The flood is falling, falling, Ofe.

Third Citizen is referring to the slain, buried Ozidi. Like a yam, he has thrown an off-shoot in the shape of a son, who, grown strong and ambitious, is threatening to avenge his father and assume his rights of kingship. Readers who detect what seems to be an echo of Elizabethan poetic language here (the verse of *A Winter's Tale* readily springs to mind) may feel that Clark's writing is affected or imitative; but the point to be seized is that Clark's fellow tribesmen do talk in this way. They bring to the English language a ready-developed sense of poetry, for the common currency of language in West Africa, as we have seen in our examination of the proverb, is highly metaphorical and pictorial. There is no gulf between the nature of Clark's stage language and the language used on the highways and byways of Nigeria, a truth which should light a beacon of hope for those who have despaired of a future for English poetic drama.[15]

Ozidi raises an interesting question of aesthetics. Sixteenth-century productions of Seneca and his imitators are boldly outstripped in this orgy of blood and horror. Decapitations on stage are not uncommon and the first Ozidi's head is served up as a dish for his newly wedded wife. Elsewhere, there are 'streams of blood in the air', and one witch seizes upon the head of another 'to bite it off with her cannibal teeth'. The same lady is described as carrying 'a crown of volcano, her teeth dripping with blood of victims she has eaten raw'. Production difficulties aside, this kind of play might bring to a western critic a whiff of decadence. African scholars would no doubt react differently, which suggests a basic aesthetic divergence that will grow wider as African writers move steadily back to indigenous norms and increasingly aim their material at African audiences.

But the importance of *Ozidi* for our study lies in the testimony which it offers to Clark's wholehearted espousal of the dramatic heritage of his own people. Although written in English, in theme, style, idiom, and inspiration, *Ozidi* is, quite simply, African.

218

Wole Soyinka

Wole Soyinka is West Africa's finest dramatist. Here is a man richly endowed with literary skill, whose work, which has poured forth abundantly in a career still in its early stages, bears the marks of a refined sensibility, stringent critical standards, and, above all, great creative energy. Educated at Ibadan and at Leeds, where he was a student of G. Wilson Knight, Soyinka worked for a time at London's Royal Court Theatre, before returning to Nigeria in 1960 to lend his support to a nation-wide dramatic awakening. Now Director of Ibadan's School of Drama, he is at the centre of a scene of theatrical ferment the like of which West Africa has never before witnessed. He is also found on occasions close to the eye of the political storms that have ravaged his country since Independence in 1960. As we have seen, by temperament a satirist, he moves about the West African scene like some marvellously gifted Malcontent, fiercely thrusting at the corruption, intrigue, and vaulting ambition which he witnesses on every side. And his blows strike home, for on two occasions he has been sent to prison.

His education and training, in Africa and the United Kingdom, partly account for his position as the West African dramatist in whom the theatrical traditions of Europe and the homeland are most successfully synthesised (though perhaps symbiosis is a more appropriate word, since both traditions are strongly alive in him). London critics have said that his roots go deep into western traditions and that he is following at a distance in the footsteps of men like Jonson and Webster. While they are right in believing that Soyinka has been receptive to such influences, it must be emphasised at the same time that his work is essentially African in material and inspiration. As our discussion of his verse revealed, Soyinka is a Yoruba who acknowledges his roots and clings to them; he is not, in any sense of the word, *déraciné*. But these are truths which he would not shout from the housetops in the manner of the negritude writers. 'You know a duiker by his elegant leap', he is once reported to have said. He has taken those elements which Yoruba Folk Opera retained – a body of religious belief, the dance, chants, songs, and ritual – and fused them with the most useful elements that western dramatists have to offer in regard to stagecraft, dramatic structure, characterisation, and physical presentation. From two traditions he has forged a species of neo-African drama which, in 1966, took London's West End by storm. Soyinka's plays were received with that same mixture of astonishment and admiration which, Traoré tells us, French West African theatre encountered in Paris during the

219

thirties; and the dramatist was awarded the Arts Council's Whiting Award for the most original plays presented on the London stage during that year. Indeed, the response to Soyinka's work has been so enthusiastic in Britain that one can be forgiven for venturing the suggestion that he represents the Commonwealth's brightest hope of actively influencing the metropolitan tradition.

The following examination of Soyinka's works is divided into three sections. The first will discuss Soyinka as a satirist and take *Dance of the Forests* and *The Road* for special treatment; the second treats of Soyinka's interest in language as an instrument of satire; and the third offers a detailed examination of the plays' synthesis of features African and western.

Soyinka as satirist

'Satire in the theatre', Soyinka observed in 1965, 'is a weapon not yet fully exploited among the contemporary dramatists of Nigeria, fertile though the social and political scene is for well-aimed barbs by the sharp, observant eye.'[16] At the same time he seized the opportunity to praise the Folk Opera Troupe of Hubert Ogunde which had become so uncomfortably contemporary in its material that the government of S. A. Akintola had banned it from performing anywhere in the Western Region. But Soyinka's interest in satire does not stem from that *annus horribilis*, 1965. One of his early poems, 'Telephone Conversation', published in 1962, was a memorable sally into this field, drawing applause from many sides, and especially from the South African critic Ezekiel Mphahlele. Even earlier, however, came *A Dance of the Forests*, written for Nigeria's Independence Celebrations, and performed by The 1960 Masks, Soyinka's own company;[17] it is the most complex satirical play which the author has so far written. Here indeed was a stroke of bold imagination that pointed up the breadth, depth and sincerity of Soyinka's vision; for in a play offered to a nation on the euphoric occasion of its Independence, the immediate victim of the satire is that nation itself; in a play ostensibly celebrating a country's birth, the talk is all of death, delusion, and betrayal. Indeed, flying in the face of all the cherished teachings of negritude, Soyinka has chosen to de-romanticise his people and their history with a boldness scarcely paralleled since the days of Synge and O'Casey.

Some light on the nature and theme of this difficult play is cast by Aroni, the Lame One, who offers the following intriguing Prologue:

I know who the Dead Ones are. They are the guests of the Human Community who are neighbours to us of the Forest. It is their

Feast, the Gathering of the Tribes. Their councillors met and said, Our forefathers must be present at this Feast. They asked us for ancestors, for illustrious ancestors, and I said to FOREST HEAD, let me answer their request. And I sent two spirits of the restless dead . . .

THE DEAD MAN, who in his former life was a captain in the army of Mata Kharibu, and the other . . . THE DEAD WOMAN, in former life, the captain's wife. Their choice was no accident. In previous life they were linked in violence and blood with four of the living generation. The most notorious of them is ROLA, now, as before, a whore. And inevitably she has regained the name by which they knew her centuries before – MADAME TORTOISE. Another link of the two dead with the present is ADENEBI, the Court Orator, oblivious to the real presence of the dead. In previous life he was COURT HISTORIAN. And I must not forget DEMOKE, the Carver. In the other life, he was a POET in the court of Mata Kharibu. AGBOREKO, the Elder of Sealed Lips, performed the rites and made sacrifices to Forest Head. His trade was the same in the court of Mata Kharibu. When the guests had broken the surface of earth, I sat and watched what the living would do.

They drove them out. So I took them under my wing. They became my guests and the Forests consented to dance for them . . .

We learn at once that Soyinka's vision ranges far beyond the present, even if this is his immediate concern; his theme is a large one, his frame of reference nothing less than the past, present, and ongoing stream of human existence. There is to be, then, a great gathering of the tribes at a momentous time in their history. It is a fitting occasion for the nation to show its medals and resurrect its trophies – a time to recall historic heroism of the sort that will provide inspiration for future endeavour. 'The accumulated heritage – that is what we are celebrating', declares Council Orator Adenebi. 'Mali, Chaka, Songhai. Glory. Empires.' Elsewhere his dream is reported in more detail (p. 32):

. . . we must bring home the descendants of our great forebears. Find them. Find the scattered sons of our proud ancestors. The builders of empires. The descendants of our great nobility. Find them. Bring them here. If they are halfway across the world, trace them. If they are in hell, ransom them. Let them symbolize all that is noble in our nation. Let them be our historical link for the season of rejoicing. Warriors. Sages. Conquerors. Builders. Philosophers. Mystics. Let us assemble them round the totem of the nation and we will drink from their resurrected glory.

Such is the spirit of the occasion; such the pride and hope of a nation at a great turning point in its history. But Soyinka possesses the satirist's passionate, almost pathological, obsession for the truth. Those heady with the excitement of the present must be bullied into setting their experience within the framework of historical fact; they must be allowed to glimpse some of the abiding truths of the human condition. Those who stand in the present and drug themselves with memories of former glories, like Orator Adenebi, whose absurd musings spiral ever further away from reality, must be faced with the grim reality behind their dreams.

The living, then, are anxious to call up from the dead a host of mighty heroes, celebrate the Gathering of the Tribes with a vision of past splendour; and in an empty clearing in the forest (with a startling piece of stagecraft), the soil breaks and there arise from the dead two pathetic human figures – a sorry link indeed 'for the season of rejoicing'. The Dead Man has behind him a wretched history of misery, thwarted hopes, and betrayal; The Dead Woman, his wife, sorrowful, and pregnant 'for a hundred generations', has an equally miserable past, and is soon to be delivered of a half-child, her baby who symbolises the future.

Soyinka allows us to see the details of their past in a Faustian recreation of the Court of Mata Kharibu, a mythical king who represents the 'glorious' history to which the living look back with nostalgia. Soyinka's purpose here is clear, for, as he observes elsewhere, the past 'clarifies the present and explains the future'.[18] As Soyinka sees it, Africa's past is a sadly inglorious one. Thus, here in this shrine of historic magnificence, in this reign to which living Africans look back with pride, we find a whore as queen, and a king unrivalled in barbaric ferocity; a king who will brook no opposition to his every whim, who fears, like all tyrants, the independent mind, and will sell into slavery even his most devoted subjects. Dead Man is one of them, sold for a cask of rum because he dared to think for himself and suggest that he and the king's warriors should only go to war in a just cause. A figure of mutating significance, Dead Man is here representative of ordinary, thinking, reasonable mankind. His treatment by Kharibu is brutal. 'I took up soldiering to defend my country', he laments, 'but those to whom I gave the power to command my life abuse my trust in them.' In Kharibu's world of perverted values, only power has significance – power that brings tyranny over less fortunate creatures, power that can speak of 'the magnificence of the destruction of a beautiful city'. When intellectual rebellion opposes such power, it must be destroyed at once, for here lies its most dangerous enemy. Listen to Kharibu anxiously

222

discussing his Warrior (our Dead Man) with a soothsayer (pp. 60–1):

Mata Kharibu: I could understand it if he aimed at my throne. But he is not even man for that. What does it mean?

What do you see for me in the future? Will there be more like him, born with this thought cancer in their heart?

Soothsayer: Mata Kharibu, have you ever seen a smudge on the face of the moon?

Mata Kharibu: What do you mean?

Soothsayer: Have you?

Mata Kharibu: No.

Soothsayer: And yet it happens. Once in every million years, one of the sheep that trail the moon in its wanderings does dare to wipe its smutty nose on the moon. Once in a million years. But the moon is there still. And who remembers the envy-ridden sheep?

Mata Kharibu: So the future holds nothing for men like him?

Soothsayer: Nothing. Nothing at all.

There is an Orwellian finality about it; the boot stamped on a human face – for ever; and the idea is driven home time and again throughout the play.

Dead Man's history also includes involvement with the slave-trade, Africa's most traumatic historical experience. Soyinka gives his audience the brutal truth that the Kharibus of Africa's past had as much blood on their hands as the white slavers. At this point in a play notable for its Janus-like viewpoint, we begin to find Africa's inglorious past pointing a finger towards the present and the future. When, for instance, Kharibu's Physician complains that the slave-dealer's ship is too small to carry the condemned Warrior and his sixty men (a mere 'finger-bowl' he calls it), the dealer assures him that he now has a new vessel capable, when the time comes, of 'transporting the whole of Kharibu's court to hell'. The Court Historian, who has just been bribed to agree, declares that this is true: 'Mata Kharibu and all his ancestors would be proud to ride in such a boat.' In the context of the play, and given the occasion for which the play was written, these words are fraught with meaning. There is a strong hint that Africa too easily accepts its chains, be they inflicted by strangers or brothers. More startling, however, is the clear implication that the chains are, and always have been, a permanent feature of the landscape. The 'new' ship in which Kharibu and all his ancestors would be proud to ride suggests modern forms of slavery that the author's fellow Africans are blindly accepting. It is as though Soyinka sees the whole of African history in the crushingly powerful image of a great slave galley sailing down the straits of time, from the dim past down to the present and on towards the horizon of the future. 'The world is old'/, the play tells us elsewhere, 'But the rust of a million years/Has left the chains un-loosened.'

And what of the present? 'The pattern is unchanged,' says Dead Man, who was 'one of those who journeyed in the market-ships of blood', and who is now visiting the modern world of the living. It is a lesson in disillusionment, for, as he is at one point reminded, 'Your wise men, casting bones of oracle/Promised peace and profit/New knowledge, new beginnings after toil . . .' Treated abominably in the past, he and his wife are abominably treated in the present. The bearers of bitter truth about an inglorious history, they are given at the Gathering of the Tribes the cold welcome of beggars at a feast. 'We were sent the wrong people', complains Old Man. 'We asked for statesmen and we were sent executioners.' It is, indeed, all rather different from Orator Adenebi's dream of purple robes, white horses dressed in gold and, as it were, a ride in triumph through Persepolis. Ill-treatment becomes sacrilege when the living decide to kill off these embarrassing spirits by fumigating the forest with the Chimney of Ereko, a fearfully battered old truck already the cause of sixty-five deaths. But, as Agboreko reminds them, 'you cannot get rid of ancestors with the little toys of children. . .' It is a measure of the subtlety of Soyinka's art that the satire here works on two levels; for this shocking treatment of guests, and, furthermore, guests from the dead (we have stressed their importance often enough), is immediately recognised as a flagrant violation of rules of conduct upon which African societies pride themselves. At a more profound level, we are meant to witness in this behaviour not only a wilful blindness to the truth about the past, but also an arrogant rejection of that past as it is enshrined in these two representative figures. The past should not be 'a fleshpot for escapist indulgence', as Soyinka has recently written, but it should be accepted, because it exists 'now, this moment; it is co-existent in present awareness', and of course, 'It clarifies the present and explains the future.'

The experience of Dead Man and his wife is clear enough. It is a case of *plus ça change*. Men treated each other appallingly in the past; they treat each other appallingly in the present; they will treat each other appallingly in the future. Indeed, the play reaches a triumphant climax of gloom when Forest Head commands that the Future be chorused, 'through lips of earth beings', and Soyinka, in writing what has a curious echo of Shelley's *Prometheus Unbound,* completes his sweep over the *via dolorosa* of human existence. Demoke, the carver, Rola, the whore, and Orator Adenebi are masked and Forest Head introduces the activities, saying (pp. 73–8):

> I take no part, but listen. If shadows,
> Future shadows form in rain-water
> Held in hollow leaves, this is the moment
> For the welcome of the dead.

As each spirit is called up, the masks become agitated and possessed, then dance and prophesy. The Spirit of the Palm is first called up, who prophesies as follows:

> White skeins wove me, I, Spirit of the Palm
> Now course I red.
> I who suckle blackened hearts, know
> Heads will fall down,
> Crimson in their bed!

At this point, however, the Half-Child, who has just been born and has appealed in vain for help from those around him, interrupts the proceedings and himself joins the roll-call of the spirits; the scene continues in the following manner:

Half-Child: I who yet await a mother
                Feel this dread,
                Feel this dread,
                I who flee from womb
                To branded womb, cry it now
                I'll be born dead
                I'll be born dead.
Interpreter: Spirit of the Dark!
Spirit of Darkness: More have I seen, I, Spirit of the Dark,
                Naked they breathe within me, fore-telling now
                How, by the dark of peat and forest
                They'll be misled
                And the shutters of the leaves
                Shall close down on the doomed
                And naked head.
Half-Child: Branded womb, branded womb . . .
Spirit of the Palm: White skeins wove me.
Spirit of Darkness: Peat and forest!

Adding to this dark picture of the future, the spirit of the Rivers foretells a drought and the Chorus of the Waters warns:

Let no man then lave his feet
In any stream, in any lake
In rapids or in cataracts
Let no woman think to bake
Her cornmeal wrapped in leaves
With water gathered of the rain
He'll think his eye deceives
Who treads the ripples where I run
In shallows. The stones shall seem
As kernels, his the presser's feet
Standing in the rich, and red, and cloying stream . . .

. . .

Let the Camel mend his leaking hump
Let the squirrel guard the hollows in the Stump.

A few moments later a group of ants rise up from the grave and this weird interlude ends with a memorable dialogue between their leader and Forest Head. The symbolic force of the ants is easily understood. They are the great anonymous mass of humanity, the sons of toil, the hewers and drawers, the ruled rather than the rulers, the hands and muscles of humanity upon whom rest the physical burdens of the world. Their experience and condition are those most germane to the African audience which Soyinka is addressing. But, not for the first time in this play, the references seem also to suggest basic truths not only about African society but about the condition of mankind at large.

When Forest Head asks who the ants are, the following dialogue ensues (pp. 77–8):

Ant Leader: We take our colour from the fertile loam
Our numbers from the hair-roots of the earth
And terror blinds them. They know
We are the children of earth. They
Break our skin upon the ground, fearful
That we guard the wisdom of Earth,
Our Mother.

Forest Head: Have you a grievance?

Ant Leader: None, Father, except great clods of earth
Pressed on our feet. The world is old
But the rust of a million years
Has left the chains unloosened.

Forest Head: Do you not walk? Talk? Bear
And suckle children by the gross?

Ant Leader: Freedom indeed we have
To choose our path

To turn to the left or the right
Like the spider in the sand-pit
And the great ball of eggs
Pressing on his back.

. . .

Forest Head: Have you a Cause, or shall I
Preserve you like a riddle?
Ant Leader: We are the ones remembered
When nations build . . .
Another: . . . with tombstones.
Another   We are the dried leaves, impaled
On one-eyed brooms.
Another: We are the headless bodies when
The spade of progress delves.

. . .

Another: Down the axis of the world, from
The whirlwind to the frozen drifts,
We are the ever legion of the world,
Smitten, for – 'the good to come'.

Such, then, is Soyinka's message for the happy occasion of Nigeria's Independence Celebrations – a sobering reminder of some basic, and abiding, truths about mankind in general and about Africans and their history in particular. Events since 1960 have proved with a vengeance the accuracy of at least that part of his vision which dealt with the future. But in addition, *A Dance of the Forests* supplies proof, if proof is needed, that Soyinka saw the need for national self-criticism six years before Achebe raised the subject as a matter of urgency in the pages of *Présence Africaine*. Soyinka's satiric vision is a curious affair – partly Swift's savage indignation, partly the Conradian 'horror', and partly the Wordsworthian lament over 'what man has made of man'. It informs every part of this difficult but remarkable play.

An equally difficult and powerful piece of satire is Soyinka's *The Road* published in 1965.[19] From the very title of the play (a work that stands in relation to pieces such as *The Lion and the Jewel* like *Hamlet* to *Twelfth Night*), one realises that here is a further exploration of a subject which has fascinated Soyinka throughout his literary career. Like the raft in Clark's most successful play, the road here is a fertile central motif. At one level it is any Nigerian road beside which the main scenes of the play are acted or danced. At another level, it is the proverbial road of life, along which all men must travel, individually or collectively as nations. Closely associated with this is the idea of the road of progress, a notion lightly ridiculed in Soyinka's poem 'Death in

227

the Dawn'. Above all, however, it is the road between life and death which runs precisely through that hazy landscape between this world and the next that so fascinates Soyinka. Along this highway the dead must travel.

Watching over the road, lurking behind all the events of the play, is Ogun, the greedy god who feeds on the butchery that the roads daily provide. Ogun lives on death and needs feeding regularly. The lorry drivers in the play are his devotees, their festival is his festival. Significantly, during their masquerade in his honour, they carry a dog tied to a stake as a sacrificial offering. Ogun's driver followers are notorious killers of dogs that stray onto the road. Samson, a driver's mate, and a sort of African Mosca, is heard to shout (p. 59):

Kill us a dog Kotonu, kill us a dog. Kill us a dog before the hungry god lies in wait and makes a substitute of me. That was a thin shave. A sensible man would see it as a timely warning, but him? I doubt it. Not for all the wealth of a traffic policeman. Dog's intestines look messy to me he says – who asked him to like it? Ogun likes it that's all that matters. It's his special meat. Just run over the damned dog and leave it there, I don't ask you to stop and scoop it up for your next dinner. Serve Ogun his tit-bit so the road won't look at us one day and say Ho ho you two boys you look juicy to me. But what's the use? The one who won't give Ogun willingly will yield heavier meat by Ogun's designing.

But Ogun shows little care for his own (one recalls the manner in which he slew his warriors when king of Ira). Hence so many of the road's 'heroes' in the play – Zorro, Akanni the lizard, Sigidi Ope, Sapele Joe, Saidu-Say, Indian Charlie, Humphrey Bogart, Cimarron Kid, Muftau, and Sergeant Burma – are dead. Hence so many of the play's central figures are probing towards death, or are actually dead and undergoing decomposition, their voices ghosting forth from this twilight zone in a most unnerving manner.

Soyinka's choice of a middle ground, a sort of no-man's land belonging neither to the world of the flesh nor the spirit, is explained in the following prefatory note For the Producer:

Since the mask-idiom employed in The Road will be strange to many, the preface poem Alagemo should be of help. Agemo is simply, a religious cult of flesh dissolution.

The dance is the movement of transition; it is used in the play as a visual suspension of death – in much the same way as Murano, the mute, is a dramatic embodiment of this suspension. He functions as an arrest of time, or death, since it was in his 'agemo' phase that the lorry knocked him down. Agemo, the mere

228

phase, includes the passage of transition from the human to the divine essence (as in the festival of Ogun in this play), as much as the part psychic, part intellectual grope of Professor towards the essence of death.

As Soyinka promises, the *Alagemo* poem helps a little. At least its opening lines further describe the area to be explored:

I heard! I felt their reach
And heard my naming named.
The pit is there, the digger fell right through
My roots have come out in the other world.

We expect, then, and find, the falling line of tragedy in the play; a steady sinking down towards the other world, visually represented by the *egungun* mask that spins and falls when Professor finally meets death in the closing scene.

This dark middle area, reminiscent of many of Soyinka's poems, effortlessly grows suggestive of ideas other than those of death and dissolution. It suggests, for example, the overall position of Africa, caught, in Mabel Segun's memorable words, 'hanging in the middle way'. Soyinka portrays a hideous mingling of cultures that he finds in this middle state, though he does so with a complexity, a subtlety, and a revulsion, unparalleled in those innumerable publications that exhibit the cultural clash through stale commonplaces.

Professor himself is the best illustration of this. With his Victorian outfit of top hat and tails, all threadbare, with his academic title, earned through prowess in forgery, with his past connection with the Christian church, and his clear leanings towards Ifa, he is a sort of amphibious creature, neither right African nor right European; neither wholly spiritually oriented nor wholly materialistic. We have mentioned already the psychological problems of modern Africa: there are definite suggestions of schizophrenia or mere lunacy in Professor, and Soyinka wants us to notice them. A veritable aura of symbolism surrounds this weird scoundrel. It is no mere chance that he is dressed in Victorian garb. In part, presumably, Soyinka is making the common joke that Africa follows absurdly, at a distance, the fashions of Europe, and never actually catches up. Similar jibes are found in Achebe and Nicol. But he is also hinting that Professor represents the first real nineteenth-century encounter with the West, and furthermore, the subsequent history of that encounter. Hence, almost everything about this creature is betwixt and between. He is partly a genuine seeker after the Word, which means here knowledge of the essence of death, and partly a genuine criminal, bold, selfish, and rapacious. It is the sort of contradiction that suggests the familiar Afro-European dichotomy. His

229

past connection with Christianity (he was learned in divinity but drummed out for thieving Church funds) and his proximity to the worshippers of Ogun, again place him in neither one camp nor the other. Notice that he chooses to sleep between the two camps, in the cemetery where he can best keep his ear to the ground for the Word.

Professor wants total knowledge of death without actually dying. 'I cannot yet believe', he says, 'that death's revelation must be total, or not at all.' He believes he can get both experience and knowledge by proxy. Hence the appalling accidents he engineers by removing road signs from dangerous points on the highway. His wayside shack AKSIDENT STORE – ALL PART AVAILEBUL, stuffed with spare parts, old shoes, and clothes, is a cloakroom at the portals of death; a place to deposit one's possessions before descending the dark tunnel to the other world. The drivers believe Professor has gone far in his research, and say so in a praise song to him; a song that also emphasises his middling position between the living and the dead (p.86):

> Professor, our being like demon
> Professor, our being like demon
> The elder above us
> The elder below
> The hand that thinks to smash me, let it pause awhile
> I have one behind me coiled snake on Mysteries
> . . .
> Who holds discourse with spirits, who dines with the
> ruler of the Forests
> He is the elder above us
> He is our elder below . . .

If Professor is an unpleasant mingling of Africa and Europe, so, too, are the play's drivers and thugs. They are men with names inspired by American crime and western films, men like Say Tokyo Kid who can affect a tough Chicago gangster's drawl ('I don give a damn for that crazy guy and he know it') yet sing traditional Yoruba praise songs and worship Ogun. With his tough talk, his alleged scorn for Professor's spiritualism (belied by his belief that there are 'a hundred spirits in every guy of timber' he carries), Say Tokyo represents an ugly fusion of the traditionally African and the hard-headed materialism of an alien culture.

Murano acts like a dumb Caliban to Professor (who first found him 'Neglected in the back of a hearse. And dying.') and seems to represent the unadulterated old order. Significantly, unlike the others, he is not a driver, a tout, or a thug, but a palm-wine tapper, the representative of a traditional rural occupation. Professor says he 'has no mind. He neither

230

speaks nor hears.' In any case he is dead and is sinking towards complete dissolution. Hence Professor's interest in him. Notice that it is Murano who puts on the *egungun* mask at the end; he is closest to the spirit world which the *egungun* professionlly deal with.

The confusion portrayed on the cultural level is mirrored also on the everyday level of speech. The language of Soyinka's play is a carefully cooked *pot pourri*. There is a mixing here of 'correct' English, pure Yoruba, the affected Americanese of Say Tokyo, and West African pidgin. The effect makes for variety of voice and character, but Soyinka is also making the cultural point again. There is the formal, Revised-version style of Professor, the brilliantly articulate figure who must always feature in Soyinka's drama. The following are fair specimens of his language (p. 88):

Observe the saintly progress of the evening communicants ... What if they were children? Is truth ever to be hidden from children? Yes, what though there was the spirit of wine upon me. It was Sunday, Palm Sunday and each child bore a cross of the tender frond, yellow and green against their innocence.

. . .

Deep. Silent but deep. Oh my friend, beware the pity of those who have no tongue for they have been proclaimed sole guardians of the Word. They have slept beyond the portals of secrets. They have pierced the guard of eternity and unearthed the Word, a golden nugget on the tongue. And so their tongue hangs heavy and they are forever silenced.

Samson, a splendid mimic, drops into pidgin when playing the role of the dead man Sergeant Burma. Here he is talking with the policeman, Particulars Joe (p. 82):

They wan' give me the King George Cross self, but you know how things be for blackman ... I say make you gi'am, blackman or no blackman – gi'am. Dey for give me dat one but when the governor for home hear wetin dey wan't do, 'e cable back say if den give me dat kind superior medal, I go return my country begin do political agitator. Haba! Justice no dey for white man world.

The linguistic confusion thus reflects the wider cultural confusion that Soyinka is portraying.

The play is also a bitter attack on Nigerian society as a whole: here is the scathing criticism of *A Dance of the Forests* in a wormier form. It is as though Soyinka, in his deliberate choice of the Agemo idea, is trying to say that he sees the whole of his contemporary society dissolving into the rottenness and stench of death. Apart from Murano, who is deaf, dumb, dead (and therefore, impotent), there is not a single undiseased

231

figure in the play. The whole dark scene is pervaded by vice and greed in all its forms. The sun never seems to rise in this play. It is a picture of unrelieved gloom and decadence, where a dog-eat-dog morality rules supreme. Kotonu, driver lately of the lorry *No Danger No Delay,* says of a former colleague (p. 21):

> Sergeant Burma was never moved by these accidents. He told me himself how once he was stripping down a crash and found that the driver was an old comrade from the front. He took him to the mortuary but first he stopped to remove all the tyres.

When Samson protests that such a man 'wasn't human', Kotonu replies, with sick humour, 'But he was. He was. A man must protect himself against the indifference of comrades who desert him.' Even Samson himself, who comes fairly close to normal decency, is heard to say, at one point (p. 92):

> Na me dat. As you see me like this, I am a quiet, peace-loving man, but when we get to motor park, I don't know my brother again.

On Professor, Kotonu makes the following comments. He is alluding to a crash that has just been engineered before the play opens (p. 21):

> You know, Professor is a bit like Sergeant Burma. He was moving round those corpses as if they didn't exist. All he cared about was re-planting that sign-post. To see him you would think he was Adam replanting the Tree of Life.

To complete this revolting picture, Soyinka ensures that a representative of all ranks of society is included: his country must be seen to be corrupt from top to bottom. The law, as represented by Particulars Joe, is corrupt in the most blatant manner; the Church stands as an empty shell behind the entire play, irrelevant and powerless. Chief-in-Town, a modern version of the traditional Oba, is a political representative who keeps a gang of thugs in hire and distributes opium. The common people, like Samson and Kotonu, prey on one another like hyenas.

The Road is Soyinka's writing on the nation's wall. He draws a society that is on the road to death and dissolution, a society for which there seems no hope. Perhaps, like Professor, who speaks of death as 'the moment of our rehabilitation', this society will have to die before it learns the truth. Rebirth is only possible after the descent from life is complete. This movement itself is foreshadowed by the mask at the end of the play which sinks slowly until 'it appears to be nothing beyond a heap of cloth and raffia.'

In *A Dance of the Forests* and *The Road*, a whole nation was under attack. In other plays, too, the satirical element has figured strongly; but there it is not a whole society but particular members of it who

232

come in for abuse. Soyinka particularly loathes those who possess power and use it dishonestly, those whose selfishness drives them to keep the people in a state of ignorance and subservience.

In *The Swamp Dwellers,* Kadiye is the target, a fat village priest who remains 'smooth and well-preserved' even in times of drought by exploiting the simple piety of those whom he represents before the local god. He lies upon the land and 'choke(s) it in the folds of a serpent'. In *The Trials of Brother Jero,* Jeroboam himself is under attack, an eloquent fraud working as a Beach Prophet and striding the boards like some strange character from mediaeval times. He cuts a striking figure with his heavily-bearded face, his rod of office, long flowing hair, white gown and fine velvet cape – all of them aids to deceit. The West African scene is alive with weird scoundrels of this sort. In a lighter vein, *The Lion and the Jewel* focuses its attack on Lakunle, a westernised schoolteacher who appears ridiculous with his modicum of book learning, his complete vacuity of wisdom and his preposterous arrogance; he is a man who feels elevated enough to call his people 'a race of savages' and sees himself as the prophet of a new order. Despising ancestral ways, he is determined to drag his community into the vulgar daylight of the modern world. Soyinka would probably call *The Lion and the Jewel* a recreational piece. But *Kongi's Harvest* appeared during the years of Nigeria's gathering storm and strikes a more urgent and 'engaged' note. At the heart of his country's afflictions he sees politicians with their lust for power and their illiberal vision. He has stated elsewhere that it is not the continent's writers but its politicians who have shaped 'the present philosophy, the present direction of modern Africa', and he asked, 'is this not a contradiction in a society whose great declaration of uniqueness to the outside world is that of a superabundant humanism?'[20] Hence *Kongi's Harvest,* theatrically a rather dull play, is a fierce onslaught on West Africa's modern breed of politicians, and especially on Kongi himself, the President of Isma and a modern version of Mata Kharibu complete with all the image-making paraphernalia of the twentieth century. What he represents is summarised in an opponent's curse 'On all who fashion chains, on farmers of terror, on builders of walls, on all who guard against the night but breed darkness by day, on all whose feet are heavy and yet stand upon the world . . .'[21] Of course the immediate satiric victim here is an African dictator; but the portrait of Kongi suggests that the dramatist's satire is once again eddying out more widely – beyond the shores of Africa and around the modern world at large. After the more general satire of *A Dance of the Forests* these, then, are some of the individual victims chosen as targets in the plays that have followed.

Language and satire

Reaping the harvest of a past dominated by the spoken word, Soyinka is deeply interested in the rhetorical arts. Hence no doubt his special penchant for the dramatic form and the appearance in each of his plays of at least one outstanding orator. We usually find, too, a carefully ordered range of linguistic styles, which not only affords Soyinka a necessary variety of voices, but constitutes a basic item in his satirical armour as well. A satirist's values are sometimes hard to determine, but the clearest signposts to Soyinka's lie in his use of language. He would agree with Buffon's terse observation, 'Le style c'est l'homme'; and, of course, other satirists have taken the same view. One recalls Jane Austen's Sir Thomas Bertram, in *Mansfield Park*, listening to the recitals of his sea-going nephew simply 'to understand the reciter, to know the young man by his histories'; and how he 'listened to his clear, simple, spirited details with full satisfaction, seeing in them the proof of good principles, professional knowledge, energy, courage, and cheerfulness – everything that could deserve or promise well'.[22] One can hardly miss the suggestion here that, details of the narration apart, the *style* of their telling is also a proof of the boy's 'good principles'. It is with the same critical attention that we must listen to Soyinka's characters, whose language accurately reflects not only their social position and education, but also their moral qualities, their honesty or affection.

As a satirist vitally concerned about language and style, Soyinka stands in line with distinguished predecessors. It is enough to recall the names of Skelton, Swift, Pope, and Sterne to establish how consistently the great satiric tradition of English letters has opposed itself to the abuse of language. The sixteenth century saw Skelton hysterically protesting at the decay of language and learning which, it seemed to him, the Renaissance was causing. The seventeenth and eighteenth centuries found the Augustan satirists lashing the scribblers of Grub Street. Dryden attacked Shadwell in 'MacFlecknoe'; Swift attacked the banal style of L'Estrange, and Pope pilloried all those hacks who were undermining literary standards. The closing lines of 'The Dunciad' offer a frightening picture of the fruits of what Pope calls the 'uncreating word'; poetic fancy dies, the fire of wit is extinguished, truth flees into hiding and philosophy no longer looks to heaven. 'Art after art goes out and all is night.' Pope's account (intended as a model of what good style should be) races to its finale of triumphant gloom:

> Religion blushing veils her sacred fires,
> And unawares morality expires.

234

Nor public flame, nor private dares to shine,
Nor human spark is left, nor glimpse divine!
Lo! thy dread empire, Chaos! is restored;
Light dies before thy uncreating word;
Thy hand, great Anarch! lets the curtain fall,
And universal darkness buries all.[23]

This is nothing less than a warning that the abuse of language can lead eventually to the complete breakdown of civilised life. As one critic put it, 'A civilisation is only as good as its language, and when literature is so debased that it has lost all its alerting power – then indeed a man like Pope may well bid civilisation a long "Good night". '[24]

Where historically the abuse of language has been decried mainly in its literary manifestations, satire in the modern world has attacked its debasement by propagandists and political machinery. George Orwell, the twentieth century's Swift, provides a useful example. In Orwell's view, the decline of a language 'must ultimately have political and economic causes'; bad politics encourage the abuse of language, and the slovenliness of our language leads to woolly thinking. Orwell believes, however, that the process is reversible: the eradication of bad habits enables one to think more clearly, and 'to think clearly is a necessary first step towards political regeneration'.[25] But in a world increasingly dominated by political machinery, we are witnessing the steady corruption of language as a means of honest communication:

> In our time it is broadly true that political writing is bad writing ... The political dialects to be found in pamphlets, leading articles, manifestos, White Papers and the speeches of under-secretaries do, of course, vary from party to party, but they are all alike in that one almost never finds in them a fresh, vivid, home-made turn of speech ...
>
> In our time, political speech and writing are largely the defence of the indefensible ... Thus political language has to consist largely of euphemism, question-begging and sheer cloudy vagueness ... A mass of Latin words falls upon the facts like soft snow, blurring the outlines and covering up all the details. The great enemy of clear language is insincerity.[26]

Orwell was convinced that the Russian, Italian, and German languages had all deteriorated in modern times as a result of dictatorship. Hence, an essential point to be seized about his novel *Nineteen Eighty Four* is his argument that language has become a prime instrument of political and cultural enslavement. His message is clear. Man's language is the precious guarantee of his liberty; let him abuse it and it will be turned against him as a weapon of tyranny. The book sets out to illustrate what could happen if the present decay of language continues. Thus, Newspeak is language in the service of ideology; language devised to narrow rather than to expand man's thought, to lay chains on his imagination rather than to let it fly free. Its purpose is 'not only to provide a medium of expression for the world-view and mental habits proper to the devotees of Ingsoc, but to make all other modes of thought impossible'. Reduction of vocabulary, therefore, is regarded as an excellent way of restricting the range of thought; and in the ultimate triumph of Ingsoc it is hoped 'to make articulate speech issue from the larynx without involving the higher brain centres at all'. Thus is the enslavement of a people contrived by the ruthless destruction of its language.

Now, Orwell and Soyinka can be taken as kindred spirits. Indeed the remarks of Orwell quoted above could be deemed required reading for those who would understand Soyinka's thinking and satire; for these men share a common view of language, a common hatred of political cant and a common hatred of oppression in all its forms. We have already cited Soyinka's complaint that 'the present philosophy, the present direction of modern Africa was created by politicians' (including men who felt it necessary on two occasions to strip him of his freedom). It is not surprising, therefore, that politicians and their abuse of language should become a theme of his plays.

Kongi's Harvest offers perhaps the best example. Here traditional African politics, which placed the power of ruling in the hands of local chieftains, is being ousted by the politics of Kongi with his passion for dictatorship in the modern style. It is a familiar case of the traditional ways in conflict with the forces of change. The old order is represented by Oba Danlola and his followers, whose choice of language sharply marks them off from Kongi's party of modernists. Their style has a concreteness of metaphor and imagery which recalls the traditional Yoruba verse discussed earlier in this chapter. Soyinka's verse here is not as rich as Ladipo's and Ijimere's, despite its greater flexibility, but it clearly springs from the same roots. Consider Danlola's remarks when Kongi's Superintendent stops his drummers (pp. 3–4):

> Good friend, you merely stopped
> My drums. But they were silenced
> On the day when Kongi cast aside
> My props of wisdom, the day he
> Drove the old Aweri from their seats.
> What is a king without a clan
> Of Elders?

236

Or his insulting words to the same individual:

> No, it is nothing new. Your betters
> Stopped the drums a long time ago
> And you the slave in khaki and brass buttons
> Now lick your master's spit and boast,
> We chew the same tobacco.

Danlola's style, a mixture of vivid metaphor, sharp observation, and pointed censure, is sustained throughout and acts like a banner of identity for the faction he represents. The abuse which he heaps on his assistants as he dresses for Kongi's great celebration is a further example of his style, taken from the second half of the play (p. 48):

> Do you dare call this a sceptre?
> This dung-stained goat-prod, this
> Makeshift sign at crossroads, this
> Thighbone of the crow that died
> Of rickets? Or did you merely
> Steal the warped backscratcher
> Of your hunchback uncle?

The difference between the era which Danlola represents and Kongi's new dispensation is seen in the play as largely one of language. Having dismissed Danlola and his followers as 'a backward superstitious lot', Kongi is firmly committed to building a political machine that is recognisably modern and recognisably western. Hence, the linguistic style which Soyinka gives to the tyrant and his minions is fraught, not with the metaphor and proverbial wisdom of Old Africa, but with the 'washer words' and politico-scientific jargon of the modern world.

We know what to expect from the outset, for Kongi is introduced as the President of 'Isma'; but in case we should miss this title's significance, it is driven home in an opening anthem sung by the friends of Danlola (p.1):

> Ism to ism for ism is ism
> Of isms and isms on absolute-ism
> To demonstrate the tree of life
> Is sprung from broken peat
> And we the rotted bark, spurned
> When the tree swells its pot
> The mucus that is snorted out
> When Kongi's new race blows
> And more, oh there's a harvest of words
> In a penny newspaper.

Thus, Kongi's harvest is to be 'a harvest of words', and Soyinka will shape his satire accordingly. Kongi has decided that there must be a deliberate break with the past – essentially a political break of course, but involving a cultural and linguistic break as well. His advisers, the Reformed Aweri Fraternity (a modernised version of the group which formerly advised Danlola) discuss this matter in one of the most comically revealing scenes of the play. They are talking together at Kongi's mountain retreat and the following pieces are taken from their conversation (pp.11–13):

FOURTH AWERI: We need an image. Tomorrow being our first appearance in public, it is essential that we find an image.

. . .

SECOND: Isn't it enough just to go in as Kongi's disciples?

FOURTH: Magi is more dignified. We hold after all the position of the wise ones. From the recognition of us as the Magi, it is one step to his inevitable apotheosis.

. . .

FIRST: I suggest we pattern ourselves on our predecessors. Oh I do admit they were a little old-fashioned, but they had er . . . a certain style. Yes, I think style is the word I want. Style. Yes, I think we could do worse than model ourselves on the old Aweri.

FIFTH: You mean, speak in proverbs and ponderous tone rhythms?

FOURTH: I'm afraid that is out anyway. Kongi would prefer a clean break from the traditional conclave of the so-called wise ones.

. . .

FIRST: The emphasis of our generation is – youth. Our image therefore should be a kind of youthful elders of the state. A conclave of modern patriarchs.

THIRD: Yes, yes. Nice word patriarch, I'm glad you used it. Has a nice, reverent tone about it. Very nice indeed, very nice.

. . .

FOURTH: We might consider a scientific image. This would be a positive stamp and one very much in tune with our contemporary situation. Our pro-

	nouncements should be dominated by a positive scientificism.
THIRD:	A brilliant conception. I move we adopt it at once.
SIXTH:	What image exactly is positive scientificism?
THIRD:	Whatever it is, it is not long-winded proverbs and senile pronouncements. In fact we could say a step has already been taken in that direction. If you've read our Leader's last publication.
FIFTH:	Ah yes. Nor proverbs nor verse, only ideograms in algebraic quantums. If the square of XQY (2bc) equals QA into the square root of X, then the progressive forces must prevail over the reactionary in the span of ·32 of a single generation.

The effort is hard to sustain, and of course Soyinka's point is that their new style is a gross affectation; but on the whole, they succeed and we hear the familiar jargon that a man like Orwell loathed so passionately. 'Progressive forces', 'a step has already been taken in that direction', 'contemporary situation', 'reactionary', 'positive stamp', 'scientific image', 'positive scientificism', 'so-called wise ones', 'clean break' – the cliches pour forth, and one half expects to hear 'consensus', 'escalation', 'dialogue', 'credibility gap', and 'all-time highs' thrown in for good measure. Though occurring here in dialogue, they are examples of the kind of language which Orwell had in mind when, in his tirade against political prose, he complained of writing which 'consists less and less of *words* chosen for the sake of their meaning, and more and more of *phrases* tacked together like the sections of a prefabricated hen-house'.[27] In the mouths of those who invented them, such expressions are simply dull; spoken by Africans who are learning them for the first time, they become comic and absurd.

Thus, Kongi's advisers are being ridiculed. Their assumed style is turned against them so that even their cliches become interesting. With much the same end in view, Soyinka gives to Kongi's secretary lines that contain slight but telling mistakes in his command of modern English idiom (pp. 14–15):

Secretary:	And your guardian and uncle, Danlola, is a pain in my neck. Now tell me, what has he up his sleeves? ·
Daodu:	Up his sleeves?
Secretary:	Up those voluminous sleeves of his. What is he hiding there in for tomorrow?

239

It is a deft touch which suffers only from Soyinka's neglect to apply it consistently.

The whole movement of the play is towards the great Festival of the New Yam, traditionally the responsibility of Danlola; Kongi plans to 'secularise' this event, ceremonially ring out the old order, and assert his supremacy as the fountainhead of all meaningful power in the country. Kongi foresees a new harmony in the making, and, in a passage that illustrates the modern style, one of his advisers describes what this means (p. 24):

FOURTH: ... The period of isolated saws and wisdoms is
            over, superseded by a more systematic formula-
            tion of comprehensive philosophies – *our* func-
            tion, for the benefit of those who still do not know
            it.
THIRD: Hear hear.
FOURTH: And Danlola, the retrogressive autocrat, will
            with his own hands present the Leader with the
            New Yam, thereby acknowledging the supremacy
            of the State over his former areas of authority
            spiritual or secular. From then on, the State will
            adopt towards him and to all similar institutions
            the policy of glamourised fossilism.
THIRD: Hear hear, very precisely put.

In the event, the show is a fiasco, and the play ends in the style of Danlola, though he is on his way into exile when the curtain falls. Before his final exit, he offers words of mocking reassurance to the Secretary whom Kongi had made responsible for the Festival's organi-sation and who is now fleeing to the nearest border-crossing (p. 88):

> But it did go well. Well, as a hurricane
> Blows well. As a bush-fire on dry
> Corn stalks burns well, and with a fine
> Crackle of northern wind behind it.

Lakunle's style in *The Lion and the Jewel* is a clear window through which we can see his worthless values.[28] This is a much less serious play than *Kongi's Harvest,* but nevertheless the style given to Lakunle represents a deliberate attempt to reflect the encroachment of western values upon African mores.

Lakunle, the torch-bearer of modernity in his community, is in love with Sidi, an unlettered village nymph; but the foxy old Bale of the village, Baroka, wants her too, and the play becomes an amusing struggle between these rivals, who represent, once again, the old order and the new. Lakunle is a fervent disciple of romantic love (that recent western import into West African society) and a champion of all those freedoms for which the feminists have struggled. He sketches for his beloved the splendid life that will be hers if only she will consent to marry him without his paying the traditional bride price. His verse is rather Audenesque in flavour, inspired by all that he feels is most alluring in western culture. It strikes us as a humorous modern-day continuation of a style of seduction verse that runs from Ovid through Marlowe and Jonson (pp. 100–1);

> When we are wed, you shall not walk or sit
> Tethered, as it were, to my dirtied heels.
> Together we shall sit at table
> – Not on the floor – and eat,
> Not with fingers, but with knives
> And forks, and breakable plates
> Like civilized beings.
> I will not have you wait on me
> Till I have dined my fill.
> No wife of mine, no lawful wedded wife
> Shall eat the leavings off my plate –
> That is for the children.
> I want to walk beside you in the street,
> Side by side and arm in arm
> Just like the Lagos couples I have seen
> High-heeled shoes for the lady, red paint
> On her lips. And her hair is stretched
> Like a magazine photo. I will teach you
> The waltz and we'll both learn the foxtrot
> And we'll spend the week-end in night-clubs at Ibadan.
> Oh I must show you the grandeur of towns
> We'll live there if you like or merely pay
>   visits.
> So choose. Be a modern wife, look me in the eye
> And give me a little kiss – like this.

Sidi of course is disgusted with this 'strange unhealthy mouthing' and retreats, leaving Lakunle to complain wearily and comically:

> It's never any use.
> Bush-girl you are, bush-girl you'll always be;
> Uncivilized and primitive – bush-girl!
> I kissed you as all educated men –
> And Christians – kiss their wives.
> It is the way of civilized romance.

This is all light satire, but it has its point. The conflict is between the champions of two worlds, and Baroka, the spokesman of tradition, wins the fight; the modern, westernised representative not only loses but is the laughing stock of the play. It is as if Soyinka, even in this gay comedy, cannot resist taking sides; as if he, in company with satirists in general, is on the side of conservatism, seeing in tradition a bedrock of sanity that will defy the swirling torrents of change and revolution. But it is not as simple as this, for Soyinka's very achievement consists in his own coming to terms, artistically, with the modern world. A clue to his real position probably lies in the fact that it is largely the trivia, the superficies of western life that Lakunle espouses – western life observed at one remove in the streets of Lagos. Thus, Soyinka is no doubt saying to his people, 'Don't throw away your heritage (which still has much to offer you) for the glossy manifestations of western life. Look at Lakunle and see how absurd it would be.'

The emptiness of Lakunle's verse, and the values which it represents, are thrown into relief by the verse of Sidi and the Bale. When Sidi offers us lines such as these (p. 114):

> See how the water glistens on my face
> Like the dew-moistened leaves on a
>   Harmattan morning
> But he – his face is like a leather
>   piece
> Torn rudely from the saddle of his
>   horse

we cannot help but contrast them, as we are meant to do, with the windy effusions of Lakunle; with lines such as the following (p. 129):

> The ruler shall ride cars, not horses
> Or a bicycle at the very least.
> We'll burn the forest, cut the trees
> Then plant a modern park for lovers
> We'll print newspapers every day
> With pictures of seductive girls.
> The world will judge our progress
> By the girls that win beauty contests.
> While Lagos builds new factories daily
> We only play 'ayo' and gossip.
> Where is our school of Ballroom dancing?
> Who here can throw a cocktail party?
> We must be modern with the rest
> Or live forgotten by the world.
> We must reject the palm wine habit
> And take to tea, with milk and sugar.

It is all patently shallow stuff, and this is never more evident than when it is set alongside the much weightier verse of Baroka, the illiterate old Bale who is Lakunle's rival. Significantly, it is the Bale who is given what one suspects are Soyinka's personal views on the idea of progress. We should not be misled by the dramatist's deliberately deceptive move of having the Bale speak them during his seduction of Sidi (p. 144):

> I do not hate progress, only its nature
> Which makes all roofs and faces look the same.
> And the wish of one old man is
> That here and there,
> Among the bridges and the murderous roads,
> Below the humming birds which
> Smoke the face of Sango, dispenser of
> The snake-tongue lightning; between this moment
> And the reckless broom that will be wielded
> In these years to come, we must leave
> Virgin plots of lives, rich decay
> And the tang of vapour rising from
> Forgotten heaps of compost, lying
> Undisturbed . . . But the skin of progress
> Masks, unknown, the spotted wolf of sameness . . .

The Trials of Brother Jero is dominated by the personality and style of the holy fraud himself, whose oratory is cultivated to deceive, whose rhetoric serves duplicity rather than divinity.[29] Here he is, magnificent in his white flowing gown and costly velvet cape, expanding on his most cherished subject – himself (p. 210):

It becomes important to stand out, to be distinctive. I have set my heart after a particular name. They will look at my velvet cape and they will think of my goodness. Inevitably they must begin to call me . . . the Velvet-hearted Jeroboam. Immaculate Jero, Articulate Hero of Christ's Crusade . . . Well, it is out. I have not breathed it to a single soul, but that has been my ambition. You've got to have a name that appeals to the imagination – because the imagination is a thing of the spirit – it must catch the imagination of the crowd. Yes, one must move with modern times. Lack of colour gets one nowhere even in the Prophet's business.

As usual, the play uses two contrasting styles. Jero's is one, and the second belongs to the plain folk who are his victims. Their language is as humble as their status, and in moments of deepest sincerity it becomes mainly West African pidgin. In the following scene on the beach, an emotional prayer session is in progress under the direction of Chume, the assistant prophet whose wife Jero has seduced. The petitions are frankly materialistic but, coming from the poor, touch-ingly human for all that. They are punctuated regularly with Amens, and the whole effort builds to a tremendous climax as these humble people whip up their emotional fervour (p. 219):

Yes, Father, make you forgive us all. Make you save us from palaver. Save us from trouble at home. Tell our wives not to give us trouble ... Tell our wives not to give us trouble. And give us money to have a happy home. Give us money to satisfy our daily necessities. Make you no forget those of us who dey struggle daily. Those who be clerk today, make them Chief Clerk tomorrow. Those who are Messenger today, make them Senior Service tomorrow. Yes Father, those who are Messenger today, make them Senior Service tomorrow. Those who are petty trader today, make them big contractor tomorrow. Those who dey sweep street today, give them their own big office tomorrow. If we dey walka today, give us our own bicycle tomorrow. I say those who dey walka today, give them their own bicycle tomorrow. Those who have bicycle today, they will ride their own car tomorrow. I say those who dey push bicycle, give them big car tomorrow. Give them big car tomorrow. Give them big car tomorrow, give them big car tomorrow.

For all its comic quaintness, and for all that Soyinka is gently mocking the materialism behind it, this is language marked by pathos and unquestionable sincerity. Jero, however, calls it 'animal jabber'. He remarks that Chume always reverts to it when he gets his spiritual excitement. It is a sign of his assistant's crudeness; but it has the advantage of ruling out any possibility of rivalry from that quarter. In the Prophet's business, sophistication and style are needed more than the crude fervour of men like Chume.

Thus we can understand Soyinka's fundamental interest in language. Language as a key to man's inner being; language as a mirror of social standing; language as an instrument of deceit and oppression; language as a device for sheer entertainment; language as a vehicle for man's deepest utterances; language as a source of comedy; language as an instrument of satire – Soyinka is keenly aware of all these facets and explores them energetically in his plays.

Soyinka's art: a meeting of traditions

Although Soyinka's work reveals a definite blending of African and western elements, the basic material out of which the plays are fashioned is overwhelmingly indigenous. The elements of African pre-drama, for instance, are here in force, as a brief survey of the plays will reveal.

Soyinka's first play was called, significantly, *A Dance of the Forests,* and its opening words indicate that it is meant to partake of the nature of a dance. The resurrected ancestors were rejected by the living 'So I took them under my wing', says Aroni. 'They became my guests and the Forests consented to dance for them.'[30] And the dance, thus, is a common feature throughout the play. The villagers dance around the totem carved for the festivities, there is the dance of the Half-Child, offspring of the Dead Woman, and a dance by the god Eshuoro and his jester, called the Dance of the Unwilling Sacrifice. Ritual is added to dance at one point when a dancer is followed by a young girl acting as an acolyte who sprinkles the dancing area as she goes. This itself is followed shortly by a solemn recitation by a dirgeman, urging everyone to stand back and 'Leave the dead/Some room to dance', and then by Agboreko's oracular consultation. At the climax of the play we find the ceremonial masking of the three 'earthly protagonists', who, ridden and possessed by the various spirits which the Interpreter calls up, 'chorus' the future in the manner of the religious masks of Egungun and Voodoo.

The Lion and the Jewel is a lively combination of dancing, singing, and drumming. A particularly memorable feature is the Dance of the Lost Traveller, a re-enactment in mime form of an important event occurring prior to the time period of the play, and about which the audience must be informed. It was the unexpected visit of a Lagos photographer whose car broke down as it passed near the village. Sidi chooses villagers to dance the different parts of 'devil horse' (car) and python; and persuades Lakunle (warmly African beneath his western veneer) to dance the part of the stranger; she chants at him:

> You are dressed like him
> You look like him
> You speak his tongue
> You think like him
> You're just as clumsy
> In your Lagos ways –
> You'll do for him![31]

The stranger's arrival and short stay in the village are then mimed, and, to simulate the car wheels, four dancers roll the upper halves of their bodies to the accompaniment of throbbing drums.

In the same play, Baroka wins Sidi by spreading abroad a rumour that he is impotent – a rumour that leads to the performance of a frankly sexual 'dance of virility', carried out exclusively by the ladies. It is a wild triumphant affair in which the Bale's sexual life from his days of great potency to his final 'defeat', is acted out with enormous gusto. Sadiku, his eldest wife, leads a dancing group of younger women in pursuit of a male, who rushes about, dancing in tortured movements as defeat draws near, and is finally 'scotched', to the unbounded delight of the ladies. It is a bold piece of theatre (made nicely ironic by having the dancers burst on stage at precisely the moment of Sidi's seduction) which not even Aristophanes could have bettered.

In the other plays, too, traditional elements feature strongly. *Kongi's Harvest,* for example, reaches a grand climax at the Yam Festival, which is a veritable orgy of feasting, dancing, chanting, and parading, all to the frenzied accompaniment of dozens of pounding pestles. As we have seen in *The Road,* Soyinka's note *For the Producer* with its reference to the mask idiom, is evidence enough of the tradition in which he is working. A play replete with dirge and praise singing, and which contains a festival in honour of Ogun, god of iron, it serves to indicate how deeply the roots of Soyinka's art are sunk in African traditional practice.

But the most interesting example of how Soyinka uses pre-dramatic material can be found in *The Strong Breed,* a dark, powerfully moving play built around the scapegoat idea, one of the most ancient conventions devised by social man for the easing of his collective conscience.[32] In the village of the play, there is a New Year's Eve ritual in which the evil of the old year is cleansed away for the beginning of the new. The theme is introduced by a sick girl, who appears dragging an effigy or 'carrier' that is to be beaten, hanged, and burnt so that it will carry away her illness. As she puts it to the village idiot (p. 243):

You will hang it up and I will set fire to it. But just because you are helping me, don't think it is going to cure you. I am the one who will get well at midnight, do you understand? It is my carrier and it is for me alone.

The adults have a parallel ceremony; with this difference, that they require a human carrier who must submit himself to merciless cruelty and degradation. They decide that Ifada, the idiot boy, is a 'godsend' for the task;[33] but Eman (a figure reminiscent of Okara's Okolo and Patrick White's Himmelfarb), a 'stranger' in the village and its schoolmaster, nobly substitutes himself and dies in the manhunt that ensues, an appalling affair accompanied by the din of banged tins, bells, dogs, and shouting.[34] Before his death, however, there is a dramatic flashback in which an old man, Eman's father, is preparing to undergo the same humiliation. It seems that in Eman's part of the country there is a slightly different custom by which the community's sins are taken

246

down to the river in a small boat and there floated away on the flood. His father has been performing the task for many years (p. 259):

> Ours is a strong breed my son. It is only a strong breed that can take this boat to the river year after year and wax stronger on it. I have taken down each year's evils for over twenty years. I hoped you would follow me.

It is a clear example of pre-drama at the heart of a most moving play.

Traditional material, then, features strongly. What of those elements borrowed from the West? Some of these are extremely simple, yet fundamental. For instance, the plays have a text, and, therefore, a fixed form, which in itself is a basic departure from traditional practice. The improvisation of the early Yoruba troupes would be unthinkable in any of the Soyinka plays which we have discussed. Again, the texts are in English and the plays are designed for western stages rather than for the traditional open square.

There are, too, several techniques learnt from European practice that give Soyinka's art a flexibility and freedom it would otherwise lack. A day in the life of Brother Jero, introduced to the audience by the Prophet himself, and then acted out by him, represents a device more likely to have been learnt from Brecht or Pirandello than from Africa. The flashback technique, for which Soyinka has been criticised by Martin Esslin, is likewise a western borrowing.[35] Salubi and Samson in *The Road* re-enact the dreadful crash scene from which the events of the play ultimately proceed, and, in *The Lion and the Jewel,* flashback combines with traditional practice when the ladies dance the history of Baroka's sex life and the villagers perform the Dance of the Lost traveller. A divided stage is used in the first section of *Kongi's Harvest,* for the play alternates between two scenes; it is a device used memorably in the Isherwood–Auden play *On the Frontier,* and, of course, it is common in films and in television plays. Soyinka might have borrowed it from any one of these sources; there is no evidence of it in the dramatic tradition inherited from his forefathers. His plots, too, reveal an ingenuity inspired more perhaps by Ben Jonson than by indigenous models. Certainly there is no plot in Yoruba Folk Opera to match the complexity of *The Lion and the Jewel* or *A Dance of the Forests.*

Western influence emerges, too, in the matter of characterisation. Soyinka's figures have a degree of psychological depth and complexity which vernacular drama has never achieved. Professor, in *The Road,* to take but one illustration, is a distinctly African personality in a distinctly African play, but the bewildering complexity of his character, the shadows of the past that enshroud it, its aura of insanity, its weird

247

admixture of the criminal and spiritual – all this is felt to have been made possible only by Soyinka's knowledge and imitation of western dramatists.

Soyinka has rapidly emerged as West Africa's most distinguished dramatist, and indeed he is beginning to claim attention as one of the foremost English-speaking playwrights of our time. As a satirist he is certainly in the front rank. As a poetic dramatist, he has few equals. This is how the London critics reacted to him in 1966, the year, so to speak, when Soyinka came to town. Of *The Road,* the *Observer's* drama critic wrote:

Wole Soyinka made himself unpopular at the festival of African arts in Dakar last April by declaring that the major obstacle faced by African artists is the patronising double standard of European criticism which hails any halting, amateurish artefact of the continent as perfectly splendid, for Africa . . . He could afford to say so – his play, *The Road,* was one of the most original and powerful works seen in London last year.[36]

The Scotsman declared that 'People are not accustomed to such eloquence in modern playwrights', while the *New Statesman* linked Soyinka with Pinter, suggesting a similarity of theme between *The Lion and the Jewel* and *The Homecoming.* However, the critic of *The Times* offered the most perceptive comment. Reviewing *The Lion and the Jewel,* he wrote:

This is the third play by Wole Soyinka to appear in London since last year, and this work alone is enough to establish Nigeria as the most fertile new source of English-speaking drama since Synge's discovery of the Western Isles. Even this comparison does Soyinka less than justice . . . to find any parallel for his work in English drama you have to go back to the Elizabethans.[37]

6. Conclusion

Against a background of problems associated with cultural turmoil, a history of colonial domination, and the basic difficulty of using a second language, the brief history of English writing in West Africa reveals a steady advance towards literary independence. Anxious to use a European tongue and yet express through it the special traits of their own culture, poets, novelists, and playwrights have found that working in a second language can have its advantages; the resistance encountered in it has been a promise of creative strength, as Balachandra Rajan once said that it might. There has also been some useful linguistic experimentation. More important than this, however, has been a definite return by these writers to indigenous sources for material and inspiration, to Africa's ancient oral traditions and to the physical details of the continent's landscape. Thus, the rich heritage of thought, experience, religion, custom, folklore and myth, carried down the ages in scores of African vernaculars, has begun to be tapped. This is the ultimate source of so much imagery in the verse of Okara and Clark; this is what accounts for the vigour and flamboyance of Soyinka's plays, for the proverb-laden narratives of Achebe and for the bizarre creations of Tutuola.

Although anglophone verse in West Africa started later than its French equivalent, it has, nevertheless, developed rapidly. It is becoming increasingly 'authentic' in flavour and content as it looks to Africa for its inspiration and themes. The temptation to imitate remains strong, but this is not necessarily unhealthy; indeed it is an essential stage through which writers universally pass on their journey towards full artistic maturity. J.P. Clark, for instance, is still young enough to delight in imitative exercises, but he is, nevertheless, free enough of enchantment with the overseas tradition to be, in the main, content with reflecting the details of his African environment. The fruits of Okara's linguistic experiments, together with the wealth of verse revealed in the vernacular plays, suggests that more translation out of the indigenous languages would be not only feasible but highly desirable.

Thus, with the strength of ancestral oral forms behind it, West African verse in English has matured rapidly and appears to be assured of an exciting future as poets cease to look overseas, cease, as the years slip by, to feel the pull of an alien tradition, and increasingly explore the wealth of material that lies waiting for a voice in the homeland.

Prose fiction, on the other hand, faces an uncertain future. After what seemed to be an auspicious beginning, it has now settled into mediocrity. That it is appearing in ever larger quantities does not disguise the fact that it lacks a sense of direction and contains little of real merit. Achebe, a good craftsman, has for the moment deserted art for journalism. Tutuola, working with the tribal myths of the Yoruba, is an eccentric without disciples. Okara's experiment with *The Voice,* an imaginative attempt to pioneer new directions, stands as an example which no one has followed. The reasons for the unhappy condition of prose fiction are not clear. But I have argued that one explanation might lie in the fact that when a society moves from oral traditions to the use of the written word, the development of a fine tradition of prose is a long and difficult process, since a basic change in the manipulation of language is involved. In this sense, prose faces much greater difficulties than do poetry and drama, those literary forms which are based on the spoken word.

Drama, as the most social or 'communal' of all literary forms, and as a form whose roots lie deep in religious and quasi-religious phenomena, finds in Africa splendidly fertile soil. Having long understood and fostered the dramatic illusion, Africa lies big with drama. Indeed, in Ijimere and Ladipo, and, to a lesser extent, in Soyinka and Clark, we have encountered drama that is scarcely one stage removed from pure ritual; and we are not surprised that Clark can talk about West African actors being 'ridden' in the way that Voodoo worshippers – those surviving West Indian practitioners of African religion – are 'ridden'. With vigour and imagination, the new dramatists have seized upon the advantages which their own traditions have offered them, and the skill of their endeavours is attested by the startled acclaim with which their work has been received in many parts of the world. What is more, we have witnessed in their plays the birth of a new species of drama, a typically African growth taking the form of a fusion of ritual, dance, song, and chant, the like of which the western stage has never seen before. With the emergence of these West African playwrights, the future of poetic drama in English looks suddenly much brighter.

The literature as a whole leaves several strong general impressions. It reflects, naturally, the society from which it springs. As Mphahlele once pointed out, and as this study has from time to time reminded us, 'Much

250

of Africa is still a land of myth . . . of people who continue to stay close enough to the earth to hear its pastoral symphonies and to feel strongly the spin of Fate's wheel and to learn to endure.' Hence we find writing that stays close to the earth, too, literature that is heavy with an intimate knowledge of the physical world that stems from long contemplation of it. And yet parallel with this vein of concern about the physical world, runs an abiding sense of the spiritual. As we have seen, respect for the gods is rivalled by devotion to the ancestors, who, though dead and departed, are still living cells of influence in the great ongoing stream of life. Though for the moment culturally restless, West Africa has preserved much of the old spiritual order. As the heir to oral traditions, the literature retains several vestiges of spoken art, which can be seen in the convoluted syntax of Tutuola, in the device of repetition in Okara, or in the love of powerful sayings in Achebe. But, while showing features which link it with the distant past, West African literature also mirrors the profound unease which afflicts contemporary Africa; it bends and buckles in sympathy with the continent's painful encounters with the western world.

A carefully selected group of images and expressions which have appeared in this study will epitomise some of the main characteristics of this society and lay a finger on the artistic position of its writers. One recalls, for instance, the meaningful image of the whirlpool that occurs in the poetry of Awoonor-Williams, in the plays of Clark, and in the prose of Okara. Awoonor-Williams, for example, talks about his people being washed in 'The whirlpool of the many river's estuary'. He also sees them as 'Caught between the anvil and the hammer'/In the forging house of a new life'. Okara summed up his own predicament in the lines 'lost in the morning mist/of an age at a riverside . . . wandering in the mystic rhythm of jungle drums and the concerto'. A rather tragic and fatalistic vein is echoed in Achebe's frequent proverbs about suffering and in, for instance, his saying that life is 'like a bowl of wormwood which one sips a little at a time world without end'. It reappears in his ponderous observation that 'man is like a funeral ram which must take whatever beating comes to it without opening its mouth; only the silent tremor of pain down its body tells of its suffering'. This stands close to a profoundly pessimistic view that lies at the heart of Soyinka's vision of mankind as a whole, and which is most vividly stated in his lines 'The world is old/But the rust of a million years/Has left the chains unloosened.' Clark, for his part, gives us the lines, 'It is enough/You know now that each day we live/Hints at why we cried out at birth.' Finally, the artistic stance of these writers in relation to the western world and modern times is pictured vividly in Awoonor-Williams' assertion 'We shall find our salvation here on the shore, asleep.'

Anglophone literature appeared later than francophone writing, but it began in a quieter, more personal strain. An indubitable fact which emerges from this study, however, is that this early calm has made way for a more strident note as the years of freedom have failed to fulfil their promise. Indeed, from negritude's avowal of the superiority of the African as a more feeling, more humane creature than the white man, we have reached a stage in which the loudest voice is Soyinka's, furiously proclaiming that, far from being in any sense superior to the white man, the African shares the profound imperfection not only of the white man but of mankind at large. Soyinka's unfortunate experiences bear silent witness to the truth of his pronouncements. But the satiric outlook is not confined to Soyinka. We have seen it in Achebe, in Okara, and even in minor poets like John Ekwere and Mabel Segun. It is part of a growing self-awareness, a developing sense of the importance of not merely reflecting African society but of dissecting and criticising it as well.

Critics talk of national literatures arising in Africa. We should accept this with caution, for while it is true that the literature of a particular area exhibits definite characteristics of its own, and may well differ from the literature of some other area of the continent, we find at the moment not so much Nigerian or Ghanaian literature, but literature in English written by a Yoruba, an Ibo, or an Ijaw. In this sense, the new writing is still tribal rather than national. True enough, writers try to offer general views, but they are more often continental or racial rather than national; and they are offered in a style and through a sensibility which have been shaped by tribal idiosyncrasies. It is perhaps too early to begin talking about national literatures.

And what of the future? With the problems of language and authenticity largely solved, a much closer relationship will develop between the author and his African audience. With the rapid spread of literacy, this audience will grow apace and the writer will meet it on common ground as he strives to stay close to indigenous modes and ceases to write with one ear turned towards the white audience of Europe and America. This will be a period of more settled styles, rather than one of continued experimentation, a period in which West African literature in English will become even more distinctive than it is at present.

Notes to the Text

Unless otherwise stated, all translations are by the author.

1. *The background*

1 Janheinz Jahn, *Muntu*, 11.
2 *Ibid*. 11.
3 'The Psychological Pressure upon Modern Africans' in *Modern Africa* (eds.) McEwan and Sutcliffe, 376.
4 Bakary Traoré, *Le Théâtre Négro-Africain et ses Fonctions Sociales*, 61.
5 Gerald Moore and Ulli Beier (eds.), *Modern Poetry from Africa*, 61. Moore and Beier are also responsible for the translations.
6 *Ibid*. 59. 'The Vultures'.
7 John Press (ed.), *Commonwealth Literature*, 204.
8 'Culture et Colonisation', *Présence Africaine*, Vol. 8, No. 10 (1956), 204. Quoted by Jahn in *Muntu*, 227.
9 The word 'metropolitan' is used throughout this study to describe the various European powers that held colonial possessions in Africa.
10 'Vernacular Languages and Cultures in Modern Africa' in *Language in Africa*, (ed.) John Spencer, 65.
11 Claude Wauthier, *The Literature and Thought of Modern Africa* (trans. Shirley Kay), 31.
12 *Ibid*. 31–2.
13 Molly Mahood, *Présence Africaine*, Vol. 32, No. 60 (1966), 29.
14 *Cultural Events in Africa*, No. 29 (April 1967), 11. My italics.
15 *Présence Africaine*, Vol. 32, No. 60, 25.
16 Wauthier, *The Literature and Thought of Modern Africa*, 37.
17 *Ibid*. 37.
18 *Ibid*. 40.
19 Press (ed.), *Commonwealth Literature*, 108.
20 Maisie Ward, *Gilbert Keith Chesterton*, London: Penguin Books, 1958, 138.
21 Wauthier, *The Literature and Thought of Modern Africa*, 66.
22 *Cultural Events in Africa*, No. 29 (April 1967), 10.
23 George Awoonor-Williams, *Rediscovery*, 10.

24 *Ibid.* 12.
25 *Ibid.* 13.
26 *Ibid.* 31.
27 Frances Ademola (ed.), *Reflections*, 65.
28 Jahn, *Muntu*, 207.
29 Wauthier, *The Literature and Thought of Modern Africa*, 103.

2. *Progress in verse*

1 Freely translated by the present author from material published by the Cuban scholar Rogelio A. Martinez Furé in his *Poesía Yoruba*, 143.
2 *Ibid.* 145.
3 S.A. Babalola, *The Content and Form of Yoruba Ijala*, vi.
4 *Ibid.* vi.
5 Published in 1963.
6 Paul Edwards (ed.), *Equiano's Travels*, 170.
7 Olumbe Bassir (ed.), *An Anthology of West African Verse*, xii.
8 Dennis Osadebay, *Africa Sings*, 11.
9 *Ibid.* 13.
10 *Ibid.* 83.
11 John Matthews, *Tradition in Exile*, 58.
12 Osadebay, *Africa Sings*, 27.
13 *Ibid.* 28.
14 Bassir (ed.), *An Anthology of West African Verse*, 56.
15 *Ibid.* 53.
16 See 'The Theme of Ancestors in Senghor's Poetry' in *Introduction to African Literature* (ed.) Beier, 95-8. He exaggerates his point about Europe. Orthodox Christianity still preaches the doctrine of the Comunion of Saints and the Mystical Body of Christ, ideas basically similar to the African view he is talking about.
17 Bassir (ed.), *An Anthology of West African Verse*, 24.
18 Moore and Beier (eds.), *Modern Poetry from Africa*, 49.
19 John Reed and Clive Wake (eds. and trans.), *Léopold Sédar Senghor: Selected Poems*, 5.
20 Ulli Beier (ed.), *Introduction to African Literature*, 98.
21 Moore and Beier (eds.), *Modern Poetry from Africa*, 23.
22 'The African Writer and his Public', *Présence Africaine*, Vol. 30, No. 58 (1966), 11.
23 Quoted by Michael Crowder in his *Senegal: A Study in French Assimilation Policy*, 35.
24 Moore and Beier (eds.), *Modern Poetry from Africa*, 23-4.

25 Federico de Onís (ed.), *Antología de Ensayos Españoles*, 168-79.
26 *Ibid*. 178.
27 Crowder, *Senegal*, 1-2.
28 Beier (ed.), *Introduction to African Literature*, x.
29 *Cultural Events in Africa*, No. 102 (undated), 4.
30 Moore and Beier (eds.), *Modern Poetry from Africa*, 94.
31 Ademola (ed.), *Reflections*, 52-3.
32 *Ibid*. 56.
33 Moore and Beier (eds.), *Modern Poetry from Africa*, 93-4.
34 John Matthews, 'The Canadian Experience' in *Commonwealth Literature* (ed) John Press, 29.
35 Ademola (ed.), *Reflections*, 60.
36 John Reed and Clive Wake (eds.), *A Book of African Verse*, 17-18.
37 'A Note on Nigerian Poetry', *Présence Africaine*, Vol. 30, No. 58 (1966), 62.
38 *Ibid*. 62.
39 Ademola (ed.), *Reflections*, 62.
40 Moore and Beier (eds.), *Modern Poetry from Africa*, 100-1.
41 Bassir (ed.), *An Anthology of West African Verse*, 27.
42 John Reed and Clive Wake (eds.), *Senghor: Prose and Poetry*, 76.
43 Reed and Wake (eds.), *A Book of African Verse*, 15-16.
44 Moore and Beier (eds.), *Modern Poetry from Africa*, 98-9. J.P. Clark first compared Osadebay's poem with Okara's in *Présence Africaine*, Vol. 30, No. 58; but he drew a different set of critical conclusions.
45 *Présence Africaine*, Vol. 30. No. 58, 64.
46 John Hayward (ed.), *T.S. Eliot: Selected Prose*. London: Peregrine Books, 1963, 26.
47 Wole Soyinka, *Idanre and other poems*, 43.
48 *Ibid*. 44.
49 *Ibid*. 14.
50 *Ibid*. 31.
51 Fela Sowande, *Ifa*, 25.
52 Soyinka, *Idanre and other poems*, 10-11.
53 *Ibid*. 45.
54 *Ibid*. 30.
55 *Ibid*. 57.
56 *Ibid*. 61.

3. *West African Prose*

1   J. Max Patrick and Robert O. Evans (eds.), *Style, Rhetoric, and Rhythm: Essays by Morris Croll,* 64.
2   Croll cites Muret as the source for this idea.
3   J.E. Stewart, 'Return to His Native Village', *Busara,* Vol. 1, No. 1 (1968), 37.
4   *Transition,* Vol. 1, No. 4 (1965), 31.
5   Collected in Neville Denny (ed.), *Pan African Short Stories,* 92–100.
6   Collected in Ademola (ed.), *Reflections,* 37–41.
7   *Ibid.* 22–5.
8   Denny (ed.), *Pan African Short Stories,* 68–78.
9   See Abioseh Nicol, *The Truly Married Woman and Other Stories,* 58–69.
10 See Ulli Beier, 'Public Opinion on Lovers' in *Black Orpheus,* No. 14 (1964), 4–16.
11 Ademola (ed.), *Reflections,* 9.
12 *Ibid.* 19.
13 Cyprian Ekwensi, *Lokotown and Other Stories.*
14 See Beier's essay on Fagunwa in *An Introduction to African Literature* (ed. Beier).
15 *Ibid.* 189.
16 *Ibid.* 190.
17 *Ibid.* 190.
18 *Ibid.* 191.
19 Reed and Wake (eds.), *Senghor: Prose and Poetry,* 88.
20 *Ibid.* 88.
21 Quoted by Wauthier in *The Literature and Thought of Modern Africa,* 74.
22 Gerald Moore, *Seven African Writers,* 39–40.
23 Amos Tutuola, *The Palm-Wine Drinkard,* 8.
24 Amos Tutuola, *My Life in the Bush of Ghosts,* 61.
25 Tutuola, *The Palm-Wine Drinkard,* 45–6.
26 *Ibid.* 25.
27 *Ibid.* 13–14.
28 Tutuola, *My Life in the Bush of Ghosts,* 131.
29 See Adrian Roscoe and Benedict Ogutu, *Keep My Words.*
30 Tutuola, *My Life in the Bush of Ghosts,* Foreword.
31 See Soyinka's article, 'The Writer in an African State', *Transition,* Vol. 6, No. 31 (1962), 11–13.
32 Talking about the dramatised version of *The Palm-Wine*

Drinkard (novels are quickly turned into plays in Nigeria), Miss Molly Mahood wrote: 'perhaps the most interesting aspect of the final production was the response of African intellectuals who had found Tutuola in English rather embarrassing, but found that Tutuola in Yoruba transported them. . .' See 'Drama in New-Born States', *Présence Africaine,* Vol. 32, No. 60, 38.

33 See *Transition,* Vol. 6, No. 31, 13.

34 Gabriel Okara, *The Voice,* 156–7. The whirlpool idea seems to be a favourite with Okara, and with other West African writers, including J.P. Clark and George Awoonor-Williams. Its implications as a symbol for Africa's modern predicament are easily felt and understood.

35 'Locale and Universe – Three Nigerian Novels', a review in the *Journal of Commonwealth Literature,* No. 3 (1967), 129. Professor Jones' main point about transliteration is that the difference between success and failure seems to depend on which items are chosen for treatment.

36 Press (ed.), *Commonwealth Literature,* 204.

37 *Présence Africaine,* Vol. 31, No. 59 (1966), 135–40.

38 *Ibid.* 139.

39 Press (ed.), *Commonwealth Literature,* 203.

40 'Rejoinder' in *Reflections,* 68. In full it reads:
> Now no more the palefaced strangers
> With unhallowed feet
> The heritage of our fathers profane;
> Now no missioned benevolent despots
> Bulldoze an unwilling race;
> No more now the foreign hawks
> On alien chickens prey –
> But we on us!

41 'Corruption' in *Reflections,* 66.

42 Leonard Doob, *Communication in Africa,* 264–5.

43 'La Tradition Gnomique', *Présence Africaine,* Vol. 8, No. 9 (1950), 325.

44 Quoted by Wauthier in *The Literature and Thought of Modern Africa,* 65–6.

45 This has always been the case, even outside Africa, and underlines the didactic side of the proverb's nature, cf. the scriptural 'These are the prouerbes of Salomon the sonne of David Kynge of Israel: to lerne wysdome, nurtoure, vnderstondinge, prudence, rightuousnesse, iudgment and equite. That the very babes might have knowledge and vnderstondinge.' *Biblia The Bible* (Coverdale), fol.

xxxviii; cited by R.E. Habenicht (ed.), *John Heywood's A Dialogue of Proverbs*. Berkeley, California: University of California, 1963.

46 Chinua Achebe, *No Longer at Ease*, 11.

47 Chinua Achebe, *Arrow of God*, 286.

48 Achebe, *No Longer at Ease*, 167.

49 Achebe, *Arrow of God*, 104-5. The illustration is used in fact to describe the coming of the white man; but to the carpenter's audience it is obviously a familiar way of looking at suffering.

50 *Ibid*. 282.

51 O.R. Dathorne offers the interesting argument that in this sense the proverb can be seen as the exact counterpart to the riddle, popular among the young, which points to the world's essential confusion and complexity. See 'Proverbs and Riddles in Africa', *Nigeria* No. 88 (1966), 70-2.

52 Edwin Muir (ed.), *The Collected Poems of Sir Thomas Wyatt*. London: Routledge and Kegan Paul, 1949, 191.

53 An illuminating account of the proverb's historical role in the educational tradition of Europe can be found in Habenicht's Introduction to *John Heywood's A Dialogue of Proverbs*.

54 Press (ed.), *Commonwealth Literature*, 205.

55 Professor Eldred Jones does a disservice to criticism and, consequently, to African writing, when he remarks that *A Man of the People* 'has qualities which invite comparison with works of stature on similar themes' and then cites *Julius Caesar, Coriolanus, Animal Farm*, and finally, *Hard Times*. (See the *Journal of Commonwealth Literature*, No. 3 (1967), 131.) Suffice it to say that *Hard Times*, to take the least absurd of the comparisons, displays quite simply all those qualities which Achebe's work lacks. It is a work of art that demands, and responds to, analysis. F.R. Leavis could certainly not make for Achebe's piece the claims he rightly made for *Hard Times*.

4. *Further Prose: children, highlifers, and politicians*

1 'A Personal View of Nigerian Independence' in *African Independence* (ed.) Peter Judd, 231-53.

2 See, for example, the cover of Ademola, *Reflections*, or Ekwensi, *An African Night's Entertainment*.

3 Kunle Akinsemoyin, *Twilight and the Tortoise*. Page references to this book will be included in the text of the discussion.

4 Drawn from Isaac Delano, *Owe L'Esin Oro: Yoruba Proverbs*.

5 Ulli Beier and B. Gbadamosi (eds. and trans.), *The Moon Cannot Fight*. The text is undated and the pages unnumbered.
6 Okenwa Olisah, *Many Things You Must Know About Ogbeufi Azikiwe and Republican Nigeria*, 6.
7 *Ibid*. 9-10.
8 *Ibid*. 22.
9 *Ibid*. 26.
10 *Zik: A Selection from the Speeches of Nnamdi Azikiwe*, 57.
11 Awolowo, *Path to Nigerian Freedom*. It was published in 1947.
12 Tai Solarin, *Thinking With You*. The contents consist of essays taken from Solarin's weekly column in the Lagos *Daily Times*.
13 Boswell's *Life of Johnson*. London: Nelson, 58-9.
14 See Judd (ed.), *African Independence*, 248-9.
15 Solarin, *Thinking With You*, 54.
16 *Ibid*. 96.
17 *Ibid*. 49-58.

5. Drama

1 Edwards (ed.), *Equiano's Travels*, 3-4.
2 See *Nigeria*, No. 82 (1964), 188-99,
3 *Ibid*. 191. *Orisha* are the traditional gods of the Yoruba.
4 'The Place of Drama in Yoruba Religious Observance', *Odu*, Vol. 3, No, 1 (1966), 88-94.
5 Doob, *Communication in Africa*, 76.
6 'Drama in New-Born States', *Présence Africaine*, Vol. 32, No. 60, 24-5.
7 *Ibid*. 25.
8 See Duro Ladipo, *Three Yoruba Plays* (ed. and trans.) Ulli Beier, 74.
9 See Obatunde Ijimere, *The Imprisonment of Obatala and Other Plays* (adapt Ulli Beier), i.
10 Ladipo, *Three Yoruba Plays*.
11 See Wole Soyinka's review 'Theatre in Nigeria' in *Cultural Events in Africa*, No. 5 (1965), i.
12 Ijimere, *The Imprisonment of Obatala and Other Plays*.
13 J. P. Clark, *Three Plays*. Critical discussion of *Song of a Goat*, *The Masquerade*, and *The Raft* is based on this volume.
14 Ships approach Forcados, wait at the bar, blow their sirens, and then pick up a bush-pilot, such as Zifa, before proceeding up the hazardous and labyrinthine creeks of the Delta towards Sapele, a hardwood-producing centre some sixty miles from the sea. During this trip, and on the return passage, the vessel's naviga-

tion is handed over to the Ijaw pilot. A non-literary note, perhaps, but a most unusual practice!

15 Of some of the West African dramatists one can repeat what Eliot said about Synge: 'The plays are based upon the idiom of a rural people whose speech is naturally poetic, both in imagery and in rhythm ... Synge wrote plays about characters whose originals in life talked poetically, so he could make them talk poetry and remain real people.' See 'Poetry and Drama', *Selected Prose*, 74.

16 'Theatre in Nigeria', *Cultural Events in Africa*, No. 5 (1965), i.

17 *A Dance of the Forests* appears in Soyinka's *Five Plays*. Page references will be to this volume.

18 'The Writer in an African State', *Transition*, Vol. 6, No. 31, 13.

19 Page references included in the text.

20 *Transition*, Vol. 6, No. 31, 12.

21 Wole Soyinka, *Kongi's Harvest*, 45.

22 Jane Austen, *Mansfield Park:* London: Nelson, 213.

23 'The Dunciad', *Poems, Epistles and Satires by Alexander Pope.* London: Everyman, 1924, 181.

24 Tony Tanner, 'Reason and the Grotesque: Pope's *Dunciad*', *Critical Quarterly*, Vol. 7, No. 2 (1965), 156,

25 'Politics and the English Language', *Inside the Whale and other Essays.* London: Penguin Books, 1967 ed., 143.

26 *Ibid.* 152-4.

27 Orwell, *Inside the Whale*, 145.

28 *The Lion and the Jewel* appears in Soyinka's *Five Plays*. Page references will be to this volume.

29 *The Trials of Brother Jero* appears in Soyinka's *Five Plays*. Page references will be to this volume.

30 Soyinka, *Five Plays*, 1. Martin Banham was mistaken when he observed that 'it is only recently that Soyinka has moved towards the utilization of music and dance'. See 'African Literature II, in *The Journal of Commonwealth Literature*, No. 3 (1967), 101. He misses the hint given by the very title of *A Dance of the Forests* and fails to notice that there are at least ten stage directions for dancing and drumming in this, the first of Soyinka's published plays.

31 Soyinka, *Five Plays*, 106.

32 Frazer offers a good deal of information on this subject, citing illustrations from all over the world. From Nigeria he draws several examples. He also distinguishes two kinds of what he calls Occasional Expulsion of Evils – one in a material, the other

in a human, vehicle. Both types are found in Nigeria, and both are found in Soyinka's play. See Frazer, *The Golden Bough,* 546-87. *The Strong Breed* appears in Soyinka's *Five Plays.* Page references are to that text.

33 Frazer writes of scapegoats being 'chosen because of some mark or bodily defect which the gods had noted and by which the victims were to be recognised'. *The Golden Bough,* 565.

34 See Patrick White's *Riders in the Chariot.* London: Penguin Books, 1964. At one point in *The Strong Breed* (p. 250) Eman, the volunteer scapegoat, remarks: 'I find consummation only when I have spent myself for a total stranger.'

35 Esslin, Head of Drama at the BBC, and author of *The Theatre of the Absurd,* London: Eyre and Spottiswode, 1962, criticised Soyinka's 'somewhat overfree, and somewhat confusing, use of flashback scenes. In practice', he writes, 'the flash-back (which is largely a cinematic technique) does not work very effectively on the stage which does not possess the subtle fade-outs of the screen; so that flash-backs as a rule involve . . . loss of continuity and easy flow of the action.' See 'Two Nigerian Playwrights' in *Introduction to African Literature,* 262. Perhaps one could argue that Soyinka's sliding about in time is at base a truly African phenomenon, and not simply a trick learnt from Western film and theatre.

36 *Cultural Events in Africa,* No. 25 (1966), 2.

37 *The Times,* 14 December 1966.

Select bibliography

Primary sources

Achebe, Chinua: *Things Fall Apart*. London: Heinemann, 1958.
No Longer at Ease. London: Heinemann, 1963.
Arrow of God. London: Heinemann, 1964.
A Man of the People. London: Heinemann, 1966.
Ademola, Frances (ed.): *Reflections*. Lagos: African Universities
Press, 1962.
Aidoo, Christina Ama Ata: *The Dilemma of a Ghost*. Accra:
Longmans, 1965.
Akinsemoyin, Kunle: *Twilight and the Tortoise*. Lagos: African
Universities Press, 1963.
Aluko, Timothy: *One Man, One Matchet*. London: Heinemann, 1964.
Kinsman and Foreman. London: Heinemann, 1966.
One Man, One Wife. London: Heinemann, 1967.
Awolowo, Obafemi: *Path to Nigerian Freedom*. London: Faber,
1947.
Awo. London: Cambridge University Press, 1960.
Awoonor-Williams, George: *Rediscovery*. Ibadan: Mbari Publica-
tions, 1964.
Azikiwe, Nnamdi: *Zik: A Selection from the Speeches of Nnamdi
Azikiwe*. London: Cambridge University Press, 1961.
Balewa, Sir Abubakar Tafawa: *Shaihu Umar*. London: Longmans,
1967.
Bassir, Olumbe (ed.): *An Anthology of West African Verse*. Ibadan:
Ibadan University Press, 1957.
Beier, Ulli (ed.): *African Poetry*. London: Cambridge University
Press, 1966.
The Origin of Life and Death. London: Heinemann, 1966.
Beier, Ulli and Gbadamosi, B. (eds. and trans.): *The Moon Cannot
Fight*. Ibadan: Mbari Publications, undated.
Not Even God is Ripe Enough. London: Heinemann, 1968.
Beier, Ulli and Moore, Gerald (eds. and trans.): *Modern Poetry from
Africa*. London: Penguin Books, 1963.

Bello, Sir Ahmadu: *My Life*. London: Cambridge University Press, 1962.

Beti, Mongo: *Mission to Kala*. London: Heinemann, 1964.

Clark, John Pepper: *Poems*. Ibadan: Mbari Publications, 1962.

Song of a Goat. Ibadan: Mbari Publications, 1962.

America, their America. London: André Deutsch, 1964.

Three Plays. London: Oxford University Press, 1964.

A Reed in the Tide. London: Longmans, 1965.

Ozidi. London: Oxford University Press, 1966.

Conton, William: *The African*. London: Heinemann, 1964.

Cook, David, *Origin East Africa*. London: Heinemann, 1965.

Damas, Léon: *African Songs of Love, War, Grief and Abuse*. Ibadan: Mbari Publications, 1961.

De Graft, Joe: *Sons and Daughters*. London: Oxford University Press, 1964.

Delano, Isaac, *Owe L'Esin Oro: Yoruba Proverbs*. London: Oxford University Press, 1966.

Denny, Neville (ed.): *Pan African Short Stories*. London: Nelson, 1965.

Echeruo, M. J. C.: *Mortality*. Nairobi: Longmans, 1968.

Edwards, Paul (ed.): *Equiano's Travels*. London: Heinemann, 1967.

Egbuna, Obi: *Wind Versus Polygamy*: London: Faber, 1964.

The Anthill. London: Oxford University Press, 1965.

Ekwensi, Cyprian: *When Love Whispers*. Onitsha: Tabansi Bookshop, 1947.

The Leopard's Claw. London: Longmans, 1950.

People of the City. London: Dakers, 1954. New ed.: Heinemann, 1963.

Passport of Mallam Ilia. London: Cambridge University Press, 1960.

The Drummer Boy. London: Cambridge University Press, 1960.

Jagua Nana. London: Hutchinson, 1961.

An African Night's Entertainment. Lagos: African Universities Press, 1962.

Beautiful Feathers. London: Heinemann, 1962.

Burning Grass. London: Heinemann, 1962.

Iska. London: Hutchinson, 1966.

Lokotown and Other Stories. London: Heinemann, 1966.

Fagunwa, D. O.: *The Forest of a Thousand Daemons* (trans. Wole Soyinka). London: Nelson, 1968.

Hughes, Langston (ed.): *An African Treasury*. New York: Pyramid Book, 1960.

263

SELECT BIBLIOGRAPHY

Ijimere, Obatunde: *The Imprisonment of Obatala and Other Plays* (adapt. Ulli Beier). London: Heinemann, 1966.

Johnston, H. A. S. (trans.): *A Selection of Hausa Stories*. London: Oxford University Press, 1966.

Ladipo, Duro: *Three Yoruba Plays* (trans. Ulli Beier). Ibadan: Mbari Publications, 1964.

Laye, Camara: *The African Child*. London: Fontana, 1960.

The Radiance of the King. London: Fontana, 1965.

Martinez, Furé, Rogelio (ed.): *Poesía Yoruba*. Havana, 1963.

Mphahlele, Ezekiel: *Down Second Avenue*. London: Faber, 1959.

African Writing Today. London: Penguin Books, 1967.

In Corner B. Nairobi: East African Publishing House, 1967.

Munonye, John: *The Only Son*. London: Heinemann, 1966.

Niane, D. T.: *Sundiata: an Epic of Old Mali* (trans. G. D. Pickett). London: Longmans, 1965.

Nicol, Abioseh: *The Truly Married Woman and Other Stories*. London: Oxford University Press, 1965.

Two African Tales. London: Cambridge University Press, 1965.

Nwankwo, Nkem: *Danda*. London: André Deutsch, 1964.

Tales Out of School. Lagos: African Universities Press, 1964.

Nwanodi, Glory: *Icheke and Other Poems*. Ibadan: Mbari Publications, 1964.

Nwapa, Flora: *Efuru*. London: Heinemann, 1966.

Nzekwu, Onuora: *Wand of Noble Wood*. London: Hutchinson, 1961.

Blade Among the Boys. London: Hutchinson, 1962.

Eze Goes to School. Lagos: African Universities Press, 1963.

Highlife for Lizards. London: Hutchinson, 1965.

Ogot, Grace: *The Promised Land*. Nairobi: East African Publishing House, 1967.

Land Without Thunder. Nairobi: East African Publishing House, 1968.

Okara, Gabriel: *The Voice*. London: André Deutsch, 1964.

Okigbo, Christopher: *Heavensgate*. Ibadan: Mbari Publications, 1962.

Limits. Ibadan: Mbari Publications, 1964.

Osadebay, Dennis: *Africa Sings*. Ilfracombe: Stockwell, 1952.

Oyono, Ferdinand: *Houseboy*. London: Heinemann, 1966.

The Old Man and the Medal. London: Heinemann, 1969.

Parkes, Frank Kobina: *Songs from the Wilderness*. London: University of London Press, 1965.

Peters, Lenrie: *Poems*. Ibadan: Mbari Publications, 1964.

The Second Round. London: Heinemann, 1966.

264

Satellites. London: Heinemann, 1967.

Reed, John and Wake, Clive (eds.): *A Book of African Verse.* London: Heinemann, 1964.

Selected Poems of L. S. Senghor. London: Oxford University Press, 1964.

Senghor: Prose and Poetry. London: Oxford University Press, 1965.

Roscoe, Adrian and Ogutu, Benedict: *Keep My Words.* Nairobi: East African Publishing House (forthcoming).

Segun, Mabel: *My Father's Daughter.* Lagos: African Universities Press, 1965.

Senghor, Léopold Sédar (ed.): *Nouvelle Anthologie de la Poésie Nègre et Malgâche.* Paris, 1948.

Solarin, Tai: *Thinking With You.* Ibadan, Longmans, 1965.

Soyinka, Wole: *A Dance of the Forests.* London: Oxford University Press, 1963.

The Lion and the Jewel. London: Oxford University Press, 1963.

Five Plays. London: Oxford University Press, 1964.

The Interpreters. London: André Deutsch, 1965.

The Road. London: Oxford University Press, 1965.

Idanre and Other Poems. London: Methuen, 1965.

Kongi's Harvest. London: Oxford University Press, 1967.

(trans.) *The Forest of a Thousand Daemons.* London: Nelson, 1968.

Tutuola, Amos: *The Palm-Wine Drinkard.* London: Faber, 1952.

My Life in the Bush of Ghosts. London: Faber, 1954.

Simbi and the Satyr of the Dark Jungle. London: Faber, 1955.

The Brave African Huntress. London: Faber, 1958.

Feather Woman of the Jungle. London: Faber, 1962.

Ajaiyi and His Inherited Poverty. London: Faber, 1967.

Whiteley, Wilfred (ed.): *A Selection of African Prose* (Oral Texts and Written Prose). London: Oxford University Press, 1964.

Writing from Onitsha, comprising:

Master of Life. *Beware of Harlots and Many Friends,* undated.

Obioha, R. I. M. *Our Modern Love Letters,* undated.

Odili, Frank E. *What is Life?,* 1961.

Okonkwo, R. *Never Trust All That Love You,* undated.

Olisah, Okenwa. *Many Things You Must Know About Ogbuefi Azikiwe and Republican Nigeria,* undated.

Stephen, Felix. *How to Get a Lady in Love,* undated.

Strong Man of the Pen. *Life, Money and Women Turn Man Up and Down,* 1964.

265

Secondary Sources

Achebe, Chinua: 'The Novelist as Teacher', *Commonwealth Literature* (ed. John Press). London: Heinemann, 1965.
'The Black Writer's Burden', *Présence Africaine,* Vol. 31, No. 59 (1966), 135–40.
Adedeji, J. A.: 'The Place of Drama in Yoruba Religious Observance', *Odu,* Vol. 3, No. 1 (1966), 88–94.
Astrachan, Anthony: 'Creative Writing', *Nigeria,* No. 79 (1963), 290–4.
'Does it Take One to Know One?', *Nigeria,* No. 77 (1963), 132–3.
Babalola, S. A.: *The Content and Form of Yoruba Ijala.* London: Oxford University Press, 1966.
Banham, Martin: 'African Literature II: Nigerian Dramatists in English and the Traditional Nigerian Theatre', The *Journal of Commonwealth Literature,* No. 3 (1967), 97–102.
Beier, Ulli (ed.): *Introduction to African Literature.* London: Longmans, 1967.
'The Agbegijo Masqueraders', *Nigeria,* No. 82 (1964), 188–99.
Césaire, Aimé: 'Culture et Colonisation', *Présence Africaine,* Vol. 8, No. 10 (1956), 204.
Clark, J. P.: 'A Note on Nigerian Poetry', *Présence Africaine,* Vol. 30, No. 58 (1966), 55–64.
'Aspects of Nigerian Drama', *Nigeria,* No. 89 (1966), 118–26.
Crowder, Michael: *Senegal: A Study in French Assimilation Policy.* London: Oxford University Press, 1962.
Dathorne, Oscar R.: 'Olaudah Equiano', *Nigeria,* No. 85 (1965), 130–1.
'Proverbs and Riddles in Africa', *Nigeria,* No. 88 (1966), 70–2.
Doob, Leonard: *Communication in Africa.* New Haven: Yale University Press, 1961.
Duffy, James: *Portugal in Africa.* London: Penguin Books, 1962.
Ekwensi, Cyprian: 'Problems of Nigerian Writers', *Nigeria,* No. 78 (1963), 217–19.
'African Literature', *Nigeria,* No. 83 (1964), 294–9.
'Literary Influences on a Young Nigerian', *Times Literary Supplement,* 4 (June 1964), 475–6.
Ellis, A. B.: *The Yoruba-speaking Peoples of the Slave Coast of West Africa.* London, 1894. New ed.: Chicago: Benin Press, 1964.
Evans-Pritchard, E. (ed.): *The Institutions of Primitive Society.* London: Oxford University Press, 1954.

SELECT BIBLIOGRAPHY

Forde, Daryll (ed.) *African Worlds*. London: Oxford University Press, 1963.

Frazer, James: *The Golden Bough*. New York: Macmillan, 1943.

Gleason, Judith I.: *This Africa*. Evanston: Northwestern University Press, 1965.

Ilogu, Edmund: 'Christianity and Ibo Traditional Religion', *Nigeria,* No. 83 (1964), 304–8.

Jahn, Janheinz: *Muntu* (trans. M. Grene). London: Faber, 1961.

The History of neo-African Literature. London: Faber, 1968.

Jones, Eldred: 'Locale and Universe – Three Nigerian Novels', *Journal of Commonwealth Literature,* No. 3 (1967), 129–31.

Judd, Peter (ed.): *African Independence*. New York: Dell, 1963.

Kane, Mohamadou: 'The African Writer and His Public', *Présence Africaine,* Vol. 30, No. 58 (1966), 10–32.

Kesteloot, Lylian: 'The West African Epics', *Présence Africaine,* Vol. 30, No. 58 (1966), 197–202.

Lambo, T. Adeoye: 'The Place of Art in the Emotional Life of the African', *Présence Africaine,* Vol. 32, No. 60 (1966), 8–22.

Liyong, Taban lo.: 'Tutuola, Son of Zinjanthropus', *Busara,* Vol. 1, No. 1 (1968), 3–8.

'Meditations in Limbo', *Busara,* Vol. 2, No. 2 (1969), 32–46.

MacKenzie, Norman H.: *The Outlook for English in Central Africa*. London: Oxford University Press, 1960.

Mahood, Molly: 'Drama in New-Born States', *Présence Africaine,* Vol. 32, No. 60 (1966), 23–39.

Matthews, John P.: *Tradition in Exile*. Toronto: University of Toronto Press, 1962.

McEwan, Peter and Sutcliffe, Robert (eds.): *Modern Africa*. New York: Cromwell, 1965.

Modisane, Bloke: 'African Writers' Summit', *Transition,* Vol. 2, No. 5 (1962), 5–6.

Moore, Gerald: *Seven African Writers*. London: Oxford University Press, 1962.

The Chosen Tongue. London: Longmans, 1969.

'The Arts in the New Africa', *Nigeria,* No. 92 (1967), 92–7.

Mphahlele, Ezekiel: *The African Image*. New York: Praeger, 1962.

'The Language of African Literature', *Harvard Educational Review,* Vol. 34, No. 2 (1964), 298–306.

Nicol, Davidson: *Africa – A Subjective View*. London: Longmans, 1964.

Nwanodi, Glory: 'Ibo Proverbs', *Nigeria,* No. 80 (1964), 61–2.

267

SELECT BIBLIOGRAPHY

Ogunba, Oyin: 'Theatre in Nigeria', *Présence Africaine,* Vol. 30, No. 58 (1966), 61–88.

Onís, Federico de (ed.): *Antología de Ensayos Españoles.* Boston, 1936.

Patrick, J. Max and Evans, Robert O. (eds.): *Style, Rhetoric, and Rhythm: Essays by Morris Croll.* London: Oxford University Press, 1966.

Press, John (ed.): *Commonwealth Literature.* London: Heinemann, 1965.

Reed, John and Wake, Clive (eds. and trans.): *Léopold Sédar Senghor: Prose and Poetry.* London: Oxford University Press, 1965.

Sowande, Fela: *Ifa.* Nigeria, Yaba East: Oja, 1964.

Smyinka, Wole: 'Theatre in Nigeria', *Cultural Events in Africa,* No. 5 (1965), i.

'The Writer in an African State', *Transition,* Vol. 6, No. 31 (1967), 11–13.

Spencer, John (ed.): *Language in Africa.* London: Cambridge University Press, 1963.

Stewart, James E. 'Return to His Native Village', *Busara,* Vol. 1, No. 1 (1968), 37–9.

Traoré, Bakary: *Le Théâtre Négro-Africaine et ses Fonctions Sociales.* Paris, 1958.

Vansina, Jan: *Oral Tradition* (trans. H. M. Wright). London: Routledge and Kegan Paul, 1965.

Wali, Obiajunwa: 'The Individual and the Novel in Africa', *Transition,* Vol. 4, No. 18 (1965), 31–3.

Wauthier, Claude: *The Literature and Thought of Modern Africa* (trans. Sheila Kay). London: Pall Mall, 1966.

Wright, Edgar: 'African Literature I: Problems of Criticism', *The Journal of Commonwealth Literature,* No. 2 (1966), 103–12.

Index